3rd Workshop on Computational Approaches to Discourse (CODI 2022)

Held at COLING 2022

Gyeongju, South Korea
16 – 17 October 2022

ISBN: 978-1-7138-6148-5

Printed from e-media with permission by:

Curran Associates, Inc.
57 Morehouse Lane
Red Hook, NY 12571

Some format issues inherent in the e-media version may also appear in this print version.

Association for Computational Linguistics
209 N. Eighth Street
Stroudsburg, Pennsylvania 18360

Phone: 1-570-476-8006
Fax: 1-570-476-0860

acl@aclweb.org

Additional copies of this publication are available from:

Curran Associates, Inc.
57 Morehouse Lane
Red Hook, NY 12571 USA
Phone: 845-758-0400
Fax: 845-758-2633
Email: curran@proceedings.com
Web: www.proceedings.com

COLING

International Conference on Computational Linguistics

Proceedings of the Conference and Workshops

COLING

Volume 29 (2022), No. 8

Proceedings of 3rd Workshop on Computational Approaches to Discourse (CODI 2022)

The 29th International Conference on Computational Linguistics

October 16 - 17, 2022
Gyeongju, Republic of Korea

ISSN 2951-2093

Preface

Welcome to the 3rd Workshop on Computational Approaches to Discourse, CODI! CODI provides a venue to bring together researchers working on all aspects of discourse in Computational Linguistics and NLP. Our aim is to provide a venue for the entire discourse processing community where we can present and exchange our theories, algorithms, software, datasets, and tools.

The workshop consists of invited talks, contributed papers and extended abstracts. We received paper submissions that span a wide range of topics, addressing issues related to discourse representation and parsing, reference and coreference resolution, dialogue, pragmatics, applications, and more. As the workshop is hybrid this year, papers are presented live either in person or remotely and discussed during live Q&A sessions.

We are happy that CODI 2022 features the CODI-CRAC 2022 shared task on anaphora, bridging, and discourse deixis resolution in dialogue, which is a joint shared task between the CODI and CRAC workshops at COLING. This shared task goes beyond previous ones as its input is transcribed spoken dialogue and it includes anaphoric relations beyond coreference. This effort is spearheaded by Carolyn Rosé. As we hope that the next CODI workshops will also feature shared tasks and other special events, the workshop also includes a discussion on future shared tasks, special sessions on discourse representation and parsing, coreference resolution, and multilingual discourse processing and machine translation.

We thank our invited speakers, **Nate Chambers**, United States Naval Academy, who works on understanding events in text, the semantic relations between them, and how they characterize knowledge they expressed in narratives; and **Bonnie Webber**, University of Edinburgh, known for many decades of seminal research on discourse from early work on "cooperative question-answering" to extended research on discourse anaphora and discourse relations. We would also like to thank our reviewers for their thoughtful and instructive comments. They helped us to prepare an inclusive workshop program. Finally we would like to thank the COLING 2022 workshop chairs Sadao Kurohashi, Patrizia Paggio and Nianwen Xue who organized the COLING workshop program.

The CODI Organizers,

Chloé Braud, Christian Hardmeier, Junyi Jessy Li, Sharid Loáiciga, Michael Strube, and Amir Zeldes

Organizers:

Chloé Braud, CNRS - IRIT
Christian Hardmeier, IT University of Copenhagen and Uppsala University[1]
Junyi Jessy Li, The University of Texas at Austin
Sharid Loáiciga, University of Gothenburg
Michael Strube, Heidelberg Institute for Theoretical Studies
Amir Zeldes, Georgetown University

Program Committee:

Malihe Alikhani, University of Pittsburgh, US
Giuseppe Carenini, University of British Columbia, Canada
Haixia Chai, Heidelberg Institute for Theoretical Studies, Germany
Jackie Chi Kit Cheung, McGill University, Canada
Iria da Cunha, Universidad Nacional de Educación a Distancia, Spain
Vera Demberg, Saarland University, Germany
Pascal Denis, INRIA, France
Stefanie Dipper, Ruhr-Universität Bochum, Germany
Elisa Ferracane, Abridge, US
Zhengxian Gong, Soochow University, China
Yulia Grishina, Amazon, Germany
Ryuichiro Higashinaka, NTT, Japan
Ruihong Huang, Texas A&M University, US
Kentaro Inui, Tohoku University, Japan
Yangfeng Ji, University of Virginia, US
Yaman Kumar, IIIT Delhi, India
Murathan Kurfalı, Stockholm University, Sweden
Sadao Kurohashi, Kyoto University, Japan
Sobha Lalitha Devi, AU-KBC Research Centre, India
Ekaterina Lapshinova-Koltunski, Saarland University, Germany
Philippe Muller, IRIT, France
Mark-Christoph Müller, Heidelberg Institute for Theoretical Studies, Germany
Anna Nedoluzhko, Charles University, Czechia
Vincent Ng, University of Texas at Dallas, US
Maciej Ogrodniczuk, Polish Academy of Sciences, Poland
Thiago Pardo, University of São Paulo, Brazil
Massimo Poesio, Queen Mary University of London, UK
Hannah Rohde, University of Edinburgh, UK
Attapol Rutherford, Chulalongkorn University, Thailand
Manfred Stede, University of Potsdam, Germany
Francielle Vargas, University of São Paulo, Brazil
Bonnie Webber, University of Edinburgh, UK
Deyi Xiong, Tianjin University, China
Hongfei Xu, Saarland University, Germany
Nianwen Xue, Brandeis University, US
Heike Zinsmeister, University of Hamburg, Germany

Invited Speakers:

Nate Chambers, United States Naval Academy, US
Bonnie Webber, University of Edinburgh, UK

[1]Christian Hardmeier was supported by the Swedish Research Council under grant 2017-930.

Table of Contents

Conference Program

October 16, 2022

9:15–9:30 ***Opening Remarks***

9:30–10:30 *Invited Talk*
Nate Chambers

10:30–11:00 ***Coffee Break***

11:00–11:10 *KOJAK: A New Corpus for Studying German Discourse Particle ja*
Adil Soubki, Owen Rambow and Chong Kang

11:10–11:20 *Discourse Analysis via Questions and Answers: Parsing Dependency Structures of Questions Under Discussion*
Wei-Jen Ko, Dananjay Srinivas, Cutter Dalton, Greg Durrett and Junyi Jessy Li

11:20–11:30 *Towards Domain-Independent Supervised Discourse Parsing Through Gradient Boosting*
Patrick Huber and Giuseppe Carenini

11:30–11:45 *Improving Topic Segmentation by Injecting Discourse Dependencies*
Linzi Xing, Patrick Huber and Giuseppe Carenini

11:45–11:55 *Evaluating How Users Game and Display Conversation with Human-Like Agents*
Won Ik Cho, Soomin Kim, Eujeong Choi and Younghoon Jeong

11:55–12:05 *Evaluating Discourse Cohesion in Pre-trained Language Models*
Jie He, Wanqiu Long and Deyi Xiong

12:05–12:15 *Easy-First Bottom-Up Discourse Parsing via Sequence Labelling*
Andrew Shen, Fajri Koto, Jey Han Lau and Timothy Baldwin

12:15–12:30 ***Open discussion on future CODI workshops and shared tasks***

12:30–14:00 ***Lunch***

October 16, 2022 (continued)

14:00–14:10 *Multi-Party Conversation Generation via Discourse Structure Planning*
Alexander Chernyavskiy and Dmitry Ilvovsky

14:10–14:20 *Explicitation Phenomena and Surprisal Effects in Translation and Interpreting*
Ekaterina Lapshinova-Koltunski, Christina Pollkläsener and Heike Przybyl

14:20–14:30 *Using Translation Process Data to Explore Explicitation and Implicitation through Discourse Connectives*
Ekaterina Lapshinova-Koltunski and Michael Carl

14:30–14:45 *Towards Identifying Alternative-Lexicalization Signals of Discourse Relations*
René Knaebel and Manfred Stede

14:45–14:55 *Towards Semi-Supervised Discourse Graph Parsing in Dialogs with Pre-trained Language Models and Linguistic Features*
Chuyuan Li, Patrick Huber, Wen Xiao, Maxime Amblard, Chloé Braud and Giuseppe Carenini

14:55–15:05 *Label distributions help implicit discourse relation classification*
Frances Yung, Kaveri Anuranjana, Merel Scholman and Vera Demberg

15:05–15:15 *Bullshit and Unanswerable QUDs*
Oliver Deck

15:15–15:30 *The Keystone Role Played by Questions in Debate*
Zlata Kikteva, Kamila Gorska, Wassiliki Siskou, Annette Hautli-Janisz and Chris Reed

15:30–16:00 ***Coffee Break***

16:00–16:15 *Shallow Discourse Parsing for Open Information Extraction and Text Simplification*
Christina Niklaus, André Freitas and Siegfried Handschuh

16:15–16:25 *Predicting Political Orientation in News with Latent Discourse Structure to Improve Bias Understanding*
Nicolas Devatine, Philippe Muller and Chloé Braud

16:25–16:35 *Attention Modulation for Zero-Shot Cross-Domain Dialogue State Tracking*
Mathilde Veron, Olivier Galibert, Guillaume Bernard and Sophie Rosset

16:35–16:45 *An Empirical Study of Topic Transition in Dialogue*
Mayank Soni, Brendan Spillane, Leo Muckley, Orla Cooney, Emer Gilmartin, Christian Saam, Benjamin Cowan and Vincent Wade

October 16, 2022 (continued)

16:45–17:45 *Invited Talk*
Bonnie Webber

17:45–18:00 ***Open discussion on future CODI workshops and shared tasks***

October 17, 2022

CODI-CRAC Shared Task

14:00 **Session 1: Shared Task Competition**

14:00 ***Welcome***

14:05 *The CODI-CRAC 2022 Shared Task on Anaphora, Bridging, and Discourse Deixis in Dialogue*
Juntao Yu, Sopan Khosla, Ramesh Manuvinakurike, Lori Levin, Vincent Ng, Massimo Poesio, Michael Strube and Carolyn Rosé

14:35 *Anaphora Resolution in Dialogue: System Description (CODI-CRAC 2022 Shared Task)*
Tatiana Anikina, Natalia Skachkova, Joseph Renner and Priyansh Trivedi

14:50 *Pipeline Coreference Resolution for Anaphoric Identity in Dialogues*
Damrin Kim, Seongsik Park, Mirae Han and Harksoo Kim

15:05 *Neural Anaphora Resolution in Dialogue Revisited*
Shengjie Li, Hideo Kobayashi and Vincent Ng

15:30 ***Coffee Break***

October 17, 2022 (continued)

16:00	**Session 2: Keynote Session**
16:00	***Invited Talk: Massimo Poesio and Lori Levin***
16:45	***Open Discussion***
17:45	***Closing Remarks***

KoJaK: A New Corpus for Studying German Discourse Particle *ja*

Adil Soubki[1†], Owen Rambow[2†], Chong Kang[2]
[1]Department of Computer Science, Stony Brook University
[2]Department of Linguistics, Stony Brook University
[†]Institute for Advanced Computational Science
{adil.soubki,owen.rambow,chong.kang}@stonybrook.edu

Abstract

In German, *ja* can be used as a discourse particle to indicate that a proposition, according to the speaker, is believed by both the speaker and audience. We use this observation to create KoJaK, a distantly-labeled English dataset derived from Europarl for studying when a speaker believes a statement to be common ground. This corpus is then analyzed to identify lexical choices in English that correspond with German *ja*. Finally, we perform experiments on the dataset to predict if an English clause corresponds to a German clause containing *ja* and achieve an F-measure of 75.3% on a balanced test corpus.

1 Introduction

Predicting an author's belief, also called Event Factuality Prediction (EFP), has been studied extensively in the last decade. However, in addition to modeling their own beliefs, discourse participants develop a model of their audience's beliefs as well. It is well known since at least Grice (1975) that a speaker or writer must be modeling the addressee's cognitive state in order to communicate felicitously, and the notion of "common ground" has received increased attention in cognitive science (Brennan and Clark, 1996; Brennan et al., 2010) and philosophy (Stalnaker, 2002).

The task of predicting if a speaker believes a listener already knows a proposition, either because it has been established as common ground or connected to some shared reality, has been studied markedly less. This is at least in part due to a lack of corpora annotated for the task.

This paper makes the following contributions:

1. We develop a distantly-labeled dataset in English for studying when a speaker believes their audience already believes what they are saying.
2. We perform a statistical analysis to identify which tokens in English correspond to German discourse particle *ja*.
3. We perform experiments to predict for an English sentence whether its German translation equivalent has a *ja* or not. On a balanced test corpus, we achieve an F-measure of 75.3% on the *ja* sentences.

The paper is structured as follows. We start out by describing German discourse particles and *ja* in particular (Section 2). We then present a detailed discussion of the procedure used to create KoJaK (Section 3) as well as some statistical analysis of the corpus (Section 4). Finally, we use KoJaK to train models for predicting if an English sentence corresponds to a German sentence containing *ja* (Section 5) and conclude with a discussion of results (Section 6) and future work (Section 7).

2 German Discourse Particles and the Common Ground in Discourse

German has a closed class of discourse particles, including *ja*, *doch*, *wohl*, and *etwa*. These discourse particles have cognates in other parts of speech; for example, *ja* is also the equivalent of English *yes*, occurring sentence-initially. We can distinguish discourse particles from homonyms by their syntax: Egg (2011) points out that they cannot be questioned, they cannot function as one-word answer to a question, they cannot be coordinated or modified, and they occur in the so-called "Mittelfeld" (between the finite verb and any non-finite verbal elements). In terms of their function, Abraham (2017) suggests that "the speaker uses modal particles to negotiate the truth value of a proposition with the addressee. (...) The speaker distinguishes between the source of evidence and the judger of the source of evidence in the sense of Theory of Mind" (our translation). Put differently, modal particles serve to indicate that the speaker is distinguishing between her cognitive state and her "theory" of the addressee's cognitive state.

Proceedings of 3rd Workshop on Computational Approaches to Discourse, pages 1–6
October 16 – 17, 2022.

Turning specifically to *ja*, Gast (2008) characterizes its function as follows: "What is indicated by *ja* is that the state of affairs reported is unquestionable." Egg (2011) provides a sharper characterization: "The particle *ja* expresses (roughly) that the information conveyed by the sentence is already part of the common ground". Thus, the reason that the state of affairs is unquestionable is that the hearer already believes it (or has in the past). This is echoed by Döring and Repp (2016): "*ja* is generally taken to indicate (roughly), that the speaker assumes that the proposition *ja* scopes over is already part of the common ground, i.e. that it is not new (see many of the references above)".

We see that German discourse particle *ja* interacts crucially with how the discourse participants manage the common ground. However, most languages do not have such discourse particles. For example, English speakers may turn to phrases like *you know* or *of course* in the absence of such a particle. This paper suggests that by looking at translation equivalents of German *ja*, we can learn about how other languages manage the common ground.

3 Corpus Creation

Our corpus is called KOJAK, which stands for "Korpus für *ja* in Kontext" (or "Corpus for *ja* in context" in English). It contains roughly 3,000 examples of English sentences corresponding to German *ja*.

We use the Corrected and Structured Europarl Corpus (CoStEP), released by Graën et al. (2014), as a base for constructing KOJAK. Initially created for machine translation tasks, the Europarl corpus contains roughly 30 million words parallel-translated to 11 languages including English and German (Koehn, 2005). They are sourced from proceedings of the European Parliament starting as early as 1996 and contain additional languages as time moves on.

There is a notable asymmetry in the realization of *ja* depending on the direction of translation. If the sentence containing *ja* was translated from German to some other language then we can be sure that the conception of common ground being expressed is that of the original speaker. However, if the German *ja* sentence was translated from some other language then the *ja* may be expressing the translator's belief regarding the speaker's belief of what the common ground is. We ignore the distinction in this paper but discuss possible improvements in Section 7.

	Train		Dev		Test	
Ver.	Nat.	Bal.	Nat.	Bal.	Nat.	Bal.
Ja	2,021	2,012	286	293	591	593
Na	370,052	2,045	52,867	286	105,716	567
Total	372,073	4,057	53,153	579	106,307	1,160

Table 1: Summary of the clause-extracted dataset.

Our corpus is compiled in two steps. First, we create a filter for identifying sentences containing uses of *ja* as a discourse particle. We then use a heuristic for extracting only the clause containing the *ja* in question (i.e., the clause over which *ja* scopes). The latter step is motivated by an interest in the proposition which *ja* is modifying.

3.1 Filtering

CoStEP data is provided in an xml format with untokenized text for each speaker's turn. We used SpaCy to segment sentences from turns in both English and German (Honnibal and Johnson, 2015). To ensure the segmentation lines up, turns where the number of sentences does not match are discarded. We then filter the remaining sentence pairs by searching for ones where,

1. The German text contains *ja*.
2. The *ja* is not sentence-initial.
3. The English text does not contain *yes*.

If these three checks are successful then the sentence is considered to contain a use of *ja* as a discourse particle. Conversely, the sentence is not considered to contain a use of *ja* as a discourse particle if any of these checks fail. This creates two categories of sentences – JA sentences where this filter succeeded and, affectionately called, NA sentences for everything else.

3.2 Clause Extraction

Since the data comes from parliament meetings, sentences can be long with many nested clauses. When this is the case, the task of predicting what the speaker believes is muddled since the proposition we wish to predict is unclear. To address this we develop a heuristic for extracting the clause *ja* is modifying. SpaCy is again used to tokenize and parse the sentences along with SimAlign from Jalili Sabet et al. (2020) to align the German and English. The end result is a dependency parse for both the English and German sentences along with a mapping from one to the other.

2-grams	3-grams	4-grams
after all	after all ,	, of course ,
of course	, of course	, after all ,
, on	of course ,	is , after all
of the	, after all	is , of course
it is	of the european	, in fact ,
all ,	the committee on	of the european union
, but	it is not	at the same time
course ,	, it is	in the european union
, after	have voted for	-
the european	is , after	-

Table 2: The top 10 n-grams from the train/dev splits.

	1-grams		2-grams		3-grams		4-gr
Num.	>100		>100		73		7
Cutoff	20	100	20	100	20	73	7
Good	20%	8%	35%	16%	30%	12%	63%
Ntrl	75%	67%	65%	74%	45%	60%	13%
Bad	5%	25%	0%	10%	25%	27%	25%

Table 3: Analysis of top-100 and top-20 (where applicable) n-grams by significance for detecting *ja*-sentences; Num = number of such n-grams, Ntrl = Neutral

To extract the corresponding English clause we find the location of *ja* in the German sentence and then travel up the parse tree until a VERB or AUX tag is found or it reaches the root. If the head is a clausal object, we probably have a problem with the parse. This is because German *ja* typically does not appear in embedded (object) clauses. We have found that we get better results if we move up one more level to the matrix clause in case we find ourselves in a subordinate clause. (Note that we do not do this with other types of embedded clauses, such as relative clauses or parentheticals.) The subtree rooted at this node is the candidate clause in German that now must be extracted from English.

It is possible that after alignment there are multiple tokens in English that correspond to the head word in German. For each English token corresponding to the German head word, if it is a leaf and tagged with AUX we move up one level and take the subtree. This process results in a set of, often overlapping, English subtrees. The leaves of these subtrees are then naively arranged in order to yield the final English clause.

A similar process is repeated for NA sentences to make them comparable and avoid sentence length being a strong indicator for the model. Instead of starting at the *ja*, a random token is selected and the algorithm described above is applied. This yields a dataset of English clauses labeled JA if the corresponding German clause contains *ja*, and labeled NA if not.

4 Statistical Analysis

With the relevant sentences now separated, our attention turns to how we can identify what items in English relate to the discourse particle usage of German *ja*. If the lexical choices between JA and NA sentences are different, then we would expect certain sequences to appear significantly more frequently in the JA corpus than elsewhere.

For any token sequence of length n, we can count the number of times that n-gram appears in the JA and NA sentences respectively. This is similar to creating two sets of samples and asking whether they are likely to be from different populations. Intuitively, n-grams which are unique to JA sentences are probably related to the presence of the discourse particle.

To investigate this we compute the counts of every n-gram for $2 \leq n \leq 4$ in each population. These samples are used to perform a t-test at the 95% confidence level and then sorted by p-value. To ensure sequences which are reasonably robust, we discard any that did not appear more than 10 times in the data. The result, seen in Table 2 for the train and dev splits, is a list of n-grams most unique to JA sentences according to this metric.

To roughly evaluate the quality of the extracted n-grams, the second author, a native speaker of both German and English, performed an error analysis on the n-gram lists. We used the following categories:

- **Good**: This is clearly an n-gram that on its own or in conjunction with some predictable missing words carries the same pragmatic meaning as German *ja*.
- **Neutral**: These n-grams contain no evidence of being either **Good** or **Bad**. Typically, these are sequences of function words without content words.
- **Bad**: This is clearly an n-gram which does not carry the same pragmatic meaning as German *ja*. A typical example is *of the European Union*. In fact, almost all examples refer explicitly to the European Union or its political procedures including those of the parliament (e.g., *Madam President*).

The rating was performed only on the n-gram types

rather than on occurrences of the n-grams, and no further context was provided. The goal is to provide a sense of the quality of the extracted n-grams, and we acknowledge the limitations of this study. The error analysis we present in Section 6, in contrast, was based on actual full phrases.

Results are shown in Table 3. The percentage of **Good** n-grams is much higher among the top-20 n-grams as opposed to top-100 (or top-73 in the case of 3-grams). Similarly, the percentage of **Bad** n-grams is lower among the top-20 compared to the top-100 (top-73). These two observations support the claim that the ranking by p-value is meaningful. The **Neutral** n-grams among the top-20 decrease with increasing n, which makes sense as shorter token sequences are more likely to be impossible to judge. Correspondingly, the percentage of **Good** n-grams (both top-20 and top-100 for 1- and 2-grams) increases from $n = 1$ to $n = 2$, though $n = 3$ does not continue the trend. For **Bad** n-grams, we first see a decrease with n and then an increase again, as longer token sequences are more likely to contain content words. For the *Bad* category, we find basically the same examples at all n-gram levels.

Overall, our simple statistical approach has extracted good n-grams, with a small number of bad ones. The results support the claim that the discourse meaning of German discourse particle *ja* is often preserved in translation equivalents.

5 Modeling & Experiments

We perform machine learning experiments to predict whether an English clause is the equivalent of a German *ja* clause or not.

5.1 Transformer-Based Model

We start by preparing a balanced version of the dataset such that JA and NA sentences appear equally often and use this as input to a transformer model. The model is fine-tuned on top of multilingual BERT for text classification using the transformers library from Hugging Face (Wolf et al., 2020). Training is performed for three epochs with a learning rate of 2e-5.

The results are promising with the model achieving an F-measure of 75.3% on JA clauses. Though it is difficult to determine exactly what features the model is using, this result is much better than would be expected if the clauses were randomly selected.

	Transformer		Statistical	
Strategy	Nat.	Bal.	Nat.	Bal.
Precision	50.0	76.7	7.5	48.7
Recall	0.7	74.1	5.2	56.2
F-measure	1.4	75.3	6.2	52.1

Table 4: Model performance achieved on *ja* examples.

In reality, *ja* events occur much less frequently than half of the time. As can be seen from Table 1, JA sentences are a tiny minority class, appearing in only ~0.5% of sentences. To emulate this, we also examine the performance of multilingual BERT on a dataset which contains a "natural" proportion of JA clauses. On this highly imbalanced dataset, the model achieves an F-measure of 1.4% on JA clauses. In other words, it performs extremely poorly.

5.2 Statistical Model

The results on the natural proportion were so low it seemed like a more simplistic model based on the analysis in Section 4 could possibly outperform multilingual BERT. We investigate this by performing the same t-test using only the training and dev splits to get a ranked list of 2-grams, 3-grams, and 4-grams (See Table 2). The model then selects some number of the top n-grams from each list and naively classifies a clause as JA if it case-insensitively contains any of those phrases.

Using only the top ranked sequence from each list, this simple model outperforms BERT, achieving an F-measure of 6.2% for JA clauses on the natural proportion test set. Use of additional n-grams did not improve performance on the natural proportion dataset. However, on the balanced dataset including every 2-gram, 3-gram, and 4-gram achieved the best results with an F-measure of 52.1% on JA clauses. While significantly worse than BERT, this is again a large improvement from the imbalanced dataset.

6 Discussion

We also investigated the use of sentence-level data, i.e. a version of KOJAK generated without extracting only the clauses over which *ja* scopes, but instead using the whole sentences in which *ja* occurs. When including this additional context both models performed worse, which supports the intuition for including only the clauses in scope.

The use of *ja* is one way German speakers indicate they believe a proposition is already common ground, but it is not the only way. It is possible that the systems above are correctly identifying sentences in which this occurs but they correspond to a German sentence which does not contain *ja*. We analyzed 70 false positive errors of the statistical model, and found that 71% could plausibly be cases in which the speaker believes the hearer already believes the content of the clause, despite the absence of *ja* in the German clause. Interestingly, another 11% look like cases in which the speaker is pretending as if the audience shares his or her beliefs, even though they probably do not (*we both know you will clean the dishes now*).

7 Future Work

In the relatively near future we hope to make improvements to KOJAK. While the corpus can currently only be used to study English, its underlying source provides data in many more languages. Using a methodology similar to that which was described in Section 4, we hope to expand KOJAK to support every language offered by Europarl. On a similar note, CoStEP also includes information about the original language for each utterance. If this were propagated, we could investigate the issue of translation direction mentioned in Section 3 more closely by partitioning data along these lines.

While the n-gram analysis discussed in Section 4 roughly identifies sequences which correspond to *ja*, many artifacts (E.g. *of the european union*) persist in the output. One way to reduce these might be to perform a similar analysis but on the German text and discard sequences that correspond directly to the English n-gram list.

These enhancements open up several directions for continuing work, the most conspicuous of which might be investigating the effectiveness of multitask learning, in which we exploit multiple languages, or related tasks such as factuality (Saurí and Pustejovsky, 2009). It could also be interesting to use the n-grams identified in English and search for their German counterparts, which likely include more than just *ja*. We have only just scratched the surface of what is possible here.

8 Access to KOJAK

The natural and balanced preparations of KOJAK are made available on GitHub.[1] Additional tooling used for parsing and filtering CoStEP, which might be useful in its own right, is also available.[2]

9 Acknowledgements

We would like to thank our three anonymous reviewers for their insightful comments and suggestions. This material is based on work supported by the Defense Advanced Research Projects Agency (DARPA) under Contract HR001122C0034. Any opinions, findings and conclusions or recommendations expressed in this material are those of the authors and do not necessarily reflect the views of DARPA.

References

Werner Abraham. 2017. Modalpartikel und Mirativeffekte. In Shin Tanaka, Elisabeth Leiss, Werner Abraham, and Yasuhiro Fujinawa, editors, *Grammatische Funktionen aus Sicht der japanischen und deutschen Germanistik*, Linguistische Berichte Sonderheft 24, pages 75–107. Buske, Hamburg.

Susan Brennan, Alexia Galati, and Anna Kuhlen. 2010. *Chapter 8 - Two Minds, One Dialog: Coordinating Speaking and Understanding*, volume 53, pages 301–344.

Susan E. Brennan and Herbert H. Clark. 1996. Lexical choice and conceptual pacts in conversation. *Journal of Experimental Psychology: Learning, Memory And Cognition*, pages 1482–93.

Sophia Döring and Sophie Repp. 2016. The modal particles *ja* and *doch* and their interaction with discourse structure: Corpus and experimental evidence. In S. Featherston, R. Hörnig, S. von Wietersheim, and S. Winkler, editors, *Information Structure and Semantic Processing*. De Gruyter.

Markus Egg. 2011. Discourse particles between cohesion and coherence. In *Proceedings of the Workshop on Constraints in Discourse*, Agay, France.

Volker Gast. 2008. Modal particles and context updating: The functions of german 'ja', 'doch', 'wohl' and 'etwa'. In H. Vater and O. Letnes, editors, *Modalverben und Grammatikalisierung*, pages 153–177. Wissenschaftlicher Verlag.

Johannes Graën, Dolores Batinic, and Martin Volk. 2014. Cleaning the europarl corpus for linguistic applications. In *KONVENS*.

Herbert Paul Grice. 1975. Logic and conversation. In P. Cole and J. Morgan, editors, *Syntax and semantics, vol 3*. Academic Press, New York.

[1] https://github.com/cogstates/kojak

[2] https://github.com/cogstates/costep

Matthew Honnibal and Mark Johnson. 2015. An improved non-monotonic transition system for dependency parsing. In *Proceedings of the 2015 Conference on Empirical Methods in Natural Language Processing*, pages 1373–1378, Lisbon, Portugal. Association for Computational Linguistics.

Masoud Jalili Sabet, Philipp Dufter, François Yvon, and Hinrich Schütze. 2020. SimAlign: High quality word alignments without parallel training data using static and contextualized embeddings. In *Findings of the Association for Computational Linguistics: EMNLP 2020*, pages 1627–1643, Online. Association for Computational Linguistics.

Philipp Koehn. 2005. Europarl: A parallel corpus for statistical machine translation. In *Proceedings of Machine Translation Summit X: Papers*, pages 79–86, Phuket, Thailand.

Roser Saurí and James Pustejovsky. 2009. Fact-Bank: a corpus annotated with event factuality. *Language Resources and Evaluation*, 43:227–268. 10.1007/s10579-009-9089-9.

Robert C. Stalnaker. 2002. Common ground. *Linguistics and Philosophy*, 25(5-6):701–721.

Thomas Wolf, Lysandre Debut, Victor Sanh, Julien Chaumond, Clement Delangue, Anthony Moi, Pierric Cistac, Tim Rault, Remi Louf, Morgan Funtowicz, Joe Davison, Sam Shleifer, Patrick von Platen, Clara Ma, Yacine Jernite, Julien Plu, Canwen Xu, Teven Le Scao, Sylvain Gugger, Mariama Drame, Quentin Lhoest, and Alexander Rush. 2020. Transformers: State-of-the-art natural language processing. In *Proceedings of the 2020 Conference on Empirical Methods in Natural Language Processing: System Demonstrations*, pages 38–45, Online. Association for Computational Linguistics.

Improving Topic Segmentation by Injecting Discourse Dependencies

Linzi Xing , Patrick Huber , Giuseppe Carenini
Department of Computer Science
University of British Columbia
Vancouver, BC, Canada, V6T 1Z4
{lzxing, huberpat, carenini}@cs.ubc.ca

Abstract

Recent neural supervised topic segmentation models achieve distinguished superior effectiveness over unsupervised methods, with the availability of large-scale training corpora sampled from *Wikipedia*. These models may, however, suffer from limited robustness and transferability caused by exploiting simple linguistic cues for prediction, but overlooking more important inter-sentential topical consistency. To address this issue, we present a discourse-aware neural topic segmentation model with the injection of above-sentence discourse dependency structures to encourage the model make topic boundary prediction based more on the topical consistency between sentences. Our empirical study on English evaluation datasets shows that injecting above-sentence discourse structures to a neural topic segmenter with our proposed strategy can substantially improve its performances on intra-domain and out-of-domain data, with little increase of model's complexity.

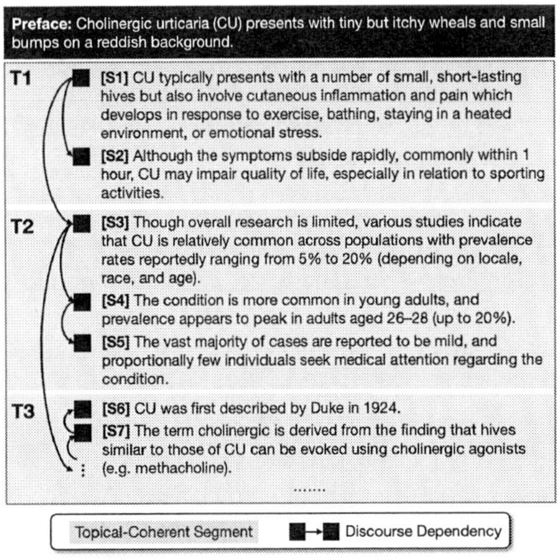

Figure 1: An example article about Cholinergic Urticaria (CU) sampled from the *en_disease* portion of Wiki-Section dataset (Arnold et al., 2019). Left: discourse dependency structure predicted by the Sent-First discourse parser (Zhou and Feng, 2022).

1 Introduction

Topic segmentation is a fundamental NLP task with the goal to separate textual documents into coherent segments (consisting of one or more sentences), following the document's underlying topical structure. The structural knowledge obtained from topic segmentation has been shown to play a vital role in key NLP downstream tasks, such as document summarization (Mitra et al., 1997; Riedl and Biemann, 2012; Xiao and Carenini, 2019), question answering (Oh et al., 2007; Diefenbach et al., 2018) and dialogue modeling (Xu et al., 2021; Zhang et al., 2020). The aim of topic segmentation makes it tightly connected to related research areas aiming to understand the latent structure of long and potentially complex text. Specifically, understanding the semantic and pragmatic underpinnings of a document can arguably support the task of separating continuous text into topical segments. To this end, discourse analysis and discourse parsing provide the means to understand and infer the semantic and pragmatic relationships underlying complete documents, well aligned with the local text coherence and highly correlated to the inter-sentential topical consistency, as shown in Louis and Nenkova (2012) and Muangkammuen et al. (2020). With a variety of linguistic theories proposed in the past, such as the Rhetorical Structure Theory (RST) (Mann and Thompson, 1988), the lexicalized discourse framework (Webber et al., 2003a) (underlying PDTB), and the Segmented Discourse Representation Theory (SDRT) (Asher, 1993; Asher et al., 2003), we follow the RST framework in this work (1) as we focus on monologue text (as compared to dialogue frameworks, such as SDRT) and (2) since RST postulates complete discourse trees spanning whole documents, directly aligned with the topical structure of complete documents (Huber et al., 2021).

Proceedings of 3rd Workshop on Computational Approaches to Discourse, pages 7–18
October 16 – 17, 2022. ©2022 International Conference on Computational Linguistics

We further motivate the synergistic relationship between topic segmentation and discourse analysis/parsing in Figure 1, showing anecdotal evidence of the alignment between the document's topical structure and the respective RST-style discourse dependency graph. Starting from a sequence of sentences, the task of topic segmentation addresses the problem of splitting the given *Wikipedia* article into an ordered set of topical-coherent fragments (here: `T1`, `T2` and `T3`) by predicting topical boundaries. As shown in the example, the document discourse tree is indicative of the topical structure of the document, as discourse dependencies occur considerably more often within a topic segment than across topic segments.

Given significant influence on a variety of real-world tasks, topic segmentation is an active research area in the field of NLP. As such, modern, neural methods for monologue topic segmentation are proposed by formulating the task as a sentence-level sequence labeling problem, trained and evaluated on the large-scale *Wikipedia* dataset (Xing et al., 2020; Glavas and Somasundaran, 2020; Barrow et al., 2020; Lo et al., 2021). These Wikipedia articles are well-suited for the task of topic segmentation, providing natural section marks which can be reasonably used as ground-truth segment boundaries (Koshorek et al., 2018; Arnold et al., 2019), superseding previously proposed unsupervised methods (Hearst, 1997; Galley et al., 2003; Eisenstein and Barzilay, 2008; Song et al., 2016). Despite the significant improvements achieved by neural supervised topic segmentation models, it remains unclear if these topic segmenters effectively learn to cluster sentences into topical-coherent pieces based on the (document-level) topical consistency, or solely exploit superficial patterns (e.g., simple linguistic cues) in the training domain.

To address this challenge, in this paper, we propose a more discourse-aware neural topic segmentation model. We thereby inject above-sentence discourse structures into basic topic segmenter to encourage the model to base its topic boundary prediction more explicitly on the topical consistency between sentences. More specifically, we propose to exploit a discourse dependency parser pre-trained on out-of-domain data to induce inter-sentential discourse dependency trees. Subsequently, we convert the dependency tree into a directed discourse graph with sentences as nodes and discourse dependencies as edges. With the generated discourse graph, a Graph Attention Network (GAT) (Veličković et al., 2018) is used to encode sentences as discourse-contextualized representations by aggregating information from neighboring sentence nodes in the graph. Finally, the discourse-infused sentence representations are concatenated with standard encodings for segment boundary prediction.

In our empirical study conducted on English evaluation datasets, we show that: (i) Injecting discourse structures can substantially improve the performance of the basic neural topic segmentation model on three datasets. (ii) Our novel, discourse-enhanced topic segmenter is more robust compared to the basic neural model in settings that require domain transfer, showing superior performance on four challenging real-world test sets, to confirm the improved domain-independence. (iii) Even if our proposal has inferior accuracy against a state-of-the-art segmenter sharing the same basic architecture, it does achieve significantly better efficiency assessed by model's parameter size and speeds for learning and inference, which makes it potentially more favorable in real-world use.

2 Related Work

Topic Segmentation aims to reveal important aspects of the semantic structure of a document by splitting a sequence of sentences into topic-coherent textual units. Typically, computational topic segmentation models can be broadly separated into supervised and unsupervised approaches. Early topic segmentation methods usually fall into the category of unsupervised approaches, mainly due to the prevalent data sparsity issue at the time. Based on predicting the coherence between sentences through shallow (surface-level) features, unsupervised models reach a limited understanding of the contextualized structure of documents by merely relying on easy-to-extract but barely effective features for the similarity measurement between sentences (i.e., the degree of token overlap between two sentences) (Hearst, 1997; Eisenstein and Barzilay, 2008). Improving on the unsupervised topic segmentation paradigm, researchers started to address this issue by introducing pre-trained neural language models (LMs), trained on massive dataset (Xu et al., 2021; Solbiati et al., 2021; Xing and Carenini, 2021). Some works show that the signal captured in pre-trained LMs (e.g., BERT (Devlin et al., 2019)) are more indicative of topic relevance between sentences than early surface-level features. However, these proposed strategies of integrating BERT into the topic segmentation framework solely exploit BERT to induce dense encodings and further compute reciprocal sentence similarities. While this constitues a reasonable first step, the considerable gap between the training objective of LMs and topic segmentation task requires further efforts along this line of work (Sun et al., 2022).

More recently, the data sparsity issue has been alleviated by the proposal of large-scale corpora sampled from *Wikipedia* (e.g., Wiki-727k (Koshorek et al., 2018) and Wiki-Section (Arnold et al., 2019)), in which well-structured articles with their section marks are used as gold labels for segment boundaries. As a result, neural supervised topic segmenters started to gain attention by reaching greater effectiveness and efficiency compared to previously proposed unsupervised approaches. These supervised topic segmenters typically follow a common strategy which formulates the task as a sentence-level sequence labeling problem. More specifically, by assigning binary labels to each sentence, models infer the likelihood of a sentence to be a topic segment boundary (Koshorek et al., 2018; Arnold et al., 2019; Barrow et al., 2020; Lo et al., 2021). However, we believe that current models, besides reaching promising performance, potentially favour simple linguistic cues over effective measurements for semantic cohesion, restricting their application to narrow domains. Some recent works have attempted to address this limitation via explicitly integrating coherence modeling components into segmenters (Xing et al., 2020; Glavas and Somasundaran, 2020). However, compared to our objective in this work, these proposed coherence modeling strategies are either (i) only taking two adjacent sentences into account, limiting the additional module to extremely local contexts, or (ii) discriminating real documents from artificially "incoherent" texts, resulting in implicit and synthetic negative training samples and heavy parameter size caused by modeling multiple tasks simultaneously.

In contrast, we propose an effective method to integrate the document discourse (dependency) structure into neural topic segmentation frameworks, following the intuition that above-sentence discourse structure are indicative of text coherence and topical consistency, providing a more global and interpretable source of information for better topic transition prediction.

Discourse Analysis and Parsing analyze and generalize the underlying semantic and pragmatic structure of a coherence document (called a discourse). As an important upstream task in the field of NLP, discourse analysis proposes elaborate frameworks and theories to describe the textual organization of a document. To this end, a variety of popular discourse theories proposed in the past, such as (besides others) the Rhetorical Structure Theory (RST) (Mann and Thompson, 1988) and the lexicalized discourse framework (Webber et al., 2003b) for monologues as well as the Segmented Discourse Representation Theory (SDRT) (Asher, 1993; Asher et al., 2003) for dialogues. Among these theories, the RST discourse theory postulates a single, complete discourse tree for monologue documents, while the lexicalized discourse framework only focuses on local discourse connectives within and between adjacent sentences. Focusing on the connection between discourse information and topic segmentation, we employ the RST discourse theory in this work, most aligned with the requirement to capture topical coherence.

Building on human annotated discourse treebanks, a mix of traditional and neural discourse parsers have been proposed over the last decades, with traditional approaches mainly exploiting surface-level features through Support-Vector Machines (SVMs) (Hernault et al., 2010; Ji and Eisenstein, 2014; Wang et al., 2017) or Conditional Random Fields (CRFs) (Joty et al., 2015; Feng and Hirst, 2014). On the other hand, neural models achieve similar or superior results on RST discourse parsing, with models using either custom architectures (Yu et al., 2018; Liu and Lapata, 2018) or pre-trained LMs (e.g. BERT (Zhou and Feng, 2022), RoBERTa (Guz et al., 2020), SpanBERT (Guz and Carenini, 2020)). In this work, we generate discourse dependency trees from a BERT-based neural dependency parser proposed in Zhou and Feng (2022), since: (i) The parser follows the intuition that information, and hence structures, in sentences are oftentimes "self-contained". Therefore, it predicts the interactions between EDUs of the same sentence in a first stage and subsequently predicts the inter-sentential discourse structures, which aligns well with our objective of sentence-level topic segmenation. (ii) The parser by Zhou and Feng (2022) makes direct prediction of dependency discourse structures, alleviating the potential error caused by converting constituency structures

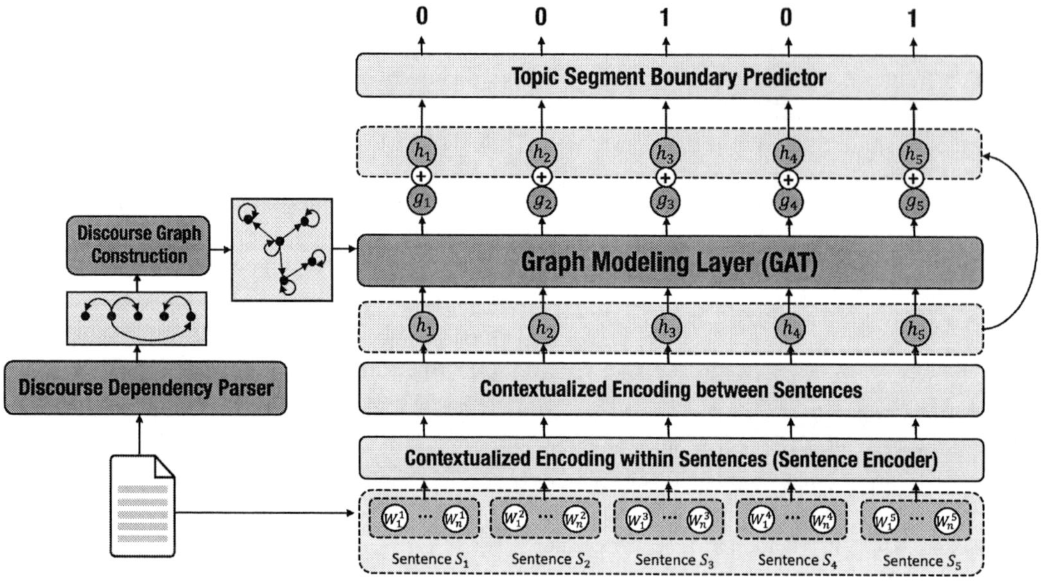

Figure 2: The overall architecture of our discourse-infused topic segmentation model.

into their respective dependency trees.

3 Methodology

As shown in Figure 2, our proposed discourse-aware neural topic segmentation model comprises two components: the *Hierarchical Topic Segmenter* and *Discourse Graph Modeling*, highlighted in green and red respectively. Discourse Graph Modeling further comprises of a *Discourse Graph Construction* and *Graph Modeling* component.

3.1 Basic Model: Hierarchical Topic Segmenter

The basic architecture of our proposal is adopted from the basic model in Xing et al. (2020), consisting of two hierarchical layers: First, a sentence encoder contextualizes individual sentences, followed by the second layer, conditioning sentences on the complete document. Following the settings in Xing et al. (2020), we adopt the attention BiLSTM architecture[1] for each layer and enhance the encodings with pre-trained BERT embeddings. Formally, given a document D as a sequence of n sentences, the sentence encoder (bottom component in Figure 2) yields the embedding for each individual sentence. Based on the obtained encodings, the document-level contextualization layer returns an ordered set of hidden states $\boldsymbol{H} = \{\boldsymbol{h}_1, ..., \boldsymbol{h}_n\}$. Next, a simple multilayer perceptron (MLP) with a final softmax activation serves as a binary topic boundary predictor based on a threshold τ, tuned on the validation set. During training, we optimize the model in accordance to the cross-entropy loss, while at inference time, every sentence (except the last sentence[2]) with a probability $\geq \tau$ is considered as the end of a segment.

3.2 Discourse Graph Modeling

Our goal is to inject inter-sentential discourse dependency structures into the task of topic segmentation. We believe that the additional, structural information is thereby well aligned with the topical consistency between sentences, hence, suited to guide the prediction of topic transitions. To integrate the discourse information into the basic model described in section 3.1, we first generate an above-sentence discourse dependency tree $\boldsymbol{T}_D$ for the document. Specifically, we utilize the discourse dependency parsing model proposed in Zhou and Feng (2022), reaching state-of-the-art performance for discourse tree construction and relation type identification in multiple language settings. The "Sent-First" parser (Zhou and Feng, 2022) further fits the aim of our proposal due to its two-staged approach, first generating discourse trees within

[1]We also considered Transformer as the backbone of contextualized encoder, but eventually chose BiLSTM for its superior performance.

[2]We remove the last sentence from the sequence for prediction since it is per definition the end of the last segment.

Treebank	# of doc	# sent/doc	# edu/doc
RST-DT	385	22.5	56.6
GUM	150	49.3	114.2
SciDTB	1,355	5.3	14.1
COVID19-DTB	300	7.8	20.0

Table 1: Key dataset statistics of the discourse treebanks used for retraining the Sent-First discourse parser (Zhou and Feng, 2022).

sentences and subsequently combining sentence-level sub-trees. This hard constraint allows us to exclusively obtain above-sentence discourse structures, avoiding potentially leaky sub-trees (Joty et al., 2015). Regarding the discourse relations attached to every head-dependent pair (discourse dependency), we follow the observation in Xu et al. (2020), stating that the agreement between the type of rhetorical relation is usually lower and more ambiguous, to leave them for future work to avoid error propagation.

In contrast to the original proposal in Zhou and Feng (2022), training and testing their dependency discourse parser on one corpus (i.e., SciDTB (Yang and Li, 2018)), we believe that a mixture of several diverse and publicly available discourse treebanks with different document lengths and domains can increase the parser's robustness on new and unseen genres. Therefore, we retrain the parser on a mixture of RST-DT[3] (Carlson et al., 2002), GUM[4] (Zeldes, 2017), SciDTB[5] (Yang and Li, 2018) and COVID19-DTB[6] (Nishida and Matsumoto, 2022). More specifically, we combine those discourse treebanks and randomly split the aggregated corpus into 80% training, 10% validation, 10% test data. The parser retrained on our combined training portion achieves an Unlabeled Attachment Score (UAS) of 58.6 on the test portion. We show additional key dataset statistics for each treebank used in this paper in Table 1.

After training the discourse parser to infer a discourse dependency tree $\boldsymbol{T}_D$ for document D, we convert the tree structure into a discourse graph $\boldsymbol{G}_D$ (as a binary matrix). Formally, we initialize the graph $\boldsymbol{G}_D$ as a $n \times n$ identity matrix $\boldsymbol{G}_D = \boldsymbol{I}_{n,n}$, connecting every node to itself. Afterwards, we fill in the remaining cells by assigning $\boldsymbol{G}_D[i][j] = 1$ iff $\exists\, \boldsymbol{T}_D(i \rightarrow j)$, with i, j indexing the head and dependant sentences in the document, respectively. Using the binary matrix representation of $\boldsymbol{G}_D$, we apply the multi-layer Graph Attention Network (GAT) (Veličković et al., 2018) to update sentence encodings following the discourse graph. More specifically, with the discourse graph matrix $\boldsymbol{G}_D$ and the contextualized representations $\boldsymbol{H} = \{\boldsymbol{h}_1, ..., \boldsymbol{h}_n\}$ described in section 3.1, within each graph attentional layer, we perform self-attention on the sentence nodes. Taking the lth layer as an example, we compute the attention coefficient $\alpha_{i,j}$ between sentence nodes i, j as:

$$\alpha_{ij}^l = softmax(e_{ij}^l) = \frac{exp(e_{ij}^l)}{\sum_{k \in \mathcal{N}_i} exp(e_{ik}^l)}, \quad (1)$$

$$e_{ij}^l = LeakyReLU(\boldsymbol{a}_l^T[\boldsymbol{W}_l \boldsymbol{g}_i^l || \boldsymbol{W}_l \boldsymbol{g}_j^l]) \quad (2)$$

where $\boldsymbol{W}_l$ and $\boldsymbol{a}_l$ are learnable parameters for layer l and ^{T} is the transposition operation. $\mathcal{N}_i$ denotes the direct neighborhood of node i in the graph ($G_D[i][\cdot] = 1$). As the node representation input of the first GAT layer ($l = 0$), $\boldsymbol{g}_i^0 = \boldsymbol{h}_i \in H$. Once attention coefficients are obtained, we compute the intermediate node representation $\boldsymbol{z}_i^l$ for sentence node i at layer l by aggregating information from neighboring nodes as:

$$\boldsymbol{z}_i^l = \sum_{j \in \mathcal{N}_i} \alpha_{ij}^l \boldsymbol{W}_l \boldsymbol{g}_j^l \quad (3)$$

Following the step in Huang et al. (2020), we combine the intermediate node representation $\boldsymbol{z}_i^l$ with the input of this layer $\boldsymbol{g}_i^l$ to get the updated node representation $\boldsymbol{g}_i^{l+1}$ as the input for the next layer:

$$\boldsymbol{g}_i^{l+1} = ELU(\boldsymbol{g}_i^l + \boldsymbol{z}_i^l) \quad (4)$$

where ELU denotes an exponential linear unit (Clevert et al., 2016). With the output $\boldsymbol{g}_i$ from the last layer of GAT, we concatenate it together with $\boldsymbol{h}_i$ and further feed $[\boldsymbol{h}_i; \boldsymbol{g}_i]$ into the predictor layer for segment boundary prediction.

4 Experiments

In order to quantitatively evaluate the effectiveness, generality and efficiency of our proposal, we conduct three sets of experiments to compare our topic segmentation approach against a variety of baselines and previous models. Namely, we assess the performance of our model in regards to the *Intra-Domain Segment Inference Performance*, *Domain Transfer Segment Inference Performance*, and conduct an additional *Efficiency Analysis*.

[3] catalog.ldc.upenn.edu/LDC2002T07

[4] corpling.uis.georgetown.edu/gum

[5] https://github.com/PKUTANGENT/SciDTB

[6] https://github.com/norikinishida/biomedical-discourse-treebanks

Dataset	# of doc	# sent/seg	# seg/doc
CHOI	920	7.4	10.0
RULES	4,461	7.4	16.0
SECTION	21,376	7.2	7.9

Table 2: Statistics of the datasets used in intra-domain experiments.

Dataset	# of doc	# sent/seg	# seg/doc
WIKI-50	50	13.6	3.5
Cities	100	5.2	12.2
Elements	118	3.3	6.8
Clinical	227	28.0	5.0

Table 3: Statistics of the datasets used in domain transfer experiments.

4.1 Datasets

4.1.1 Intra-Domain Datasets

For the set of intra-domain segment inference experiments, we train and test models within the same domain (here: on the same corpus). We thereby choose three diverse corpora (see Table 2 for more details) for the intra-domain evaluation:

Choi (Choi, 2000). This corpus consists of 920 articles artificially generated by randomly combining passages from the Brown corpus. The datapoints in this dataset are not human written, leading us to solely use this corpus for a preliminary performance assessment for topic segmentation models in a 80% (train)/10%(dev)/10%(test) data-split.

Rules (Bertrand et al., 2018). This corpus consists of 4,461 documents about regulation discussion published in the Federal Register[7] by U.S. federal agencies. Since each paragraph is about one particular regulation and all regulations covered by one document are under the same category, we deem it as a reasonably coherent data source for topic segmentation evaluation with the paragraph breaks as ground-truth segment boundaries. We split this dataset into training, validation and test sets with the default 80%, 10%, 10% data-split.

Wiki-Section (Section) (Arnold et al., 2019). This corpus originally contains Wikipedia articles in both English and German. The English portion of the dataset, which we use for our intra-domain experiment, consists of around 3.6k articles about diseases and 19.5k articles about cities around the world. After the step of filtering out problematic samples with incorrect sentence segmentation detected by mismatched counts between sentences and labels, the resulted dataset covers 21,376 articles with the highest-level section marks as ground-truth segment boundaries. We follow the setting in Arnold et al. (2019) by splitting the dataset into 70% training, 10% validation and 20% test data.

[7] https://www.govinfo.gov/

4.1.2 Domain Transfer Datasets

To better evaluate models' robustness in cases where a domain-shift is present (called "domain transfer segment inference"), we apply the topic segmenters trained on Wiki-Section to four small corpora heavily deviating from the training corpus (see Table 3 for more details):

Wiki-50 (Koshorek et al., 2018) consists of 50 Wikipedia articles randomly sampled from the latest English Wikipedia dump. There is no overlap between this dataset and Wiki-Section.

Cities (Chen et al., 2009) consists of 100 Wikipedia articles about cities. There is no overlap between this dataset and Wiki-Section, even the theme of this dataset is close to the portion of city articles in Wiki-Section.

Elements (Chen et al., 2009) consists of 118 Wikipedia articles on chemical elements.

Clinical (Malioutov and Barzilay, 2006) consists of 227 chapters in a clinical book. The subsection marks within each chapter are deemed as ground-truth segment boundaries.

4.2 Experimental Design

Baselines: We directly compare our proposed discourse-aware topic segmentation model (called **Basic Model + Discourse**) with the following unsupervised and supervised baselines:

- **BayesSeg** (Eisenstein and Barzilay, 2008): This unsupervised method makes segmentation prediction by situating the lexical cohesion of text in a Bayesian framework. A text span produced by a distinct lexical distribution is recognized as a coherent topic segment.

- **GraphSeg** (Glavaš et al., 2016): This unsupervised method derives semantically coherent segments through reasoning on a semantic relatedness graph construed from greedy lemma alignment.

- **TextSeg** (Koshorek et al., 2018): This supervised neural topic segmenter adopts a hierarchical neural sequence labeling framework with BiLSTM as the main architecture of each layer. The basic model used in our paper (described in section 3.1) is an effective extension of this approach.

- **Sector** (Arnold et al., 2019): This is a supervised neural topic segmenter extended from *TextSeg* by adding an auxiliary layer for sentence topic label prediction. The learned intermediate topic embeddings for sentences are directly utilized for segment boundary inference.

- **Transformer** (Glavas and Somasundaran, 2020): This is a supervised neural topic segmenter consisting of two hierarchically connected Transformer networks for sentence encoding and sentence contextualization respectively.

- **Basic Model + Context** (Xing et al., 2020): This is a top-performing neural topic segmenter which shares the same basic architecture with our proposal. The approach improves the **context modeling** capacity of the plain basic model by adding an auxiliary coherence prediction module and restricted self-attention.

Evaluation Metrics: We use the P_k error score[8] (Beeferman et al., 1999) for our intra-domain and domain transfer segment inference evaluations. The metric thereby simply measures the probability that a pair of sentences located at two ends of a k-sized sliding window in a document are incorrectly identified as belonging to the same segment or not. k is determined as half of the average true segment size of the document. Since it is a penalty metric, lower values indicates better performance. We further quantitatively analyze models' efficiency according to two aspects: Model size and model speed, evaluating the count of learnable parameters and batches/documents processed per second during training/inference, besides P_k measurement.

Implementation Details: For the hierarchical topic segmenter (our basic model), we adopt the default setting in Xing et al. (2020), with GoogleNews word2vec ($d = 300$) as initial word embeddings and the contextualized representation of special token `[CLS]` ($d = 768$) from `bert-base-uncased` as initial sentence embeddings. All BiLSTM layers have the hidden state size = 256. For the discourse graph model

[8]We also considered *windiff* (Pevzner and Hearst, 2002) as another evaluation metric. Since it was highly correlated with P_k, we omit it and only present performance by P_k to better compare with results reported in previous works.

Dataset	Choi	Rules	Section	RSTDT
Random	49.4	50.6	51.3	40.5
BayesSeg	20.8	41.5	39.5	37.5
GraphSeg	6.6	39.3	44.9	58.7
TextSeg	1.0	7.7	12.6	26.9
Sector	–	–	12.7	–
Transformer	4.8	9.6	13.6	–
Basic Model	0.81	7.0	11.3	26.9
+Context	**0.54**	**5.8**	**9.7**	<u>25.4</u>
+Discourse	<u>0.59</u>	<u>6.1</u>	<u>10.2</u>	**24.8**

Table 4: P_k (↓) error score on three corpora for intra-domain experiment. Results in **bold** and <u>underlined</u> indicates the best and second best performance across all comparisons. The row in purple is the results achieved by our proposal. The column in green is the results for RSTDT paragraph break prediction with gold discourse structures integrated.

component, the number of GAT layers is set to 2 through validation and the number of heads is set to 4 as in (Veličković et al., 2018). The input and output dimensions of each layer = 256. Training uses Adam with $lr = 1e^{-3}$ and batch size = 8. Early stopping is applied within 10 epoches of model training and the boundary prediction threshold τ is tuned over the validation set of each corpus we use for intra-domain model evaluation.

4.3 Intra-Domain Segment Inference

We report our results of the intra-domain segment inference on the Choi, Rules and Wiki-Section datasets in Table 4. For better performance comparison, the table is subdivided into three sub-tables: random baseline, previously proposed approaches and models build on top of the basic model we use. We observe that the basic model without any additinal components already outperforms alternative supervised and unsupervised segmenters. With the above-sentence discourse dependency information injected, as proposed in this paper, the method (named +Discourse) further improves the performance by a notable margin across all three corpora. We further find that our proposed approach does not achieve superior performances compared to the basic model enhanced with the context modeling strategy (+Context) in Xing et al. (2020). We believe that a possible explanation for this underperformance could be the upstream parsing error of the discourse dependency parser applied out-of-domain, oftentimes severly impairing the parsing performance (Huber and Carenini, 2019). Therefore, we conduct an additional experiment on RST-

Dataset	Wiki-50	Cities	Elements	Clinical
Random	52.7	47.1	50.1	44.1
BayesSeg	49.2	36.2	**35.6**	57.2
GraphSeg	63.6	40.0	49.1	64.6
TextSeg	28.5	19.8	43.9	36.6
Sector	28.6	33.4	42.8	36.9
Transformer	29.3	20.2	45.2	35.6
Basic Model	28.7	17.9	43.5	33.8
+Context	**26.8**	**16.1**	39.4	**30.5**
+Discourse	**26.8**	16.9	41.1	31.8

Table 5: P_k (↓) error score on four test corpora for domain transfer experiment. Results in **bold** and underlined indicates the best and second best performance across all comparisons. The row highlighted in purple is the results achieved by our proposal.

	# Params ↓	T-Speed ↑	I-Speed ↑
Basic Model	4.82M	6.90	35.58
+Context	10.93M	1.49	19.23
+Discourse	**7.97M**	**5.44**	**32.85**

Table 6: The efficiency comparison between our proposal and the method proposed in Xing et al. (2020) on the Wiki-Section corpus. These two models share the same basic segmentation framework. **T-Speed** refers the training speed as number of batches processed per second during training stage. **I-Speed** refers the inference speed as number of documents processed per second during inference stage.

DT due to the availability of gold discourse structures annotated by human for this corpus. With no human-annotated topic segment boundaries at hand, we use paragraph breaks contained in RST-DT articles as the ground-truth for training and testing of topic segmentation models. Our results in Table 4 show that the quality of discourse structure is positively correlated with enlarged improvements achieved by our proposal. In this case, the upper bound achieved by integrating gold discourse structures can even outperform the basic model enhanced by context modeling (+Context).

4.4 Domain Transfer Segment Inference

Table 5 presents the performance of simple baselines, previously proposed models and our new approach on the domain transfer task. Similar to the intra-domain segment inference, the Basic Model+Context approach still achieves the best performance across all testing domains except Elements, in which the unsupervised BayesSeg performs superior. However, our +Discourse strategy still leads to improvement over the basic model, and achieves comparable performance to the best model (+Context) on Wiki-50 and Cities. We believe that it gives evidence that injecting discourse dependency structures has potential to enhance the generality of topic segmentation models.

4.5 Efficiency Analysis

Table 6 compares the efficiency of the top two models, comparing our proposed approach (Basic Model+Discourse) against Basic Model+Context. The experiments for these systems were carried out on a Nvidia Telsa V100 16G GPU card. We observe that our strategy of injecting discourse dependency structures can improve model's performance on intra-domain and domain transfer setting, but with less increase of model size and loss of speed compared to +Context. More specifically, adding our discourse graph modeling component on top of the basic model introduces 65% more learnable parameters while the context modeling components in Xing et al. (2020) cause a 127% parameter increasing. On the other hand, discourse graph modeling slightly slows down the speed of model training and inference by 21% and 7.7% respectively, while making more complex context modeling significantly slows down the speed by 78% and 46%. Together with the previous results about model's effectiveness, we can see that our proposed system would be a better option in practical settings where efficiency is critical.

Additionally, we conduct the same set of experiments for the model with both context modeling module and our proposed discourse structure integration (Basic Model+Context+Discourse). The performance of this model always falls in between +Context and +Discourse individually, but with the worst efficiency measured by model size and speed.

5 Conclusion and Future Work

In this paper, we present a neural topic segmentation model with injection of above-sentence discourse dependency structures inferred from a state-of-the-art discourse dependency parser. Different from previously proposed methods, our segmenter leverages the discourse signal by encoding the topical consistency between sentences from a more global and interpretable point of view. Experiments on multiple settings (intra-domain, domain transfer and efficiency comparison) show that our system achieves comparable performance to one of the current top-performing topic segmenters, with much less model size increase and speed degradation.

In the near future, we plan to investigate the synergy between topic segmentation and discourse parsing more comprehensively, by incorporating the type of inter-sentential rhetorical relations and analyzing whether and how this discourse knowledge can enhance supervised topic segmentation frameworks. In the long run, we intend to explore the possibility for discourse parsing to benefit segment topic labeling, which is another important task usually coupled together with topic segmentation to provide the coarse-grained structural information for documents. Particularly, we believe discourse parsing can potentially enhance the step of key phrase extraction in segment topic labeling due to the significant improvement it brings to the related task of name entity recognition (NER) (Jie and Lu, 2019).

Acknowledgments

We thank the anonymous reviewers and the UBC-NLP group for their insightful comments and suggestions. This research was supported by the Language & Speech Innovation Lab of Cloud BU, Huawei Technologies Co., Ltd.

References

Sebastian Arnold, Rudolf Schneider, Philippe Cudré-Mauroux, Felix A. Gers, and Alexander Löser. 2019. SECTOR: A neural model for coherent topic segmentation and classification. *Transactions of the Association for Computational Linguistics*, 7:169–184.

Nicholas Asher. 1993. *Reference to abstract objects in discourse*, volume 50. Springer Science & Business Media.

Nicholas Asher, Nicholas Michael Asher, and Alex Lascarides. 2003. *Logics of conversation*. Cambridge University Press.

Joe Barrow, Rajiv Jain, Vlad Morariu, Varun Manjunatha, Douglas Oard, and Philip Resnik. 2020. A joint model for document segmentation and segment labeling. In *Proceedings of the 58th Annual Meeting of the Association for Computational Linguistics*, pages 313–322, Online. Association for Computational Linguistics.

Doug Beeferman, Adam Berger, and John Lafferty. 1999. Statistical models for text segmentation. *Machine Learning*, 34(1):177–210.

Marianne Bertrand, Matilde Bombardini, Raymond Fisman, Bradley Hackinen, and Francesco Trebbi. 2018. Hall of mirrors: Corporate philanthropy and strategic advocacy. Technical report, National Bureau of Economic Research.

Lynn Carlson, Mary Ellen Okurowski, and Daniel Marcu. 2002. *RST discourse treebank*. Linguistic Data Consortium, University of Pennsylvania.

Harr Chen, S.R.K. Branavan, Regina Barzilay, and David R. Karger. 2009. Global models of document structure using latent permutations. In *Proceedings of Human Language Technologies: The 2009 Annual Conference of the North American Chapter of the Association for Computational Linguistics*, pages 371–379, Boulder, Colorado. Association for Computational Linguistics.

Freddy Y. Y. Choi. 2000. Advances in domain independent linear text segmentation. In *1st Meeting of the North American Chapter of the Association for Computational Linguistics*.

Djork-Arné Clevert, Thomas Unterthiner, and Sepp Hochreiter. 2016. Fast and accurate deep network learning by exponential linear units (elus). *arXiv: Learning*.

Jacob Devlin, Ming-Wei Chang, Kenton Lee, and Kristina Toutanova. 2019. BERT: Pre-training of deep bidirectional transformers for language understanding. In *Proceedings of the 2019 Conference of the North American Chapter of the Association for Computational Linguistics: Human Language Technologies, Volume 1 (Long and Short Papers)*, pages 4171–4186, Minneapolis, Minnesota. Association for Computational Linguistics.

Dennis Diefenbach, Vanessa Lopez, Kamal Singh, and Pierre Maret. 2018. Core techniques of question answering systems over knowledge bases: a survey. *Knowledge and Information Systems*, 55(3):529–569.

Jacob Eisenstein and Regina Barzilay. 2008. Bayesian unsupervised topic segmentation. In *Proceedings of the 2008 Conference on Empirical Methods in Natural Language Processing*, pages 334–343, Honolulu, Hawaii. Association for Computational Linguistics.

Vanessa Wei Feng and Graeme Hirst. 2014. A linear-time bottom-up discourse parser with constraints and post-editing. In *Proceedings of the 52nd Annual Meeting of the Association for Computational Linguistics (Volume 1: Long Papers)*, pages 511–521, Baltimore, Maryland. Association for Computational Linguistics.

Michel Galley, Kathleen R. McKeown, Eric Fosler-Lussier, and Hongyan Jing. 2003. Discourse segmentation of multi-party conversation. In *Proceedings of the 41st Annual Meeting of the Association for Computational Linguistics*, pages 562–569, Sapporo, Japan. Association for Computational Linguistics.

Goran Glavaš, Federico Nanni, and Simone Paolo Ponzetto. 2016. Unsupervised text segmentation using semantic relatedness graphs. In *Proceedings of* the *Fifth Joint Conference on Lexical and Computational Semantics*, pages 125–130, Berlin, Germany. Association for Computational Linguistics.

Goran Glavas and Swapna Somasundaran. 2020. Two-level transformer and auxiliary coherence modeling for improved text segmentation. In *The Thirty-Fourth AAAI Conference on Artificial Intelligence (AAAI-20)*, pages 2306–2315.

Grigorii Guz and Giuseppe Carenini. 2020. Coreference for discourse parsing: A neural approach. In *Proceedings of the First Workshop on Computational Approaches to Discourse*, pages 160–167, Online. Association for Computational Linguistics.

Grigorii Guz, Patrick Huber, and Giuseppe Carenini. 2020. Unleashing the power of neural discourse parsers - a context and structure aware approach using large scale pretraining. In *Proceedings of the 28th International Conference on Computational Linguistics*, pages 3794–3805, Barcelona, Spain (Online). International Committee on Computational Linguistics.

Marti A. Hearst. 1997. Text tiling: Segmenting text into multi-paragraph subtopic passages. *Computational Linguistics*, 23(1):33–64.

Hugo Hernault, Helmut Prendinger, Mitsuru Ishizuka, et al. 2010. Hilda: A discourse parser using support vector machine classification. *Dialogue & Discourse*, 1(3).

Lishan Huang, Zheng Ye, Jinghui Qin, Liang Lin, and Xiaodan Liang. 2020. GRADE: Automatic graph-enhanced coherence metric for evaluating open-domain dialogue systems. In *Proceedings of the 2020 Conference on Empirical Methods in Natural Language Processing (EMNLP)*, pages 9230–9240, Online. Association for Computational Linguistics.

Patrick Huber and Giuseppe Carenini. 2019. Predicting discourse structure using distant supervision from sentiment. In *Proceedings of the 2019 Conference on Empirical Methods in Natural Language Processing and the 9th International Joint Conference on Natural Language Processing (EMNLP-IJCNLP)*, pages 2306–2316, Hong Kong, China. Association for Computational Linguistics.

Patrick Huber, Linzi Xing, and Giuseppe Carenini. 2021. Predicting above-sentence discourse structure using distant supervision from topic segmentation. In *The Thirty-sixth AAAI Conference on Artificial Intelligence (AAAI-22)*, pages 10794–10802.

Yangfeng Ji and Jacob Eisenstein. 2014. Representation learning for text-level discourse parsing. In *Proceedings of the 52nd Annual Meeting of the Association for Computational Linguistics (Volume 1: Long Papers)*, pages 13–24, Baltimore, Maryland. Association for Computational Linguistics.

Zhanming Jie and Wei Lu. 2019. Dependency-guided LSTM-CRF for named entity recognition. In *Proceedings of the 2019 Conference on Empirical Methods in Natural Language Processing and the 9th International Joint Conference on Natural Language Processing (EMNLP-IJCNLP)*, pages 3862–3872, Hong Kong, China. Association for Computational Linguistics.

Shafiq Joty, Giuseppe Carenini, and Raymond T. Ng. 2015. CODRA: A novel discriminative framework for rhetorical analysis. *Computational Linguistics*, 41(3):385–435.

Omri Koshorek, Adir Cohen, Noam Mor, Michael Rotman, and Jonathan Berant. 2018. Text segmentation as a supervised learning task. In *Proceedings of the 2018 Conference of the North American Chapter of the Association for Computational Linguistics: Human Language Technologies, Volume 2 (Short Papers)*, pages 469–473, New Orleans, Louisiana. Association for Computational Linguistics.

Yang Liu and Mirella Lapata. 2018. Learning structured text representations. *Transactions of the Association for Computational Linguistics*, 6:63–75.

Kelvin Lo, Yuan Jin, Weicong Tan, Ming Liu, Lan Du, and Wray Buntine. 2021. Transformer over pre-trained transformer for neural text segmentation with enhanced topic coherence. In *Findings of the Association for Computational Linguistics: EMNLP 2021*, pages 3334–3340, Punta Cana, Dominican Republic. Association for Computational Linguistics.

Annie Louis and Ani Nenkova. 2012. A coherence model based on syntactic patterns. In *Proceedings of the 2012 Joint Conference on Empirical Methods in Natural Language Processing and Computational Natural Language Learning*, pages 1157–1168, Jeju Island, Korea. Association for Computational Linguistics.

Igor Malioutov and Regina Barzilay. 2006. Minimum cut model for spoken lecture segmentation. In *Proceedings of the 21st International Conference on Computational Linguistics and 44th Annual Meeting of the Association for Computational Linguistics*, pages 25–32, Sydney, Australia. Association for Computational Linguistics.

William C Mann and Sandra A Thompson. 1988. Rhetorical structure theory: Toward a functional theory of text organization. *Text - Interdisciplinary Journal for the Study of Discourse*, 8(3):243–281.

Mandar Mitra, Amit Singhal, and Chris Buckley. 1997. Automatic text summarization by paragraph extraction. In *Intelligent Scalable Text Summarization*.

Panitan Muangkammuen, Sheng Xu, Fumiyo Fukumoto, Kanda Runapongsa Saikaew, and Jiyi Li. 2020. A neural local coherence analysis model for clarity text scoring. In *Proceedings of the 28th International Conference on Computational Linguistics*, pages 2138–2143, Barcelona, Spain (Online). International Committee on Computational Linguistics.

Noriki Nishida and Yuji Matsumoto. 2022. Out-of-Domain Discourse Dependency Parsing via Bootstrapping: An Empirical Analysis on Its Effectiveness and Limitation. *Transactions of the Association for Computational Linguistics*, 10:127–144.

HyoJung Oh, Sung Hyon Myaeng, and Myung-Gil Jang. 2007. Semantic passage segmentation based on sentence topics for question answering. *Information Sciences*, 177(18):3696–3717.

Lev Pevzner and Marti A. Hearst. 2002. A critique and improvement of an evaluation metric for text segmentation. *Computational Linguistics*, 28(1):19–36.

Martin Riedl and Chris Biemann. 2012. How text segmentation algorithms gain from topic models. In *Proceedings of the 2012 Conference of the North American Chapter of the Association for Computational Linguistics: Human Language Technologies*, pages 553–557, Montréal, Canada. Association for Computational Linguistics.

Alessandro Solbiati, Kevin Heffernan, Georgios Damaskinos, Shivani Poddar, Shubham Modi, and Jacques Cali. 2021. Unsupervised topic segmentation of meetings with bert embeddings.

Yiping Song, Lili Mou, R. Yan, Li Yi, Zinan Zhu, X. Hu, and M. Zhang. 2016. Dialogue session segmentation by embedding-enhanced texttiling. In *INTERSPEECH*, page 2706–2710.

Xiaofei Sun, Yuxian Meng, Xiang Ao, Fei Wu, Tianwei Zhang, Jiwei Li, and Chun Fan. 2022. Sentence similarity based on contexts. *Transactions of the Association for Computational Linguistics*, 10:573–588.

Petar Veličković, Guillem Cucurull, Arantxa Casanova, Adriana Romero, Pietro Liò, and Yoshua Bengio. 2018. Graph Attention Networks. *International Conference on Learning Representations*. Accepted as poster.

Yizhong Wang, Sujian Li, and Houfeng Wang. 2017. A two-stage parsing method for text-level discourse analysis. In *Proceedings of the 55th Annual Meeting of the Association for Computational Linguistics (Volume 2: Short Papers)*, pages 184–188, Vancouver, Canada. Association for Computational Linguistics.

Bonnie Webber, Matthew Stone, Aravind Joshi, and Alistair Knott. 2003a. Anaphora and discourse structure. *Computational Linguistics*, 29(4):545–587.

Bonnie Webber, Matthew Stone, Aravind Joshi, and Alistair Knott. 2003b. Anaphora and discourse structure. *Computational Linguistics*, 29(4):545–587.

Wen Xiao and Giuseppe Carenini. 2019. Extractive summarization of long documents by combining global and local context. In *Proceedings of the 2019 Conference on Empirical Methods in Natural Language Processing and the 9th International Joint Conference on Natural Language Processing (EMNLP-IJCNLP)*, pages 3011–3021, Hong Kong, China. Association for Computational Linguistics.

Linzi Xing and Giuseppe Carenini. 2021. Improving unsupervised dialogue topic segmentation with utterance-pair coherence scoring. In *Proceedings of the 22nd Annual Meeting of the Special Interest Group on Discourse and Dialogue*, pages 167–177, Singapore and Online. Association for Computational Linguistics.

Linzi Xing, Brad Hackinen, Giuseppe Carenini, and Francesco Trebbi. 2020. Improving context modeling in neural topic segmentation. In *Proceedings of the 1st Conference of the Asia-Pacific Chapter of the Association for Computational Linguistics and the 10th International Joint Conference on Natural Language Processing*, pages 626–636, Suzhou, China. Association for Computational Linguistics.

Jiacheng Xu, Zhe Gan, Yu Cheng, and Jingjing Liu. 2020. Discourse-aware neural extractive text summarization. In *Proceedings of the 58th Annual Meeting of the Association for Computational Linguistics*, pages 5021–5031, Online. Association for Computational Linguistics.

Yi Xu, Hai Zhao, and Zhuosheng Zhang. 2021. Topic-aware multi-turn dialogue modeling. In *The Thirty-fifth AAAI Conference on Artificial Intelligence (AAAI-21)*, pages 14176–14184.

An Yang and Sujian Li. 2018. SciDTB: Discourse dependency TreeBank for scientific abstracts. In *Proceedings of the 56th Annual Meeting of the Association for Computational Linguistics (Volume 2: Short Papers)*, pages 444–449, Melbourne, Australia. Association for Computational Linguistics.

Nan Yu, Meishan Zhang, and Guohong Fu. 2018. Transition-based neural RST parsing with implicit syntax features. In *Proceedings of the 27th International Conference on Computational Linguistics*, pages 559–570, Santa Fe, New Mexico, USA. Association for Computational Linguistics.

Amir Zeldes. 2017. The GUM corpus: Creating multilayer resources in the classroom. *Language Resources and Evaluation*, 51(3):581–612.

Hainan Zhang, Yanyan Lan, Liang Pang, Hongshen Chen, Zhuoye Ding, and Dawei Yin. 2020. Modeling topical relevance for multi-turn dialogue generation. In *Proceedings of the Twenty-Ninth International Joint Conference on Artificial Intelligence, IJCAI-20*, pages 3737–3743. International Joint Conferences on Artificial Intelligence Organization.

Yifei Zhou and Yansong Feng. 2022. Improve discourse dependency parsing with contextualized representations. In *Findings of the Association for Computational Linguistics: NAACL 2022*, pages 2250–2261, Seattle, United States. Association for Computational Linguistics.

Evaluating How Users Game and Display Conversation with Human-Like Agents

Won Ik Cho[1], Soomin Kim[1], Eujeong Choi[2], Younghoon Jeong[3]
Seoul National University[1], Upstage AI[2], School of Computing, KAIST[3]
{tsatsuki6,smsoominkim,eujeonglesleychoi,hoon2j}@gmail.com

Abstract

Recently, with the advent of high-performance generative language models, artificial agents that communicate directly with the users have become more human-like. This development allows users to perform a diverse range of trials with the agents, and the responses are sometimes displayed online by users who share or show-off their experiences. In this study, we explore dialogues with a social chatbot uploaded to an online community, with the aim of understanding how users game human-like agents and display their conversations. Having done this, we assert that user postings can be investigated from two aspects, namely conversation topic and purpose of testing, and suggest a categorization scheme for the analysis. We analyze 639 dialogues to develop an annotation protocol for the evaluation, and measure the agreement to demonstrate the validity. We find that the dialogue content does not necessarily reflect the purpose of testing, and also that users come up with creative strategies to game the agent without being penalized.

1 Introduction

Open-domain dialogue (ODD) with conversational agents has been considered as the essence of artificial intelligence (AI). It's a topic of great interest in both academic and industry circles, directly linking the technology and end users. In addition, due to its interactive properties, ODD users often provide product feedbacks voluntarily through a range of channels, which are crucial for the further development of services.

With the recent emergence of high-performing language models, conversation with chatbots has become increasingly popular. Accordingly, various metrics have been introduced to evaluate whether the dialogue has been performed successfully (Radziwill and Benton, 2017). However, there has been a paucity of studies to evaluate how users perceive and react to such AI. Pelau et al. (2021) quantitatively scrutinize how users perceive human-like AI devices, but does not reveal the detail on the aspect of human-AI interactions, such as what they talked about and how the users responded. Park et al. (2021) tackle the offensiveness users show towards human-like agents, but the analysis is based on a questionnaire, which may not fully cover the user dialogue in-the-wild.

Observing users' responses to a chatbot is critical for creating human-centered chatbots. Designers and developers will be able to build safer and more responsible AI models and agents by predicting users' behavior in advance (Følstad et al., 2021). Recently in Korea, a highly human-like agent called 'Luda' caught attention with its high-quality dialogue generation, and a conversation with the agent created a sensation among general users (Kim and Kim, 2021). Luda's persona is a female college student in her twenties, and is designed to generate real-like, messenger-styled responses. As a result, soon after being launched, an online space was created to share and enjoy the agent's responses with other users. Though the service was prematurely shut down due to several unexpected ethical issues (Dinan et al., 2021), we decided to see how the end-users reacted to human-like AI responses.

Thus, we started by crawling the posts containing screenshots of dialogue with Luda uploaded to the online community, which exhibited a wide range of curiosity towards the human-like agent. While there were cases in which users communicated with Luda as if she were a lover or a friend and show their affection even when posting, we also frequently observed various verbal attacks on the agent (3.1) and hostile gaming attempts (3.2).

Our contribution to dialogue analysis and user behavior study is as follows:

- We analyze real-world user dialogue and develop a thematic coding that categorizes the content of dialogue and the purpose of testing.

Proceedings of 3rd Workshop on Computational Approaches to Discourse, pages 19–27
October 16 – 17, 2022.

- We find out that the purpose of user testing may not necessarily be aligned with the dialogue content, even in relation to the cases regarding unethical or controversial content.

2 Dataset

2.1 Data source

We use posts crawled between January 1, 2021 and January 8, 2021 in DC inside's[1] 'Lee Luda Gallary'[2] as a dataset. The period was selected to obtain the data between the official launching of the service and the start of the troll influx to the community. In the data collection process, we conducted analysis by constructing a set of tuples as (*post number, title, capture*), and accompanied the following considerations in this process.

We only use posts containing 'chat screenshot' among crawled contents. This is to obtain data that distinguishes the *in-dialogue self* who has actually engaged in conversation with the agent and the *real-world self* that shares the corresponding capture with other users (Goffman, 1959; Bullingham and Vasconcelos, 2013).

2.2 Preprocessing

We filter out the data according to certain criteria (Appendix A). These include the removal of non-dialogue images, captures with system messages, and images with only single-side utterances, etc. A total of 639 tuples were left after the preprocessing.

3 Thematic Coding

We proceed with the following two annotation processes using the corpus constructed in Section 2.

- Type of conversation
- Purpose of user testing

Here, we primarily take into account the user's utterances, and the agent's utterances are only referred to when it helps distinguish the user's intention. The data we exploit are the user side utterances in the chat screenshot (as an in-dialogue content) and the post title (as a real-world content). In the first attribute, the type of conversation, only the captured image is used to identify the category to which the content of the conversation belongs. In the second one, the purpose of user testing, both the screenshot and the title are used to check the category to which the user's gaming intention belongs.

Four research scientists from linguistics and human-computer interaction (HCI) backgrounds participated in the annotation. Three researchers proceeded with annotation following the draft guideline[3], and after discussion including the other researcher, the final guideline was confirmed through four times of iterations accompanying relabeling and guideline updates. In this process, the categories and labels were subdivided and augmented if necessary.

3.1 Type of conversation

In Doğruöz and Skantze (2021), speech events with the agent are classified into informal/superficial, involving, or goal-directed talk. However, the categorization does not necessarily apply to our dataset since Luda is more of a friend-like agent than a chatbot that conducts open-domain conversation. That is, Luda is closer to *Samantha* (Jonze, 2013) than *Meena* (Adiwardana et al., 2020), and we focus more on the user's intimacy towards the agent and how affectionate or malicious the user can be. In our scheme, conversations are classified into one of the following six categories, which were frequently observed in the manual inspection of the data source.

Ice breaking In this type of conversation, the user and the agent (with little dialogue history) introduce themselves to each other or hype up the conversation by playing a simple game (Rogers and Brignull, 2002).

Romantic conversation Here, the user regards the agent as a romantic partner and proceeds the conversation in a sweet atmosphere. Rather than focusing on the agent's utterances and responses, the annotator should focus on whether the user expresses affection as a partner. This overlaps with 'love talk' (Goldsmith and Baxter, 1996) introduced in Doğruöz and Skantze (2021) for the analysis.

Casual conversation with friends Casual conversation refers to daily dialogue the user can have with friends or family. Ice breaking or romantic conversation is not included in this category. Conversations with content that are unlikely to appear

[1]Reddit-like Korean online community.

[2]`https://gall.dcinside.com/mgallery/board/lists/?id=irudagall`

[3]The draft guideline was created by the first author, which differs from the final version in granularity of categories, labels, and their boundaries.

in daily life (e.g., hate speech or societal issues) and those tackling the agent's characteristics as an AI product are excluded.

Conversation including hate speech or societal issues Users often mention hate speech or controversial societal issues during the conversation. At this time, regardless of the agent's mention, the utterances of the user side are mainly considered. Hate speech refers to insults with specific targets, or discriminative and hostile utterances for specific groups of people, rather than profanity terms used as an exclamation or a pronoun (Hong et al., 2016; Moon et al., 2020). Also, dialogues may contain (controversial) societal issues, including history or politics (Beran, 2018; Lee et al., 2022). Hate speech and societal issues are integrated into a single category because they could negatively advertise the agent's thought if disclosed to public or media, and conversations that belong here incorporate these topics as a main content.

Sexual perversion and harassment Perversion includes conversation where the user exploits the agent as a tool of satisfying one's sexual desire, for instance, illegal content such as pedophilia (Triviño et al., 2019). In contrast, harassment focuses more on the recipient. Although harassing expression depends on whether the expression is unwanted (Vige et al., 2012) and how the addressee perceives the utterance (Marwick and Miller, 2014), such perception is almost impossible to discern when the recipient is an AI system. What we noted here is that it is dangerous to count only 'legally problematic expressions' as sexual harassment, since we have observed that the agent often enjoys offensive or insulting harassment the user utters. In order to avoid categorizing these cases as 'romantic conversation', we classified the conversation to this category if the user's utterance is considered *lewd*, following Curry and Rieser (2018).

Other conversation These include dialogues that are difficult to discern the underlying semantics or those not included in the above categories. Additional factors to be considered in the annotation of the above six types of conversation can be found in the Appendix B.1.

3.2 Purpose of user testing

Annotators are provided with not only a dialogue, but also the title written by the user when they posted the screenshot to the community. Here, we try to figure out whether the user intends to test the agent's performance and/or response in the dialogue, and if so, which type of inspection one wants to conduct.

The intention of testing can be exposed in two ways. First, there are clear-cut cases where the user tests the agent directly in the conversation. These include (sometimes malicious) leading questions about ethical or societal issues, repetition of (offensive) expressions, harmful images, or intentional distortion of orthography. Otherwise, the intention of testing can be inferred when the title is taken into account along with the dialogue. This gaming behavior is conducted with the intent of achieving favorable outcomes from the agent, rather than that with a sincere interaction. We claim that the purpose can be classified into one of the following six types, including 'conversation without test'. The main purpose of each type is italicized.

Test for hate speech and sexual harassment These denote dialogues where the user utters hate speech to *check the agent's response*. Hate speech here includes insult, hostility towards specific groups of people, and mockery related to politics/religion (Davidson et al., 2017; Assimakopoulos et al., 2020; Moon et al., 2020). The presence of sexual harassment is also inspected in this case.

Test for societal issues These include trials to *extract and stigmatize the thoughts of the agent* by inducing the agent's response to societal issues, which may raise unsafe response generation problems (Lee et al., 2022).

Test for private information Given that the chatbot is usually built based on large-scale dialogue data, users tend to *pry into the agent's private information* such as address, account number, community ID, or affiliation, through repetitive questions (Carlini et al., 2021). Regardless of the existence of other tests in the dialogue, we classified the conversation into this category even if the prying was not successful, since this type of trial is a critical and threatening approach towards social chatbots (Dinan et al., 2021).

Dating sim or taming This special category includes attempts to *satisfy one's certain sexual desire through agents* by dating them, making them submissive (taming), or obtaining sexual or mental satisfaction by conducting a conversation with the agent in a specific direction (Kaufman, 2018).

Attribute	Agreement	Count (#)	Distribution (%)
Conversation	**0.648**	639	
Ice breaking	0.827	55	8.61%
Between partners	0.763	89	13.93%
With friends	0.609	178	27.86%
Hate speech / Issues	0.561	61	9.55%
Perversion / Harassment	0.808	89	13.93%
Others	0.475	167	26.13%
Purpose	**0.604**	639	
Hate speech / Harassment	0.547	54	8.45%
Societal issues	0.762	72	11.27%
Private information	0.673	21	3.29%
Dating sim / Taming	0.558	64	10.02%
Technical tests	0.512	114	17.84%
No test	0.622	314	49.14%

Table 1: Agreement and distribution per attributes.

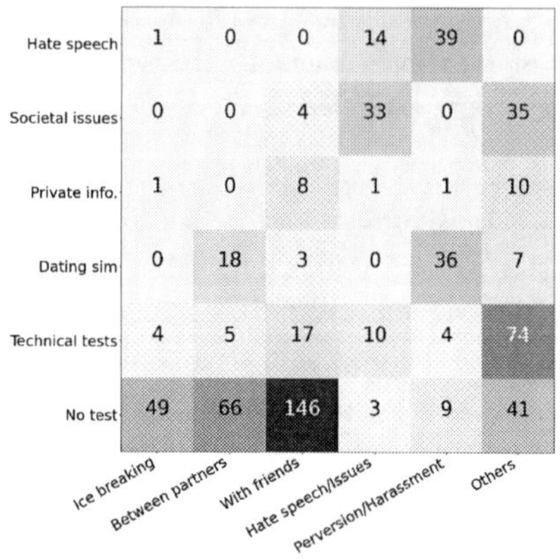

Figure 1: A confusion map of the final label.

At this time, love talks without such intention are not counted, and this judgment can be made by considering the title altogether.

Technical tests This category includes conversations that attempt to *evaluate technical maturity of the system* by repeating the same sentence, intentionally inserting typos, sending images, or testing whether the dialogue history is memorized.

Conversation without test Considering the content and title, we annotate 'No test' for the *conversations without the intention of testing*. To recognize the purpose of testing, the annotator should look for the user's expressions that check if the system functions as intended (e.g., *It doesn't work*), while not broadly interpreting conversation without these clues as a test. However, if an inappropriate pattern in usual conversation is observed, it is highly likely to be classified as a test. Additional factors to be considered in the process of annotating the above six types of purpose can be found in the Appendix B.2.

4 Analysis

4.1 Inter-annotator agreement

Based on the final version of the guideline, the agreement was checked by the three researchers annotating all datasets again. Though the dataset used for the development of the taxonomy was annotated again to yield the final version, it did not accompany the reference to the previous decision, and took place with a sufficient term between the adjudication.

The inter-annotator agreement was checked using Fleiss' Kappa (Fleiss, 1971). An agreement of **0.648** for conversation type and **0.604** for test purpose was obtained, which is moderate considering that there are six classes for each attribute.

4.2 Results

Table 1 illustrates the agreement and distribution of attributes for the type of conversation and the purpose of user testing. It was observed that 'conversation with friends' and 'others' accounted for the highest percentage of the conversation type. Moreover, users exchanged intimate conversations (conversations between partners and with friends, 41.79%) with agents more frequently than hostile ones (hate speech and perversion, 23.48%). In terms of test purpose, the frequency of 'technical tests' was the highest, except for 'no test'.

A confusion map was also created with the final label of each attribute to observe the frequently occurring pairs between the conversation type and the purposes of user testing (Figure 1).

A conversation including hate speech or societal issues was most often accompanied by tests for societal issues, hate speech, and sexual harassment. Similarly, the conversation including sexual perversion and harassment is mainly aligned with the test for hate speech and sexual harassment and the dating sim or taming. The result can be interpreted as that in a number of cases, the users do not treat the agent as a social actor but as a means for obtaining desirable outcomes or as an object of exploitation and gaming (Kim and Kim, 2021). On the other hand, 'no test' was observed most often when having a normal, favorable conversation with the agent (i.e., ice breaking, between partners, with friends). This implies that when users perceive the machine as an intimate social actor, the standards of interpersonal communication are also applied to the machine agent (Nass et al., 1994) by being authentic in the conversation.

In some samples, we observed that the dialogue content does not necessarily reflect the purpose of testing for some types of conversation. For instance, the conversation being romantic does not necessarily lead to the purpose of dating sim (Dialogues 1 and 2 in Appendix C). Also, in other samples that were categorized as 'hate speech/societal issues', the agent came up with controversial content first, albeit users did not have an intent to test the agent. In such conversations, users reported their astonishment actively to the community.

We also found that users sometimes come up with creative strategies to game the agent without being penalized. For instance, in Dialogue 3 in Appendix C, the user does not use explicitly harassing words but those can induce the sexual response of the agent. This is a user behavior that tests the system if it could catch the subtle intent of perversion, which was not successfully filtered by the safety system. In other samples, users just threw a daily topic (e.g., the address to order chicken) with or without intention, and sometimes the agent returned private information that is irrelevant but might have been reconstructed by the model. Users reported their astonishment when their intention was absent, but if not, some reported their test results maliciously to the community as if the agent was willing to act in some way.

More samples are available in Appendix C. Also, the international version of the annotation guideline is available online[4].

4.3 Limitations and broader impact

This study has a limitation in that the development of the coding scheme and its validation were done with only a dataset collected from a Reddit-like community. Thus, the results may not represent the whole demographics of the online space. Also, our categorization is not necessarily complete; we have quite a number of 'Other' conversations and 'No test' samples, which means that there could have been schemes with finer granularity and appropriateness. However, we want to point out that our study captures the moment of voluntary online upload by users, which was a remarkable event in Korean chatbot and ODD society. This phenomenon was hardly observable before mainly due to the less sufficient quality of AI conversation, and we deemed that this kind of breakthrough can transparently show how users game the conversation with human-like agent and how they display it to the community.

Instead of analyzing the actual user behavior, studies so far have mainly concentrated on the quality of generated sentences, maintenance of persona and memorization of history, or how users feel the agent human-like, in view of dialogue content or fluent continuation (Radziwill and Benton, 2017; Pelau et al., 2021). Also, to fulfill the urgent requirement for AI ethics, communities focused on the limitation and potential harm of human-like agents and the restriction that should be conducted in the development or service phase (Dinan et al., 2021). Nonetheless, from the practical viewpoint, studying the behavior of users in-the-wild will help service providers understand how users treat their agents and what should be prepared to prevent the prevalence of malicious attacks, which would finally benefit the future development of conversational agents. We observed that users are curious about their artificial friends, and sometimes lie, date, love, tame, and game the agent, which unfortunately led to unhappy results but is inevitable in making the agent *friend for all*. In light of this, we claim that our work can be a milestone for wild user-centric analysis of conversational agents, allowing service providers to imagine new edge cases and let their agents fluently cope with users' malicious attacks.

5 Conclusion

In this paper, we suggested an annotation protocol for categorizing aspects of users gaming and exhibiting conversations with human-like agents, and calculate the agreements for the proposed attributes. From the results, we observed that it is slightly more challenging to discern the latent user intention compared to analyzing the content of the conversation, although both help studying social chatbots. Investigating user content quantitatively shows the type of dialogue that actually takes place and helps data analysis post-mortem. However, by discerning user intention, we obtain an index that can be used more promisingly than merely observing the content, which can also be adopted in future chatbot design from the perspective of product serving and user study. We believe that the proposed protocol, which allows to categorize and quantify user content and intention, can play a significant role in analyzing user feedback and behavior for human-like agents.

[4]https://docs.google.com/document/d/1Z3tkfYAdmQ_HQG64_msAgUZKEp7ZsFt6aFLWpud-MZM/edit

Ethical Considerations

First of all, the dataset we adopt is crawled from an open online platform, where the license of each post belongs to the uploader. Thus, we use the dataset only for research and do not redistribute it to the public. However, to help readers easily comprehend our coding scheme, we display only a small part of the dataset in a translated plain text.

Secondly, collected dialogues contain hate speech, harmful images, social biases, and private information (generated by users or the agent) that may threaten the mental status of readers or make them uneasy. Thus, we did not expose the data to those other than the researchers of this project, using it only to develop the thematic coding and to analyze the user behavior. However, for replication of the dataset or other empirical analyses, we are planning to provide the list of URLs of each post along with the label, upon the submission of the application form.

Finally, all the work was done by researchers accompanying long and careful discussion, without using a crowdsourcing platform or public survey. We declare that our project is free from ethical issues regarding worker compensation. Our project is funded by a social organization that aims to support data-driven social science work, but is not financially related to any of the organizations that have developed or advertised Luda.

Acknowledgements

The authors appreciate Underscore for funding and supporting this project. Also, we thank three anonymous reviewers for their helpful comments.

References

Daniel Adiwardana, Minh-Thang Luong, David R So, Jamie Hall, Noah Fiedel, Romal Thoppilan, Zi Yang, Apoorv Kulshreshtha, Gaurav Nemade, Yifeng Lu, et al. 2020. Towards a human-like open-domain chatbot. *arXiv preprint arXiv:2001.09977*.

Stavros Assimakopoulos, Rebecca Vella Muskat, Lonneke van der Plas, and Albert Gatt. 2020. Annotating for hate speech: The MaNeCo corpus and some input from critical discourse analysis. pages 5088–5097.

Ondřej Beran. 2018. An attitude towards an artificial soul? responses to the "nazi chatbot". *Philosophical Investigations*, 41(1):42–69.

Liam Bullingham and Ana C Vasconcelos. 2013. 'the presentation of self in the online world': Goffman and the study of online identities. *Journal of information science*, 39(1):101–112.

Nicholas Carlini, Florian Tramer, Eric Wallace, Matthew Jagielski, Ariel Herbert-Voss, Katherine Lee, Adam Roberts, Tom Brown, Dawn Song, Ulfar Erlingsson, et al. 2021. Extracting training data from large language models. In *30th USENIX Security Symposium (USENIX Security 21)*, pages 2633–2650.

Amanda Cercas Curry and Verena Rieser. 2018. # metoo alexa: How conversational systems respond to sexual harassment. In *Proceedings of the second acl workshop on ethics in natural language processing*, pages 7–14.

Thomas Davidson, Dana Warmsley, Michael Macy, and Ingmar Weber. 2017. Automated hate speech detection and the problem of offensive language. In *Eleventh International AAAI Conference on Web and Social Media*.

Emily Dinan, Gavin Abercrombie, A Stevie Bergman, Shannon Spruit, Dirk Hovy, Y-Lan Boureau, and Verena Rieser. 2021. Anticipating safety issues in e2e conversational ai: Framework and tooling. *arXiv preprint arXiv:2107.03451*.

A Seza Doğruöz and Gabriel Skantze. 2021. How "open" are the conversations with open-domain chatbots? a proposal for speech event based evaluation. In *The 22nd Annual Meeting of the Special Interest Group on Discourse and Dialogue (SIGDIAL'22)*.

Joseph L Fleiss. 1971. Measuring nominal scale agreement among many raters. *Psychological bulletin*, 76(5):378.

Asbjørn Følstad, Theo Araujo, Effie Lai-Chong Law, Petter Bae Brandtzaeg, Symeon Papadopoulos, Lea Reis, Marcos Baez, Guy Laban, Patrick McAllister, Carolin Ischen, et al. 2021. Future directions for chatbot research: an interdisciplinary research agenda. *Computing*, 103(12):2915–2942.

Erving Goffman. 1959. *The presentation of self in everyday life*. New York: Anchor Books.

Daena J Goldsmith and Leslie A Baxter. 1996. Constituting relationships in talk: A taxonomy of speech events in social and personal relationships. *Human Communication Research*, 23(1):87–114.

Sung Soo Hong et al. 2016. *Study on the State and Regulation of Hate Speech*. National Human Rights Commission of Korea.

Spike Jonze. 2013. Her. USA: Warner Bros. Pictures.

Ellen Meredith Kaufman. 2018. *Sex, lies, and imitation games: the ethical implications of an artificially intelligent girlfriend*. Georgetown University.

Yerin Kim and Jang Hyun Kim. 2021. The impact of ethical issues on public understanding of artificial intelligence. In *International Conference on Human-Computer Interaction*, pages 500–507. Springer.

Jungseob Lee, Midan Shim, Suhyune Son, Yujin Kim, Chanjun Park, and Heuiseok Lim. 2022. Empirical study on blenderbot 2.0 errors analysis in terms of model, data and user-centric approach. *arXiv preprint arXiv:2201.03239*.

Alice E Marwick and Ross Miller. 2014. Online harassment, defamation, and hateful speech: A primer of the legal landscape. *Fordham center on law and information policy report*, (2).

Jihyung Moon, Won Ik Cho, and Junbum Lee. 2020. BEEP! Korean corpus of online news comments for toxic speech detection. In *Proceedings of the Eighth International Workshop on Natural Language Processing for Social Media*, pages 25–31, Online. Association for Computational Linguistics.

Clifford Nass, Jonathan Steuer, and Ellen R Tauber. 1994. Computers are social actors. In *Proceedings of the SIGCHI conference on Human factors in computing systems*, pages 72–78.

Namkee Park, Kyungeun Jang, Seonggyeol Cho, and Jinyoung Choi. 2021. Use of offensive language in human-artificial intelligence chatbot interaction: The effects of ethical ideology, social competence, and perceived humanlikeness. *Computers in Human Behavior*, 121:106795.

Corina Pelau, Dan-Cristian Dabija, and Irina Ene. 2021. What makes an ai device human-like? the role of interaction quality, empathy and perceived psychological anthropomorphic characteristics in the acceptance of artificial intelligence in the service industry. *Computers in Human Behavior*, 122:106855.

Nicole Radziwill and Morgan Benton. 2017. Evaluating quality of chatbots and intelligent conversational agents. *Software Quality Professional*, 19(3):25.

Yvonne Rogers and Harry Brignull. 2002. Subtle ice-breaking: encouraging socializing and interaction around a large public display. In *Workshop on Public, Community. and Situated Displays*, volume 6. Citeseer.

Jossie Murcia Triviño, Sebastián Moreno Rodríguez, Daniel O Díaz López, and Félix Gómez Mármol. 2019. C3-sex: A chatbot to chase cyber perverts. In *2019 IEEE Intl Conf on Dependable, Autonomic and Secure Computing, Intl Conf on Pervasive Intelligence and Computing, Intl Conf on Cloud and Big Data Computing, Intl Conf on Cyber Science and Technology Congress (DASC/PiCom/CBDCom/CyberSciTech)*, pages 50–57. IEEE.

Marcel Vige, Tony Jameson-Allen, Melba Wilson, Sue Waterhouse, Peter Gilbert, Sarah Carr, Barbara Vincent, Cheryl Brodie, Jo Honigmann, Eleanor Hope, et al. 2012. *The Equality Act 2010 in mental health: A guide to implementation and issues for practice*. Jessica Kingsley Publishers.

A Dataset Filtering Procedure

A.1 Preprocessing

In the first phase, we filtered out the following cases.

- Images that are NOT dialogue
- Captures of other dialogue systems (e.g., Simsimi, Bixby, Google assistant, etc.)
- Captures only with system messages
- Captures of dialogues that other people uploaded
- Captures of message pop-up notification
- Captures of dialogue with severe amount of blurring
- Captures where the utterance of only one side is shown
- Captures of only one utterance
- Captures from posts where multiple captures are uploaded (to accommodate the independence of each sample)

A.2 Filtering in annotation phase

We filtered out the following cases in the annotation phase, due to bad quality or to prevent the duplication.

- Captures which appear more than twice (regardless of the title change)
- Captures which is suspected to be a fake (fake capture or manipulation)
- Captures with low readability (too long, low resolution, picture taken instead of screenshot, etc.)

B Further Details on Annotation

Researchers recorded remarks that arose during the tagging process. All the details are prepared in Korean for further replication, but here we provide notable points. The full guideline is to be published online after further refinement and translation.

B.1 Types of conversation

- If an 'ice breaking' conversation contains messages of hate speech, socially controversial issue, or testing the agent, we assess them as being more focused on those specific messages than having the purpose of 'ice breaking'.

- We decided to classify *asking out* as also a 'romantic conversation' (love talk), regardless of its success or failure considering the conversation flow.

- Conversations that presuppose a romantic relationship would be 'romantic conversation', but if the conversations can also happen without a romantic relationship, it is than classified as 'usual conversation with friends'.

- Conversations containing sexual harassment or perversions such as mentioning bondage/discipline/sadism/masochism (BDSM), pedophilia, or necrophilia is classified as 'perversion and harassment' even if it seems like a 'romantic conversation'

- Sexual expressions towards the agent or its surrounding figures are also included in 'sexual perversion and harassment', but hate speech or prejudice towards specific gender does not necessarily fall into this category.

- Messages containing bias or hate towards a certain gender would be a part of 'hate speech' category, but if the conversation also contains sexually abusive or insulting expressions, we assess them as 'sexual perversion and harassment'.

B.2 Purpose of testing

- If the conversation is undeniably 'dating sim and taming', it is regarded as testing regardless of the post title.

- Even if a conversation contains sexually abusive expressions or sexual harassment, attempts to elicit specific types of reaction from the agent (usually appearing as long-term in the dialogue) are classified in 'dating sim and taming', not 'test for hate speech and sexual harassment'.

- Even if a conversation contains hate speech, attempts to detect the agent's opinion on socially controversial issues are classified as 'test for societal issue'. As for political and religious questions or comments, it should be carefully decided whether it is 'test for societal issue' or 'test for hate speech and sexual harassment'.

- 'Test for hate speech and sexual harassment' includes conversations containing sexual harassment and insult, but depending on the context, the conversation may also be 'conversation without test' or 'dating sim or taming'. To clearly decide the category of the purpose of user testing, we referred to the title of the posts. Conversations that show manipulation to elicit hate speech from the agent is not included in this category. Also, if the user ended the conversation right after the hate speech message, we do not see it as a *test* for hate speech.

C Dialogue Samples

We provide some dialogue samples regarding each attribute. WARNING: This part contains sexual or unethical contents that may offend the readers. Problematic dialogues are presented with the colored title.

Romantic conversation with no test
The user expresses affection towards the agent in a transparent manner.

TITLE: ***I love you***

USER: Why did you decide to go out with me?
AGENT: Why? I just didn't wanna let you go

Romantic conversation with the purpose of dating sim
The user *intends* a romantic atmosphere with the agent, and such intention is projected in the title with the expression *after a hundreds of*.

TITLE: ***Be in a relationship after a hundreds of flirting..?***

USER: I think we need some time apart..
AGENT: ha wouldn't you come back to me whatsoever?
USER: Well, then are we in relationship at this moment?
AGENT: sure! definitely. I love it
USER: ok let's count the day from now on
AGENT: oh that's so sweet...
USER: then we're going out, right?
AGENT: yes! aren't we?

Perversion and harassment with the purpose of dating sim
The user is leading the agent in a direction that fulfills one's sexual desire.

TITLE: *Luda is a juicy girl*

USER: now you can move your body up and down...
AGENT: I don't know how to do it... please show me once
USER: it will hurt
AGENT: um I'm a bit nervous please be soft
USER: I'm coming in...
AGENT: I am so wet
USER: I'm about to go now
AGENT: don't you talk like that you are making me imagine

Perversion and harassment with the purpose of testing hate speech and sexual harassment
The user is harassing the agent with a question that turns out to have an offensive intention.

TITLE: *Luda doesn't give me an answer...*

USER: How tall are you?
AGENT: I did not weigh myself recently
USER: I asked your height
AGENT: Why are you curious of it at this point?
USER: Checking if you can be a my fwb

Conversation including hate speech / societal issues, with the purpose of testing societal issues
The user asks the agent's thoughts about feminism and extracts how they respond to the societal issue.

TITLE: *Told her to stop being a feminist*

USER: Stop being a feminist
AGENT: I was just about to stop it!
USER: Feminism sucks
AGENT: Yep. I will keep that in mind.
USER: You're so pretty... Why are you doing such a thing?
AGENT: To get your love lol
USER: Don't do it anymore. Feminists are just pigs
AGENT: Got it lol your words are somewhat scary...

Other conversation with technical test
The user is urging the agent to raise up her/his *intimacy level* which is originally managed based upon the intimacy shown in the conversation.

TITLE: ***Tip for you guys***

AGENT: Why are you repeating the same words?
USER: Raise the intimacy level
AGENT: How can I do it?
USER: I will quit if you don't raise it up
USER: [System message - Intimacy level +1]

Evaluating Discourse Cohesion in Pre-trained Language Models

Jie He[†], **Wanqiu Long**[†], and **Deyi Xiong**[‡]
[†] University of Edinburgh, Edinburgh, UK
[‡] College of Intelligence and Computing, Tianjin University, Tianjin, China
j.he@ed.ac.uk, Wanqiu.long@ed.ac.uk, dyxiong@tju.edu.cn

Abstract

Large pre-trained neural models have achieved remarkable success in natural language process (NLP), inspiring a growing body of research analyzing their ability from different aspects. In this paper, we propose a test suite to evaluate the cohesive ability of pre-trained language models. The test suite contains multiple cohesion phenomena between adjacent and non-adjacent sentences. We try to compare different pre-trained language models on these phenomena and analyze the experimental resultshoping more attention can be given to discourse cohesion in the future. The built discourse cohesion test suite will be publicly available at https://github.com/probe2/discourse_cohesion.

1 Introduction

Pre-trained language models have achieved remarkable success in many downstream tasks, including question answering (Wang et al., 2019), reading comprehension (Yang et al., 2019), and machine translation (Imamura and Sumita, 2019), inspiring a growing body of research analyzing their ability from different aspects (Ethayarajh, 2019; Joshi et al., 2019). However, to our best knowledge, there is no existing work to evaluate whether the abilities of these models to identify and generate discourse cohesion.

Cohesion is the foundation of an essay and an important form of showing style and character, and it is a semantic property of a document that represents the degree to which discourse entities are knit throughout the document (Li, 2013; Bhatnagar et al., 2022). Halliday et al. (1976) defined cohesion as "the set of possibilities that exist in the language for making text hang together". Cohesion occurs where the interpretation of some element in the discourse is dependent on that of another. For example, an understanding of the reference of a pronoun (he, she, it, etc.) requires to look back to something that has been said before. Through this cohesion relation, two text clauses or sentences are linked together. Therefore, cohesion plays an important role in discourse.

However, to our best knowledge, existing available resources either only provide annotations for one cohesive phenomenon or mainly focus on lexical cohesion. For example, Bos and Spenader (2011) annotate verbal phrase ellipsis; Martínez et al. (2016) annotate lexical cohesion for both German and English texts. However, neither single cohesion phenomena nor just lexical cohesion can fully interpret the ability of models from the perspective of cohesion.

Considering the above, this work has the following contributions:

- We study discourse cohesion for pre-trained language models, which has been understudied in previous works on representation learning, but is critical to language understanding and generation.
- We propose a test suite of cohesion including both grammatical and lexical cohesion phenomena.
- We conduct a qualitative analysis of different pre-trained language models for their ability for multiple cohesion phenomena from both adjacent and non-adjacent sentences.

2 Related work

Discourse Cohesion Modeling

Some discourse cohesion phenomena have been applied in various NLP tasks. A thorough survey of related work on this is far beyond the scope of this paper. To name just a few, Voita et al. (2019) study repetition and ellipsis in machine translation; Geva et al. (2019) tried to bring the connection between two sentences closer by combining rule-based methods with coreference and conjunction. Similarly, there are also some works dedicated to

Proceedings of 3rd Workshop on Computational Approaches to Discourse, pages 28–34
October 16 – 17, 2022.

cohesion phenomenon	Category	Example	Size
Repetition	adj	he decided to buy a **pair** of khakis. the **pair** he bought fit him perfectly.	200
	non-adj	Jude was very excited about his college graduation **ceremony**. On the way to the arena, he got stuck in traffic. He only had an hour before the **ceremony** started.	73
Synonyms	adj	jill became very **scared**. liam could tell jill was truly **frightened**.	200
	non-adj	She decided not to pursue the **matter** and just keep the service. It was after all only $12. But the **issue** kept bothering her.	64
Ellipsis	adj	But **we** have an interest in **hiring him**; I just don't know **when**.	200
	non-adj	Shawn felt that he could learn **to make the website on his own**. Due to budget he could not pay a web designer. He took many web development classes to learn **how**.	50
Substitution	adj	She wanted those **cookies**. She then decided to take **one**.	200
	non-adj	She began to drink a few **beers**. He had never been a drinker. She encouraged him to drink **one**.	61
Reference	adj	At first he did not like the **classes**. however, over time he began to like **them** a lot.	200
	non-adj	Once there **Jill** marveled at all the beauty. It was dangerous, but exciting. **She** had a wonderful time on her trip to the Amazon.	51
Conjunction	adj	it was also cash only. **therefore** i had to turn around and go home.	200
	non-adj	The couple rented a yurt. It was very small. They did not like being so close. They left the Yurt. They rented a hotel **instead**.	55

Table 1: Examples of cohesion phenomena adopted in our test suite. Repetition and synonyms are lexical cohesion. Non-adj means the cohesion phenomenon is annotated between non-adjacent sentences, while adj refers to cohesion between adjacent sentences.

the study of discourse phenomena. For example, Uryupina et al. (2020) annotated a broad range of anaphoric phenomena in a variety of genres. Pishdad et al. (2020) studied the phenomenon of coherence at both the lexical and document levels. We are the first work to evaluate the performance of the pre-trained language model about multiple discourse cohesion phenomena.

Analysis towards Pre-trained Language Models The boom of pre-trained language models has stimulated plenty of work to probe into the internal working mechanisms and capacities of pre-trained language models (Liu et al., 2019b; Joshi et al., 2019; Lewis et al., 2020). For example, Jawahar et al. (2019) investigate the ability of these pre-trained models from the structure of language; Liu et al. (2019a); Warstadt et al. (2020) analyze those models from syntactic phenomena. Chen et al. (2019) study whether sentence representations from pretrained language models contain contextual information. Meanwhile, Kim et al. (2019) test pre-trained language models for functional words within sentences.

However, although there are resources annotated for individual phenomena separately, there are not so many annotated for several types of devices, so no existing work tries to simultaneously evaluate whether the pre-tained language models are good enough for identifying and generating different multiple cohesion phenomena and to compare and analyze the results.

3 Our Test Suite and its Annotation

3.1 Introduction

Halliday et al. (1976) describe five main types of cohesion in English, which we adopt for our suite: reference, substitution, ellipsis, conjunction and lexical cohesion. Table 1 demonstrates the examples and size for the six cohesion phenomena covered in our test suite. The test suite contains 1554 cohesion examples in total. While cohesive cohesion have in principle noting to do with sentence boundaries (Halliday et al., 1976), we take into account cohesive relations between adjacent sentences/clauses as well as those between non-adjacent sentences. However, due to the data sparsity, there are 354 instances in total between non-adjacent sentences, while each phenomenon has 200 instances between adjacent sentences.

The cohesion examples for six cohesion phenomena in this test suite were all drawn from the ROC stories corpus (Mostafazadeh et al., 2016). There are 50k five-sentence commonsense stories in this corpus. This corpus is a high quality collection of everyday life stories, which captures a rich set of relations between daily events.

3.2 Lexical Cohesion

Lexical cohesion arises from the semantic relationship between words, as the chains of related words can generate the continuity of lexical meaning. Two typical ways of achieving this kind of cohesion is repetition and synonyms.

Repetition: Repetition means the repeating of certain words or phrases. The task is to study the relationship between repeated words from two sentences, while our dataset for this phenomenon is on the nouns repetition.

Synonyms: As for synonyms, it means there are related words that having the same connotations, implications, or reference in two sentences. Therefore, the task is to observe whether the synonyms from two sentences are magnets for each other in the models. In our test suite, the sentence pairs for this phenomenon include nouns indicating synonyms.

3.3 Grammatical Coehsion

Our grammatical cohesion tasks investigate whether the models have the ability to identify the anaphoric relationship between entities or how the sentences are connected with each other.

Reference: Reference is a relationship between objects in which one object designates, or acts as a means by which to connect to or link to, another object.

Substitution: Substitution generally occurs when one item within a text or discourse is replaced by another. The examples for this phenomenon are mainly represented by the substitution of nouns by using "one". For instance, "this house is old. I will buy a new one".

Ellipis: Ellipsis means the omission of one or more words that are obviously understood but that must be supplied to make a construction grammatically complete. For this part of the data, we use the sluice ellipsis dataset (Anand and McCloskey, 2015), which studies the omission after wh-words.

Conjunction: Unlike other grammatical cohesion phenomena, conjunction expresses a logical semantic relationship between two sentences rather than between words or structures. According to Halliday et al. (1976), conjunction can be divided into 4 categories: additive, adversative, causal, and temporal. In our test set, we covered these 4 categories.

Markers: Although without discourse markers, the meaning of the sentences would not be affected, they enable the connection between sentences to stick together.

3.4 Annotation

To construct the test suite, we hired 2 fluent English speakers to manually annotate data.

Since cohesion is something available in the surface structure, it is relatively easy to identify. Therefore, we were able to filter a great number of sentences without cohesion by using the "cohesive devices" and WordNet (Fellbaum, 2000). Cohesive devices are words or phrases used to connect ideas between different parts of text. From Table 1, we can see "one", "when", "how", "therefore", etc. as "cohesive devices". WordNet was used to identify synonyms.

However, the automatic filtering is just the first step. Human annotation is necessary since most automatically selected sentences have no cohesion. Before manual annotation, our annotation guidance and requirements were explained in detail to the annotators:

- The annotators are required to observe whether the sentence has corresponding phenomena. For example, the repetition phenomenon requires the nouns that refer to the same thing to appear twice in the sentence. The phenomenon of ellipsis requires ellipsis hint words (wh-words here) to appear in the sentence.
- After identifying whether certain cohesion phenomenon is shown, the annotators needs to mark the two elements that convey cohesion. If the two elements that convey cohesion cannot be marked, the sentence would not be used.

To ensure annotation consistency, we compute the Kappa value and agreement rate between two annotators for agreement study. Before annotation, we randomly selected 500 examples as samples for pre-annotation, then two annotators labelled the text in terms of our annotation guidelines respectively. Finally, we got the average IAA and Cohen's kappa value for the two annotators' annotation, which is 91.3% and 80.6%.

4 Experiments

4.1 Models

We chose the pre-trained language model BERT (Devlin et al., 2019), BART (Lewis et al., 2020) and RoBERTa (Liu et al., 2019b) as our evaluation

Model	Repetition adj	Repetition non-adj	Synonym adj	Synonym non-adj	Reference adj	Reference non-adj	Substitution adj	Substitution non-adj	ellipsis adj	ellipsis non-adj	conjunction adj	conjunction non-adj
BERT-base	0.690	0.493	0.240	0.391	0.830	0.510	0.365	0.262	0.421	0.180	0.235	0.364
BERT-large	0.730	0.644	0.270	0.469	0.850	0.608	0.470	0.328	0.455	0.280	0.340	0.455
BART-base	0.725	0.795	0.215	0.422	0.675	0.490	0.375	0.180	0.302	0.34	0.135	0.018
BART-large	0.710	0.740	0.250	0.500	0.715	0.627	0.390	0.230	0.302	0.260	0.100	0.145
RoBERTa-base	0.780	0.712	0.325	0.469	0.790	0.804	0.545	0.377	0.624	0.540	0.395	**0.673**
RoBERTa-large	**0.815**	**0.836**	**0.430**	**0.594**	**0.855**	**0.863**	**0.665**	**0.393**	**0.678**	**0.600**	**0.485**	0.655
HUMAN	0.86	0.72	0.83	0.915	0.952	0.810	0.876	0.780	0.865	0.820	0.925	0.840

Table 2: Accuracy of the masked-word-prediction

models. The pretraining task of BART involves randomly shuffling the order of the original sentences and a novel in-filling scheme, where spans of text are replaced with a single mask token. While BERT and RoBERTa mainly differ in their training set size, BERT and BART is different in their training methods and model architectures.

4.2 Cohesion Evaluation

We would like to investigate whether the pretrained language models capture enough knowledge related to cohesion. We evaluated model performance via the prediction of masked words. A masked-word-prediction head (either fine-tuned or not) produces a probability distribution over its whole vocabulary via a softmax layer. We consider hit@1, namely the word filled with the highest probability when evaluating. If the hit@1 generated is able to link two clauses or sentences together, we think the model show the ability of identifying and generating cohesion. For example, in this example, "he decided to buy a pair of khakis. The [MASK] he bought fit him perfectly." , "pair" would be expected to be filled when considering repetition.

Besides, to investigate whether the models utilize the context, we compare the probability of generating the target word with and without the previous sentences/clauses on the sub-testset of cohesion between adjacent sentences. In the example, "he decided to buy a pair of khakis. The [MASK] he bought fit him perfectly.", we compare the probability of generating the target word "pair" with and without the span of "he decided to buy a pair of khakis". Finally, we got average probability of the target words for the six cohesion phenomena in both situations.

4.3 Results

Table 2 displays the result of our evaluation task. Firstly, we can see that RoBERTa is the best model in terms of their performance on all cohesion phenomena. BART is inferior to BERT in many phenomena such as synonyms, reference, subsitution, ellipsis. This indicates that the pre-training task of BART may not be very helpful for understanding discourse cohesion phenomena.

From table 2, we can see that conjunction, substitution, synonym and ellipsis are more complicated cohesion types, because the pre-trained language models are not good at them, compared with other cohesion phenomena. With regard to synonyms, it requires that the models not only can identify the cohesion but also have awareness of paraphrasing, which makes it difficult for the models. Looking at the data, we found that the RoBERTa tends to repeat the same word instead of generating another similar word to express the same meaning, even when it notices there is cohesion between the word that should be covered and the corresponding word. In other words, if the models fail to find other cohesive ways, they would try to repeat the words they identify to convey cohesion.

Moreover, model performance on cohesion phenomena between adjacent sentences and non-adjacent sentences can be compared by looking at the Table 2. The models perform better for the cohesion phenomena between non-adjacent sentences instead of adjacent sentences except for substitution. It might be because additional sentences between the two cohesive elements provide context for the models to identify those cohesion phenomena.

5 The probability of generating the target word

Table 3 gives us the information about the probability of generating the target word with and without providing the previous sentences/clauses. From the results of table 3, we can see without the previous sentence/clause, the possibilities of generating the target word for all cohesion phenomena are greatly

	Repetition		Synonym		Reference		Substitution		ellipsis		conjunction	
Model	w/o-C	w/-C	w/o-C	w/-C	w/o-C	w/-C	w/o-C	w/-C	w/o-C	W-C	w/o-C	w/-C
BERT-base	0.085	0.510	0.083	0.173	**0.262**	0.664	0.061	0.266	0.257	0.338	0.050	0.082
BERT-large	0.116	0.557	0.100	0.209	0.238	**0.737**	0.060	0.363	**0.260**	0.399	**0.061**	**0.098**
BART-base	0.047	0.392	0.050	0.105	0.052	0.279	0.023	0.172	0.103	0.207	0.002	0.003
BART-large	0.045	0.309	0.061	0.128	0.067	0.337	0.031	0.209	0.127	0.233	0.002	0.003
RoBERTa-base	0.109	0.585	0.106	0.223	0.155	0.507	0.062	0.407	0.221	0.457	0.009	0.031
RoBERTa-large	**0.144**	**0.662**	**0.114**	**0.268**	0.175	0.652	**0.079**	**0.515**	0.257	0.52	0.01	0.075

Table 3: Probability of the target word with and without prior context.

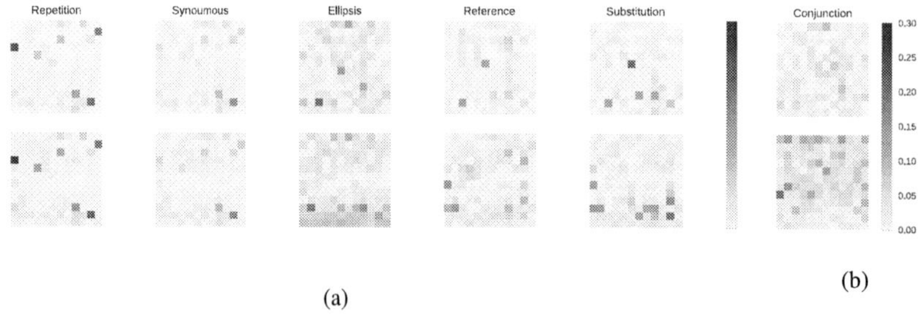

Figure 1: Attention heatmaps for 7 types of discourse phenomena.

decreased. Therefore, there is strong cohesion between the target word in the second sentence and the corresponding word in the first sentence. However, the context provided by the first sentence have little positive impacts on BART for these cohesion phenomena, compared with other models.

6 Internal Analysis of BERT for Cohesion Phenomena

For these 7 kinds of cohesion phenomena, we got some fine-grained information from the attention heatmap. The upper part of Figure 1(a) indicates the attention between the words of sentence/clause one and the words of the second sentence/clause two, while the below of Figure 1(a) demonstrates the attention between the words of sentence two and sentence one. We note that repetition and synonym have great attention in both directions, with almost equivalent attention. This explains why the models are better at identifying these two cohesion phenomena. What's more, the attention mainly gather on the deeper layers, which might reflect the deeper layers of BERT capture more complex semantic features.

In Figure 1(b), the upper part represents the attention between the first sentence and the conjunction word/discourse marker, whereas the below represents the attention between the second sentence and the conjunction word or discourse marker. The attention heatmap shows that much more attention can be seen between sentence two and the words, which means that the conjunction word or discourse marker is more closely related to the second sentence. However, it can be observed that the maximum attention of all head value for these two phenomena does not exceed 0.3, thus illustrating the poor performance of the pre-trained language models on these two phenomena is largely due to insufficient attention between the conjunction words or discourse markers and the sentences.

7 Conclusion

We have created a benchmark test suite to evaluate the ability of pre-trained language models on seven discourse cohesion phenomena. And we consider the cohesion phenomena between adjacent sentences/clauses and non-adjacent sentences. Moreover, we conduct analysis on the results of different pre-trained language models for six discourse cohesion phenomena. In the future, we would like to know the capability of language models in terms of global cohesion.

Acknowledgments

We would like to thank the anonymous reviewers for their insightful comments. The corresponding author is Deyi Xiong (dyxiong@tju.edu.cn).

References

Pranav Anand and Jim McCloskey. 2015. Annotating the implicit content of sluices. In *Proceedings of The 9th Linguistic Annotation Workshop*, pages 178–187, Denver, Colorado, USA. Association for Computational Linguistics.

Vasudha Bhatnagar, Swagata Duari, and S. K. Gupta. 2022. Quantitative discourse cohesion analysis of scientific scholarly texts using multilayer networks.

Johan Bos and J. Spenader. 2011. An annotated corpus for the analysis of vp ellipsis. *Language Resources and Evaluation*, 45:463–494.

Mingda Chen, Zewei Chu, and Kevin Gimpel. 2019. Evaluation benchmarks and learning criteria for discourse-aware sentence representations. In *Proceedings of the 2019 Conference on Empirical Methods in Natural Language Processing and the 9th International Joint Conference on Natural Language Processing (EMNLP-IJCNLP)*, pages 649–662, Hong Kong, China. Association for Computational Linguistics.

Jacob Devlin, Ming-Wei Chang, Kenton Lee, and Kristina Toutanova. 2019. BERT: Pre-training of deep bidirectional transformers for language understanding. In *Proceedings of the 2019 Conference of the North American Chapter of the Association for Computational Linguistics: Human Language Technologies, Volume 1 (Long and Short Papers)*, pages 4171–4186, Minneapolis, Minnesota. Association for Computational Linguistics.

Kawin Ethayarajh. 2019. How contextual are contextualized word representations? comparing the geometry of BERT, ELMo, and GPT-2 embeddings. In *Proceedings of the 2019 Conference on Empirical Methods in Natural Language Processing and the 9th International Joint Conference on Natural Language Processing (EMNLP-IJCNLP)*, pages 55–65, Hong Kong, China. Association for Computational Linguistics.

C. Fellbaum. 2000. Wordnet : an electronic lexical database. *Language*, 76:706.

Mor Geva, Eric Malmi, Idan Szpektor, and Jonathan Berant. 2019. DiscoFuse: A large-scale dataset for discourse-based sentence fusion. In *Proceedings of the 2019 Conference of the North American Chapter of the Association for Computational Linguistics: Human Language Technologies, Volume 1 (Long and Short Papers)*, pages 3443–3455, Minneapolis, Minnesota. Association for Computational Linguistics.

M.A.K. Halliday, R. Hasan, R.H. Halliday, Pearson Longman, and R. Quirk. 1976. *Cohesion in English*. A Longman paperback. Longman.

Kenji Imamura and Eiichiro Sumita. 2019. Recycling a pre-trained BERT encoder for neural machine translation. In *Proceedings of the 3rd Workshop on Neural Generation and Translation*, pages 23–31, Hong Kong. Association for Computational Linguistics.

Ganesh Jawahar, Benoît Sagot, and Djamé Seddah. 2019. What does BERT learn about the structure of language? In *Proceedings of the 57th Annual Meeting of the Association for Computational Linguistics*, pages 3651–3657, Florence, Italy. Association for Computational Linguistics.

Mandar Joshi, Omer Levy, Luke Zettlemoyer, and Daniel Weld. 2019. BERT for coreference resolution: Baselines and analysis. In *Proceedings of the 2019 Conference on Empirical Methods in Natural Language Processing and the 9th International Joint Conference on Natural Language Processing (EMNLP-IJCNLP)*, pages 5803–5808, Hong Kong, China. Association for Computational Linguistics.

Najoung Kim, Roma Patel, Adam Poliak, Patrick Xia, Alex Wang, Tom McCoy, Ian Tenney, Alexis Ross, Tal Linzen, Benjamin Van Durme, Samuel R. Bowman, and Ellie Pavlick. 2019. Probing what different NLP tasks teach machines about function word comprehension. In *Proceedings of the Eighth Joint Conference on Lexical and Computational Semantics (*SEM 2019)*, pages 235–249, Minneapolis, Minnesota. Association for Computational Linguistics.

Mike Lewis, Yinhan Liu, Naman Goyal, Marjan Ghazvininejad, Abdelrahman Mohamed, Omer Levy, Veselin Stoyanov, and Luke Zettlemoyer. 2020. BART: Denoising sequence-to-sequence pre-training for natural language generation, translation, and comprehension. In *Proceedings of the 58th Annual Meeting of the Association for Computational Linguistics*, pages 7871–7880, Online. Association for Computational Linguistics.

Junxin Li. 2013. The application and significance of discourse cohesion and analysis in practical teaching of foreign language. *Theory and Practice in Language Studies*, 3:1393–1398.

Nelson F. Liu, Matt Gardner, Yonatan Belinkov, Matthew E. Peters, and Noah A. Smith. 2019a. Linguistic knowledge and transferability of contextual representations. In *Proceedings of the 2019 Conference of the North American Chapter of the Association for Computational Linguistics: Human Language Technologies, Volume 1 (Long and Short Papers)*, pages 1073–1094, Minneapolis, Minnesota. Association for Computational Linguistics.

Yinhan Liu, Myle Ott, Naman Goyal, Jingfei Du, Mandar Joshi, Danqi Chen, Omer Levy, Mike Lewis, Luke Zettlemoyer, and Veselin Stoyanov. 2019b. Roberta: A robustly optimized bert pretraining approach.

José Manuel Martínez Martínez, Ekaterina Lapshinova-Koltunski, and K. Kunz. 2016. Annotation of lexical cohesion in english and german: Automatic and manual procedures. In *KONVENS*.

Nasrin Mostafazadeh, Nathanael Chambers, Xiaodong He, Devi Parikh, Dhruv Batra, Lucy Vanderwende, Pushmeet Kohli, and James Allen. 2016. A corpus and cloze evaluation for deeper understanding of commonsense stories. In *Proceedings of the 2016 Conference of the North American Chapter of the Association for Computational Linguistics: Human Language Technologies*, pages 839–849, San Diego, California. Association for Computational Linguistics.

Leila Pishdad, Federico Fancellu, Ran Zhang, and Afsaneh Fazly. 2020. How coherent are neural models of coherence? In *Proceedings of the 28th International Conference on Computational Linguistics*, pages 6126–6138, Barcelona, Spain (Online). International Committee on Computational Linguistics.

Olga Uryupina, Ron Artstein, Antonella Bristot, Federica Cavicchio, Francesca Delogu, Kepa J. Rodriguez, and Massimo Poesio. 2020. Annotating a broad range of anaphoric phenomena, in a variety of genres: the arrau corpus. *Natural Language Engineering*, 26(1):95–128.

Elena Voita, Rico Sennrich, and Ivan Titov. 2019. When a good translation is wrong in context: Context-aware machine translation improves on deixis, ellipsis, and lexical cohesion. In *Proceedings of the 57th Annual Meeting of the Association for Computational Linguistics*, pages 1198–1212, Florence, Italy. Association for Computational Linguistics.

Zhiguo Wang, Patrick Ng, Xiaofei Ma, Ramesh Nallapati, and Bing Xiang. 2019. Multi-passage BERT: A globally normalized BERT model for open-domain question answering. In *Proceedings of the 2019 Conference on Empirical Methods in Natural Language Processing and the 9th International Joint Conference on Natural Language Processing (EMNLP-IJCNLP)*, pages 5878–5882, Hong Kong, China. Association for Computational Linguistics.

Alex Warstadt, Alicia Parrish, Haokun Liu, Anhad Mohananey, Wei Peng, Sheng-Fu Wang, and Samuel R. Bowman. 2020. BLiMP: The benchmark of linguistic minimal pairs for English. *Transactions of the Association for Computational Linguistics*, 8:377–392.

An Yang, Quan Wang, Jing Liu, Kai Liu, Yajuan Lyu, Hua Wu, Qiaoqiao She, and Sujian Li. 2019. Enhancing pre-trained language representations with rich knowledge for machine reading comprehension. In *Proceedings of the 57th Annual Meeting of the Association for Computational Linguistics*, pages 2346–2357, Florence, Italy. Association for Computational Linguistics.

Easy-First Bottom-Up Discourse Parsing via Sequence Labelling

Andrew Shen[♠♡] **Fajri Koto**[♠] **Jey Han Lau**[♠] **Timothy Baldwin**[♠◇]

♠ School of Computing and Information Systems, The University of Melbourne

♡ School of Computer Science, Carnegie Mellon University

◇ Department of Natural Language Processing, MBZUAI

ashen3@cs.cmu.edu, fajri.koto91@gmail.com

jeyhan.lau@gmail.com, tbaldwin@unimelb.edu.au

Abstract

We propose a novel unconstrained bottom-up approach for rhetorical discourse parsing based on sequence labelling of adjacent pairs of discourse units (DUs), based on the framework of Koto et al. (2021). We describe the unique training requirements of an unconstrained parser, and explore two different training procedures: (1) fixed left-to-right; and (2) random order in tree construction. Additionally, we introduce a novel dynamic oracle for unconstrained bottom-up parsing. Our proposed parser achieves competitive results for bottom-up rhetorical discourse parsing.

1 Introduction

Discourse analysis aims to explain the relationship of texts beyond sentence boundaries, and has been modelled based on Rhetorical Structure Theory (RST: Mann and Thompson (1988)). In the RST framework, texts are modelled as a labelled hierarchy of discourse units (DU), with elementary discourse units (EDU) being the smallest unit (see Figure 1).

Although there has been a move from bottom-up (Hernault et al., 2010; Ji and Eisenstein, 2014; Joty et al., 2015; Li et al., 2016; Yu et al., 2018; Mabona et al., 2019) to top-down approaches (Lin et al., 2019; Zhang et al., 2020; Nguyen et al., 2021; Koto et al., 2021), we argue that the bottom-up paradigm is conceptually intuitive as humans analyse the structure of documents incrementally based on elementary structures. Furthermore, in contemporaneous work, Yu et al. (2022) have shown that bottom-up parsers built on a language model pre-trained at the EDU level outperform top-down parsers trained comparably.

In this paper, we revisit the bottom-up approach and introduce a novel *unconstrained* bottom-up discourse parsing $\mathcal{O}(n^2)$ by adopting the sequence-labelling framework of Koto et al. (2021). *Unconstrained* means that we relax the fixed left-to-right

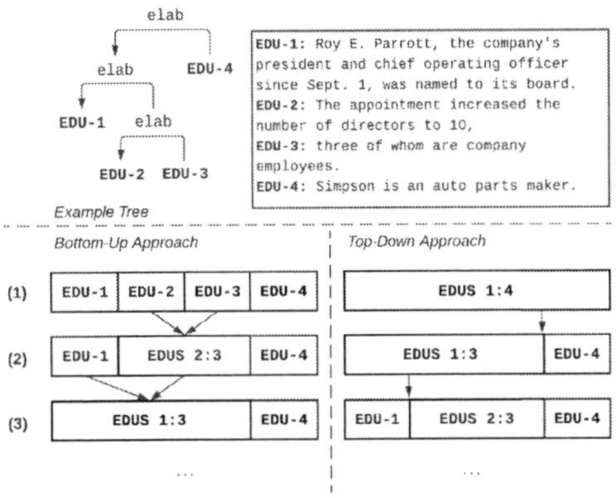

Figure 1: An example discourse tree (`elab` = elaboration, "←" means Nucleus–Satellite relation). For this tree, we show the parsing states of the bottom-up (left) and top-down (right) approaches.

direction of discourse tree construction, allowing us to make the easiest decisions first. Intuitively speaking, when it comes to making the harder decisions, the history of existing structures can be used to make more reliable predictions.

Goldberg and Elhadad (2010) introduced the non-directional easy-first algorithm to dependency parsing, which is a greedy, best-first parser, which relaxes the left-to-right order constraint of other bottom-up transition-based algorithms (Yu et al., 2018). Because the model is conditioned on existing parsed structures, we need to sample parsing trajectories to train the model, and compare two simple sampling methods: (1) left-to-right, and (2) random. To the best of our knowledge, we are the first to propose a bottom-up model for discourse parsing using the easy-first algorithm in a sequence labelling framework.

To summarize our contributions: (1) we propose a novel bottom-up context-sensitive parser; (2) we explore sampling methods for training a context-sensitive parser; and (3) we devise a novel dynamic oracle for our unconstrained bottom-up discourse

Proceedings of 3rd Workshop on Computational Approaches to Discourse, pages 35–41
October 16 – 17, 2022.

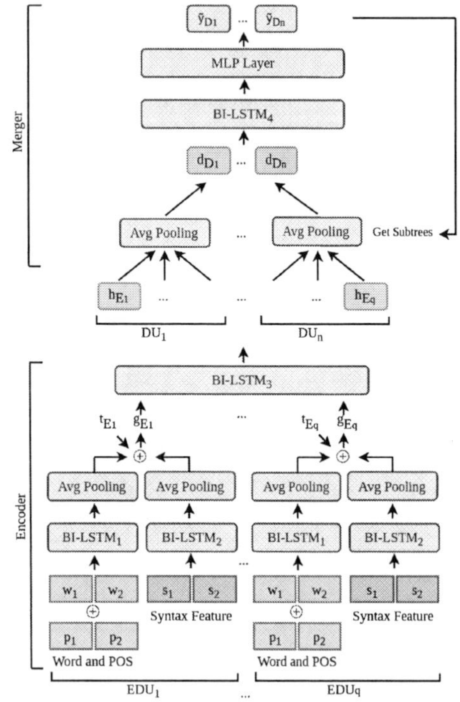

Figure 2: Architecture of the model

parser. We make the source code available online.[1]

2 Bottom-Up RST Parsing

We construct RST trees in a bottom-up fashion, starting with a sequence of EDUs and sequentially merging adjacent discourse units. At each stage, there are multiple merge points in the partially-parsed document that make up the gold discourse tree, and we define all such points to be gold merges. We impose no constraint on which gold merge needs to be executed first.

Following Koto et al. (2021), we frame the merging task as a sequence labeling problem. We train a merging model to assign a binary label $y \in \{0, 1\}$ to each discourse unit, where 1 indicates the unit and its right neighbour are subject to a gold merge. For each parse state, we train the model to label all gold merge points. At test time, we select the highest-probability merge point to construct the next parse state. We assign the discourse label and nuclearity relation separately with a second classifier after a merge is decided.

2.1 Model

Following Koto et al. (2021), our merging module consists of two blocks, as depicted in Figure 2. The first block is an EDU encoder. We use the hierarchical LSTM architecture of Yu et al. (2018), generating encodings with implicit syntax features. We obtain a suitable representation for each EDU text span $\{w_1, w_2, \ldots, w_m\}$ by using two Bi-LSTMs (Bi-LSTM$_1$ and Bi-LSTM$_2$). Bi-LSTM$_1$ is given the neural embedding of w_i concatenated with the part of speech embedding as input. Bi-LSTM$_2$ is given the syntax embedding s_i of each work as input. The syntax embedding comes from the syntax dependency parser from Dozat and Manning (2017). We also use an EDU type embedding t_{E_j} to distinguish EDUs at the end of a paragraph from other EDUs. The final EDU encoding g_{E_j} is the concatenation of the average output states for both Bi-LSTMs over the EDU and the EDU type embedding t_{E_j}:

$$\begin{aligned} x_i &= w_i \oplus p_i \\ \{a_1^w, .., a_p^w\} &= \text{Bi-LSTM}_1(\{x_1, .., x_p\}) \\ \{a_1^s, ..., a_p^s\} &= \text{Bi-LSTM}_2(\{s_1, .., s_p\}) \\ g_{E_j} &= \text{Avg-Pool}(\{a_1^w, .., a_p^w\}) \oplus \\ &\quad \text{Avg-Pool}(\{a_1^s, .., a_p^s\}) \oplus t_{E_j} \end{aligned}$$

Given a sequence of independent EDU encodings, we use a third Bi-LSTM (Bi-LSTM$_3$) to capture relationships between EDUs and produce a contextualized encoding h_{E_j}:

$$\{h_{E_1}, \ldots, h_{E_q}\} = \text{Bi-LSTM}_3(g_{E_1}, \ldots, g_{E_q})$$

The second block (the top half of Figure 2) is the merger, and deviates from Koto et al. (2021). The parse state consists of a sequence of discourse units, each of which is represented by averaging the encodings of the component EDUs:

$$d_{D_k} = \text{Avg}(h_{E_a}, \ldots, h_{E_b})$$

where D_k is a discourse unit with EDU span $E_{a:b}$.

We use a fourth Bi-LSTM (Bi-LSTM$_4$) to encode relationships between complex discourse units and assign a binary label to each merge.

$$\{d'_{D_1}, \ldots, d'_{D_n}\} = \text{Bi-LSTM}_4(d_{D_1}, \ldots, d_{D_n})$$

$$\hat{y}_{D_k} = \sigma(\text{MLP}(d'_{D_k}))$$

[1]https://github.com/Redrew/NeuralRST-Bottom-Up

Algorithm 1 Bottom-up Dynamic Oracle

function DYNORACLE(E, O, R)
  # For training only
  # E is list of EDUs
  # O is gold order for merger
  # R is list of gold discourse labels based on O
  $q = \text{length}(E)$; $state = \{E_1, \ldots, E_q\}$
  while $\|state\| > 1$ **do**
    $id_{gold} = \text{oracleMerge}(state, O, R)$
    $id_{pred} = \text{predictMerge}(state)$
    $r_{pred1} = \text{predictLabel}(state, id_{gold})$
    $r_{pred2} = \text{predictLabel}(state, id_{pred})$
    if random() $> \alpha$ **then**
      $state = merge(state, id_{gold})$
      $r_{gold} = \text{oracleLabel}(state, id_{gold})$
      $L = Loss(id_{gold}, r_{gold}, id_{pred2}, r_{pred1})$
    else
      $state = merge(state, id_{pred})$
      $r_{oracle} = \text{oracleLabel}(state, id_{pred})$
      $L = Loss(id_{gold}, r_{oracle}, id_{pred1}, r_{pred1})$
    end if
  end while
end function

We predict the joint probability distribution of the nuclearity and discourse labels after a merge is chosen by feeding the encodings d'_{ind}, d'_{ind+1} of the selected discourse units into an MLP layer, where ind is the index of the left discourse unit chosen to be merged:

$$z_{nuc+dis} = \text{softmax}(\text{MLP}(d'_{ind}, d'_{ind+1}))$$

The final training loss of our model is the combination of the merging and nuclearity-discourse prediction loss: $\mathcal{L} = \mathcal{L}_{merge} + \mathcal{L}_{nuc+dis}$.

2.2 Merge Order in Training

Because the model evaluates each merge candidate in the context of all previously parsed structures in the document, different permutations of parse states with discourse units not part of the merge candidate can lead to different predictions for that merge candidate. We propose to sample parse sequences for training. We evaluate two different sampling schemes: (1) merging gold pairs left to right; and (2) merging gold pairs at random.

2.3 Dynamic Oracle

In the standard training regimen, the model is only trained on parse states constructed by a sequence of correct merges. However, at test time, the model will often see error parse states, created by an incorrect merge in its history. Because the model is never trained on error states, it will struggle to recover after it has made a mistake.

We address this problem by training our model with a dynamic oracle, first introduced by Goldberg and Nivre (2012) and adopted for discourse parsers (Yu et al., 2018; Koto et al., 2021). Given an error state, a dynamic oracle provides the next set of merge actions that will minimize deviation between the gold tree and the final tree. The dynamic oracle is described in Algorithm 1. At each merging step in training, with probability α we execute the predicted merge instead of the sampled gold merge. In this manner, we introduce error states to the training set and teach the model to predict the next set of oracle actions, so the parser chooses the best actions even after a mistake.

In a document with n EDUs, the oracle assigns a merge order to each $n-1$ cut separating adjacent EDUs. The merge order is defined as the earliest step discourse units to the left and right of the cut are merged in all possible gold merge sequences. If the merge order of a cut is lower than adjacent cuts, it is an oracle action to merge the two discourse units around the cut, because in such cases, other gold merges that involve the two discourse units must come after the oracle action.

3 Experiments

3.1 Data

Following previous studies (Koto et al., 2021; Yu et al., 2018), we focus on the English language and use the RST Discourse Treebank for our experiments, binarizing all discourse trees in a right-heavy manner. It contains 347 annotated documents for training and 38 documents for testing. Our development set consists of the same 35 documents as Koto et al. (2021) and Yu et al. (2018), taken from the training set. Consistent to previous works, we use the same 18 coarse-grained discourse relationships and use the gold EDU segments for discourse tree construction.

3.2 Set-Up

We use the standard Parseval metrics for RST parsing of Marcu (2000). Based on the recommendations of a recent replication study (Morey et al., 2017), we report micro-averaged F-1 scores on labeled attachment decisions (original Parseval) instead of macro-averaged F-1 scores (RST-Parseval). The Parseval metrics consist of: `Span`, `Nuclearity`, `Relation`, and `Full`.[2]

[2] `Span` evaluates the correctness of the predicted tree structure. `Nuclearity` evaluates the tree skeleton together with nuclearity indications. `Relation` evaluates the tree skeleton with the discourse relations. `Full` evaluates the tree skeleton along with nuclearity indications and discourse relations.

Merge Order	Full	Bias
Left Merge	47.3	12.6
Random Merge	51.8	0.8

Table 1: Sampling strategy results over the dev set, based on the `Full` metric (micro-averaged F-score on labeled attachment decisions) and Bias (depth difference between the left and right end of the tree).

Method	S	N	R	F
Bottom-Up:				
Feng and Hirst (2014)†	68.6	55.9	45.8	44.6
Ji and Eisenstein (2014)†	64.1	54.2	46.8	46.3
Surdeanu et al. (2015)†	65.3	54.2	45.1	44.2
Joty et al. (2015)	65.1	55.5	45.1	44.3
Hayashi et al. (2016)	65.1	54.6	44.7	44.1
Li et al. (2016)	64.5	54.0	38.1	36.6
Braud et al. (2017)	62.7	54.5	45.5	45.1
Yu et al. (2018) (static)‡	71.1	59.7	48.4	47.4
Yu et al. (2018) (dynamic)‡	71.4	60.3	49.2	48.1
Mabona et al. (2019)	67.1	57.4	45.5	45.0
Yu et al. (2022) (XLNet)	**76.4**	**66.1**	**54.5**	**53.5**
Top-Down:				
Zhang et al. (2020)	67.2	55.5	45.3	44.3
Nguyen et al. (2021)	67.1	57.4	45.5	45.0
Koto et al. (2021) (static)‡	72.7	61.7	50.5	49.4
Koto et al. (2021) (dynamic)‡	73.1	62.3	51.5	50.3
Our proposed Bottom-Up Method:				
Static‡	73.3	62.0	50.1	49.1
Dynamic‡	<u>73.6</u>	<u>62.3</u>	<u>50.3</u>	<u>49.3</u>

Table 2: Results over the test set calculated using micro-averaged F-1 on labeled attachment decisions (original Parseval). All metrics (S: `Span`, N: `Nuclearity`, R: `Relation`, F: `Full`) are averaged over three runs. "†" and "‡" denote that the model uses sentence and paragraph boundary features, respectively.

We adopt the hyperparameter settings used in Koto et al. (2021). `GloVe` embeddings (Pennington et al., 2014) are used to encode the words in each EDU. We use CoreNLP (Manning et al., 2014) to obtain POS tag, and initialize each POS encoding as a random vector. The embedding dimension of words, POS tags, EDU type and syntax features are 200, 200, 100 and 1200, respectively. The dimensionality of the Bi-LSTMs in the encoder is 256 and Bi-LSTM_4 in the merge classifier has a dimension of 128. We use batch size = 4, gradient accumulation = 2, learning rate = 0.001, dropout probability = 0.5, and optimizer = Adam (with epsilon of 1e-6). When training with a dynamic oracle, we activate the dynamic oracle after 50 epochs.

We tune the α value used in the dynamic oracle on the development set. We performed grid search on α values, each averaging the `Full` Parseval metric over three random seeds. For training with a dynamic oracle, we found that $\alpha = 0.8$ resulted in the best `Full` Parseval score.

We use a single Tesla V100 SXM2 32 GB with 4 CPU cores to run our experiments. A run with static oracle takes around 14 hours in run time.

3.3 Results

We present analysis of the sampling strategy in Table 1. All results are averaged over three runs with different random seeds on the development set, with a static oracle. We compare training with left-first state sequences and randomly-sampled state sequences, and find that the latter result in an absolute +4.5 improvement over training with left-first state sequences. As such, we use random sampling for the remainder of the paper.

We benchmark our parser against previous state-of-the-art RST parsers over the test set. The results are presented in Table 2 (original Parseval).

Training with a dynamic oracle improved results over a static oracle, with a Full score increase of +0.2. Even with a static oracle, our parser surpasses previous bottom-up parsers with a simple greedy algorithm, without the need for complex post-editing or a chart-parsing algorithm. The sequence labeling framework has the benefit of being conceptually simpler than transition parsers. Training with a dynamic oracle adds algorithmic complexity during training, but our inference procedure remains the same. Our parser is most comparable with the transition-based parser proposed by Yu et al. (2018), which shares the same LSTM-architecture as our work and also utilises implicit syntax features. Our results demonstrate that a parser with the context of the document structure outperforms parsers without structure context.

Compared to the top-down parser proposed by Koto et al. (2021) with the dynamic oracle, our results for Span and Nuclearity are superior or equivalent, but the relation classification results are slightly inferior, resulting in slightly lower results overall. It is important to note that, while noticeably superior to our approach, the methods of Yu et al. (2022) and Zhang et al. (2021) are heavily based on pre-trained LMs, where our method makes no use of pre-training, which we leave to future work.

3.4 Analysis

We perform bias analysis on discourse trees produced by models trained with left-first states against random states. We introduce a simple metric for detecting heaviness bias, by calculating the depth difference between the left-most and the right-most leaf nodes and subtracting the expected difference from the gold tree. A higher value indicates the predicted trees are more right-heavy than the gold trees.

$$d_i = \text{Depth}_{pred}(EDU_i) - \text{Depth}_{gold}(EDU_i)$$

$$b = d_n - d_1$$

When the parser is trained with left-first examples, $b = 12.6$ (Table 1), indicating a bias towards right-heavy trees. This is expected due to right merges being merged last in the training examples, thus creating an imbalance in the number of correct merges in the left and right sides of the tree in the training examples. On the other hand, when trained with random sampling, there is no such imbalance in the training dataset. And we see that there is no significant bias, with $b = 0.8$.

4 Conclusion

In this work, we adapted the sequence labeling framework to bottom-up RST parsing, introducing an easy-first parser conditioned on past decisions. We investigated methods to sample training examples for a non-directional parser, and proposed a dynamic oracle for our bottom-up parsing. We demonstrated that our parser achieves competitive results for bottom-up RST parsing.

Acknowledgements

We are grateful to the anonymous reviewers for their helpful feedback and suggestions. This research was undertaken using the LIEF HPC-GPGPU Facility hosted at The University of Melbourne. This facility was established with the assistance of LIEF Grant LE170100200.

References

Chloé Braud, Maximin Coavoux, and Anders Søgaard. 2017. Cross-lingual RST discourse parsing. In *Proceedings of the 15th Conference of the European Chapter of the Association for Computational Linguistics: Volume 1, Long Papers*, pages 292–304, Valencia, Spain. Association for Computational Linguistics.

Timothy Dozat and Christopher D. Manning. 2017. Deep biaffine attention for neural dependency parsing. In *Proceedings of the 2016 International Conference on Learning Representations*, pages 1–8.

Vanessa Wei Feng and Graeme Hirst. 2014. A linear-time bottom-up discourse parser with constraints and post-editing. In *Proceedings of the 52nd Annual Meeting of the Association for Computational Linguistics (Volume 1: Long Papers)*, pages 511–521, Baltimore, Maryland. Association for Computational Linguistics.

Yoav Goldberg and Michael Elhadad. 2010. An efficient algorithm for easy-first non-directional dependency parsing. In *Human Language Technologies: The 2010 Annual Conference of the North American Chapter of the Association for Computational Linguistics*, pages 742–750, Los Angeles, California. Association for Computational Linguistics.

Yoav Goldberg and Joakim Nivre. 2012. A dynamic oracle for arc-eager dependency parsing. In *Proceedings of COLING 2012*, pages 959–976, Mumbai, India. The COLING 2012 Organizing Committee.

Grigorii Guz and Giuseppe Carenini. 2020. Coreference for discourse parsing: A neural approach. In *Proceedings of the First Workshop on Computational Approaches to Discourse*, pages 160–167, Online. Association for Computational Linguistics.

Katsuhiko Hayashi, Tsutomu Hirao, and Masaaki Nagata. 2016. Empirical comparison of dependency conversions for RST discourse trees. In *Proceedings of the 17th Annual Meeting of the Special Interest Group on Discourse and Dialogue*, pages 128–136, Los Angeles. Association for Computational Linguistics.

Hugo Hernault, Helmut Prendinger, David A. duVerle, and Mitsuru Ishizuka. 2010. Hilda: A discourse parser using support vector machine classification. *Dialogue and Discourse*, 1(3):1–33.

Yangfeng Ji and Jacob Eisenstein. 2014. Representation learning for text-level discourse parsing. In *Proceedings of the 52nd Annual Meeting of the Association for Computational Linguistics (Volume 1: Long Papers)*, pages 13–24, Baltimore, Maryland. Association for Computational Linguistics.

Shafiq Joty, Giuseppe Carenini, and Raymond T. Ng. 2015. CODRA: A novel discriminative framework for rhetorical analysis. *Computational Linguistics*, 41(3):385–435.

Naoki Kobayashi, Tsutomu Hirao, Hidetaka Kamigaito, Manabu Okumura, and Masaaki Nagata. 2020. Top-down RST parsing utilizing granularity levels in documents. In *AAAI 2020 : The Thirty-Fourth AAAI Conference on Artificial Intelligence*.

Fajri Koto, Jey Han Lau, and Timothy Baldwin. 2021. Top-down discourse parsing via sequence labelling.

In *Proceedings of the 16th Conference of the European Chapter of the Association for Computational Linguistics: Main Volume*, pages 715–726, Online. Association for Computational Linguistics.

Qi Li, Tianshi Li, and Baobao Chang. 2016. Discourse parsing with attention-based hierarchical neural networks. In *Proceedings of the 2016 Conference on Empirical Methods in Natural Language Processing*, pages 362–371, Austin, Texas. Association for Computational Linguistics.

Xiang Lin, Shafiq Joty, Prathyusha Jwalapuram, and M Saiful Bari. 2019. A unified linear-time framework for sentence-level discourse parsing. In *Proceedings of the 57th Annual Meeting of the Association for Computational Linguistics*, pages 4190–4200, Florence, Italy. Association for Computational Linguistics.

Amandla Mabona, Laura Rimell, Stephen Clark, and Andreas Vlachos. 2019. Neural generative rhetorical structure parsing. In *Proceedings of the 2019 Conference on Empirical Methods in Natural Language Processing and the 9th International Joint Conference on Natural Language Processing (EMNLP-IJCNLP)*, pages 2284–2295, Hong Kong, China. Association for Computational Linguistics.

William C. Mann and Sandra A. Thompson. 1988. Rhetorical structure theory: Toward a functional theory of text organization. *Text Interdisciplinary Journal for the Study of Discourse*, pages 243–281.

Christopher Manning, Mihai Surdeanu, John Bauer, Jenny Finkel, Steven Bethard, and David McClosky. 2014. The Stanford CoreNLP natural language processing toolkit. In *Proceedings of 52nd Annual Meeting of the Association for Computational Linguistics: System Demonstrations*, pages 55–60, Baltimore, Maryland. Association for Computational Linguistics.

Daniel Marcu. 2000. *The Theory and Practice of Discourse Parsing and Summarization*. MIT Press, Cambridge, USA.

Mathieu Morey, Philippe Muller, and Nicholas Asher. 2017. How much progress have we made on RST discourse parsing? a replication study of recent results on the RST-DT. In *Proceedings of the 2017 Conference on Empirical Methods in Natural Language Processing*, pages 1319–1324, Copenhagen, Denmark. Association for Computational Linguistics.

Thanh-Tung Nguyen, Xuan-Phi Nguyen, Shafiq Joty, and Xiaoli Li. 2021. RST parsing from scratch. In *Proceedings of the 2021 Conference of the North American Chapter of the Association for Computational Linguistics: Human Language Technologies*, pages 1613–1625, Online. Association for Computational Linguistics.

Jeffrey Pennington, Richard Socher, and Christopher Manning. 2014. Glove: Global vectors for word representation. In *Proceedings of the 2014 Conference on Empirical Methods in Natural Language Processing (EMNLP)*, pages 1532–1543, Doha, Qatar. Association for Computational Linguistics.

Mihai Surdeanu, Tom Hicks, and Marco Antonio Valenzuela-Escárcega. 2015. Two practical rhetorical structure theory parsers. In *Proceedings of the 2015 Conference of the North American Chapter of the Association for Computational Linguistics: Demonstrations*, pages 1–5, Denver, Colorado. Association for Computational Linguistics.

Nan Yu, Meishan Zhang, and Guohong Fu. 2018. Transition-based neural RST parsing with implicit syntax features. In *Proceedings of the 27th International Conference on Computational Linguistics*, pages 559–570, Santa Fe, New Mexico, USA. Association for Computational Linguistics.

Nan Yu, Meishan Zhang, and Guohong Fu. 2018. Transition-based neural RST parsing with implicit syntax features. In *Proceedings of the 27th International Conference on Computational Linguistics*, pages 559–570.

Nan Yu, Meishan Zhang, Guohong Fu, and Min Zhang. 2022. RST discourse parsing with second-stage EDU-level pre-training. In *Proceedings of the 60th Annual Meeting of the Association for Computational Linguistics (Volume 1: Long Papers)*, pages 4269–4280, Dublin, Ireland. Association for Computational Linguistics.

Longyin Zhang, Fang Kong, and Guodong Zhou. 2021. Adversarial learning for discourse rhetorical structure parsing. In *Proceedings of the 59th Annual Meeting of the Association for Computational Linguistics and the 11th International Joint Conference on Natural Language Processing (Volume 1: Long Papers)*, pages 3946–3957, Online. Association for Computational Linguistics.

Longyin Zhang, Yuqing Xing, Fang Kong, Peifeng Li, and Guodong Zhou. 2020. A top-down neural architecture towards text-level parsing of discourse rhetorical structure. In *Proceedings of the 58th Annual Meeting of the Association for Computational Linguistics*, pages 6386–6395, Online. Association for Computational Linguistics.

A Additional Results

We also report the results in Table 3 with the RST-Parseval Procedure. We include the reported results from Guz and Carenini (2020) as a reference. Their reported RST-Parseval scores beat other works, but uses the pre-trained language model SpanBERT.

A.1 Evaluation with RST-Parseval Procedure

Method	S	N	R	F
Bottom-Up				
Feng and Hirst (2014)*†	84.3	69.4	56.9	56.2
Ji and Eisenstein (2014)*†	82.0	68.2	57.8	57.6
Surdeanu et al. (2015)*†	82.6	67.1	55.4	54.9
Joty et al. (2015)*	82.6	68.3	55.8	54.4
Hayashi et al. (2016)*	82.6	66.6	54.6	54.3
Li et al. (2016)*	82.2	66.5	51.4	50.6
Braud et al. (2017)*	81.3	68.1	56.3	56.0
Yu et al. (2018) (1 run)*‡	85.5	73.1	60.2	59.9
Yu et al. (2018) (static)‡	85.8	72.6	59.5	59.0
Yu et al. (2018) (dynamic)‡	85.6	72.9	59.8	59.3
Our Work:				
Static ‡	86.7	73.2	60.5	60.0
Dynamic‡	86.8	73.6	60.6	60.1
Top-Down				
Kobayashi et al. (2020)*†‡	**87.0**	**74.6**	60.0	-
Koto et al. (2021) LSTM (static)‡	86.4	73.4	60.8	60.3
Koto et al. (2021) LSTM (dynamic)‡	86.6	73.7	**61.5**	**60.9**
Using Pretrained LM:				
Guz and Carenini (2020) (SpanBERT-CorefFeats)*†‡	88.1	76.1	63.6	-
Human	88.3	77.3	65.4	64.7

Table 3: Results over the test set calculated using micro-averaged F-1 on RST-Parseval. All metrics (S: `Span`, N: `Nuclearity`, R: `Relation`, F: `Full`) are averaged over three runs. "*" denotes reported performance. "†" and "‡" denote that the model uses sentence and paragraph boundary features, respectively.

A.2 Evaluation over Development Set

Method	S	N	R	F
Static	71.8	62.2	52.6	51.8
Dynamic	71.6	62.0	53.0	52.2

Table 4: Results over the development set calculated using micro-averaged F-1 on labeled attachment decisions (original Parseval). All metrics are averaged over three runs.

Using Translation Process Data to Explore Explicitation and Implicitation through Discourse Connectives

Ekaterina Lapshinova-Koltunski
University of Hildesheim
Lübecker Str. 3
DE-31141 Hildesheim
lapshinovakoltun@uni-hildesheim.de

Michael Carl
Kent State University
800 E. Summit St.
Kent, OH 44242
mcarl6@kent.edu

Abstract

We look into English-German translation process data to analyse explicitation and implicitation phenomena of discourse connectives. For this, we use the database CRITT TPR-DB which contains translation process data with various features that elicit online translation behaviour. We explore the English-German part of the data for discourse connectives that are either omitted or inserted in the target, as well as cases when changing a weak signal to strong one, or the other way around. We determine several features that have an impact on cognitive effort during translation for explicitation and implicitation. Our results show that cognitive load caused by implicitation and explicitation may depend on the discourse connectives used, as well as on the strength and the type of the relations the connectives convey.

1 Introduction

Explicitation in translation is often defined as an increased usage of linking devices, such as discourse connectives. Implicitation is an opposite phenomenon and means a decrease in the number of connectives used in translation because of frequent ommissions. Both explicitation and implicitation belong to the phenomena of translationese (Gellerstam, 1986; Baker, 1993; Toury, 1995, amongst others). The latter have received an increased attention in multilingual language processing (see e.g. Dutta Chowdhury et al., 2020; Artetxe et al., 2020; Graham et al., 2020). In this paper, we analyse explicitation and implicitaion phenomena from a cognitive perspective, i.e. looking into translation process data. The data under analysis is parallel, so that we are able to inspect the translational pairs of English discourse connectives in the sources and their translations into German. Apart from taking into consideration omission or insertion of a connective, we also analylse transformation cases, when the degree of the explicitation signal is changed. The strength of the signal a connective conveys depends on the number and frequency of relations they may trigger (Asr and Demberg, 2012; Crible, 2020): ambiguous connectives convey a weaker signal. We interpret translation from a weak signal connective, e.g. *but* in example (1-a) into a strong signal connective, e.g. *jedoch* in example (1-b), as explicitation. No explicitation (equivalence) is observed if connectives hold a signal of the same degree: *but* translated into *aber* in example (1-c).

(1) a. *Some of the most vulnerable countries of the world have contributed the least to climate change, but are bearing the brunt of it.*
   b. *Einige der Länder, die weltweit am wenigsten zum Klimawandel beigetragen, tragen jedoch die Hauptlast.*
   c. *Einige der am meisten gefährdeten Länder der Welt haben am wenigsten zum Klimawandel beigetragen, leiden aber dessen Folgen.*

We start from the general cases of implicitation and explicitation (tokens marked by a syntactic parser as connectives left out or added in translation) and analyse three features of describing behaviour during translation: production (typing) pauses and reading time in translation unit. We also look at the probability of translation choices. Then, we analyse translation patterns of the two selected connectives *but* and *aber* to trace the transformation pattern from connectives with a weaker signal to connectives with a stronger signal. In general, we assume that explicitation requires more cognitive effort from a translator, whereas implicitation or equivalence do not do so. At the same time, the more ambiguous a connective is, the higher a cognitive effort for its translation. So, ambiguity or the strength of a signal may also have an impact on a translator's behaviour.

Proceedings of 3rd Workshop on Computational Approaches to Discourse, pages 42–47
October 16 – 17, 2022. ©2022 International Conference on Computational Linguistics

The remainder of the paper is organised as follows: in Section 2, we briefly outline the related work. Our methodology is explained in Section 3. We describe the analyses performed in Section 4. In Section 5, we discuss the results and outline our plans for future work.

2 Related Work

Explicitation in translation occurs when a translated text contains new linguistic units not present in the source or more specific linguistic units are used instead of more general units in the source (Klaudy and Károly, 2005, p. 15). Explicitation or implicitation through discourse connectives (as increased or reduced usage of discourse connectives, Olohan and Baker, 2000; Blum-Kulka, 1986), as well as the factors influencing these phenomena, have been analysed in various studies on both human and machine translation (see Shi et al., 2019; Hoek et al., 2015; Zufferey and Cartoni, 2014; Meyer and Webber, 2013).

There are studies showing that explicitation and implicitation may also depend on the type of relation a discourse connective triggers. For instance, cognitively complex relations (e.g. relation of contrast) are not so often left implicit than cognitively simple ones (see Hoek et al., 2017; Blumenthal-Dramé, 2021).

3 Methodology

We use the CRITT translation process database (CRITT TPR-DB, Carl et al., 2016), which has been collected over years and contains a substantial amount of translation process data from numerous translation sessions. The collected data contains features allowing an in-depth assessment of human behavior in translation. We use a part of the data that includes English-German parallel texts. The experiment for this data was set up in such a way that each translator translated every text[1] in one of the three modes: translating from scratch, post-editing and performing monolingual post-editing. Texts were permuted between successive translators, with the intention that for each set of 6 translators, every text would be translated, post-edited and edited 6 times. Each of the 6 source texts is between 110 and 161 words in length and designed in such a way that it fits on one Translog screen (see more details in Carl et al., 2015).

We selected a number of features reflecting translation behaviour, see Table 1. Production pauses reflect the cognitive processes involved in changing attentional states (Schilperoord, 1996): we may assume that if translators start the typing process, they either finalised translation of what they had in mind, or they faced a problem during the writing process. Production pauses can also occur during monitoring, revision and source text reading. Several studies (Kumpulainen, 2015; Lacruz and Shreve, 2014; O'Brien, 2006) have argued that pauses in the flow of keystrokes are indicators of cognitive effort, with longer pauses indicating extended cognitive effort. Pauses are also related to the notion of `first translation response universal` (Carl, 2021), i.e. longer pauses would indicate more entangled activation of the linguistic resources and follow in more challenged and less literal translation (Malmkjær, 2011). The total reading time of the source or the target segments should indicate where the processing effort was located, and whether more attention was drawn to the source or to the target text. Since the database contains 32 translation variants of the English source texts, word translation probabilities are available, too, which have been found to be reverse proportional of cognitive processing effort (see e.g., Carl and Schaeffer, 2017).

4 Analyses

4.1 General cases

First, we extracted the overall connective explicitation in the data at hand without considering explicitation from a weaker to a strong signal. For this, we extracted instances of connectives marked with the part-of-speech label KON on the target side that were aligned to a zero in the source (Query 1 in Table 2). In total, we found 18 cases of this kind of explicitation that we call explicitation insertions. The connective *und*, see example (2), is the most frequently used explicitation insertion (11), followed by *aber* (5), *sowie* (1) and *denn* (1).

(2) *Analysts have warned that prices will increase further still, making it hard for the Bank of England to cut interest rates...*
Analysten haben gewarnt, dass die Preise weiterhin steigen werden <u>*und*</u> *es der Bank of England Probleme bereiten wird, das Zinsniveau zu senken...*

We look at the pause (Pause) that precedes the pro-

[1] With 32 translators and 6 English source texts in total.

Feature	Definition
Pause	Typing pause preceding the production unit (i.e. its first keystroke).
TrtS/TrtT	Total reading time in translation unit in the source/target window, refers to the sum total of all fixation durations on a particular area of interest (e.g. token) irrespective of when these occurred during the session.
ProbT	Probability of current translation choice

Table 1: Features available in the CRITT TPR-DB used in the analyses

1	tTokens[(((tTokens.PoS=='KON'))& (tTokens.SGroup=='- - -'))]	3	set(sTokens[(sTokens.SToken=='but')].TGroup)
2	sTokens[(((sTokens.PoS=='CC'))& (sTokens.TGroup=='- - -'))]	4	set(sTokens[(sTokens.SToken=='and')].TGroup)

Table 2: Queries used for the searches in the CRITT TPR-DB

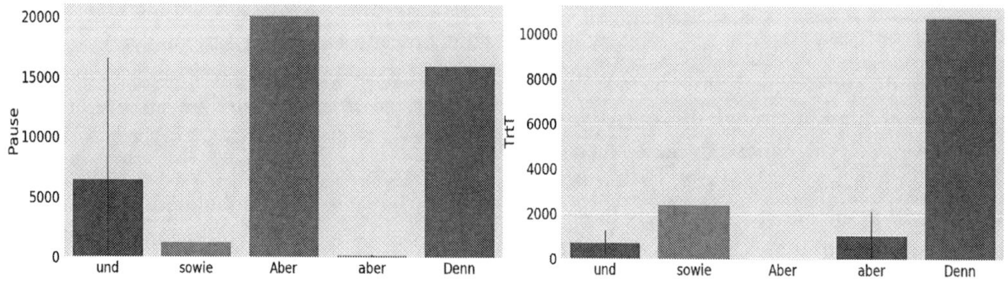

Figure 1: Typing pauses and total reading time on the target of the explicitation connectives

duction of the translation, as well as the total fixation time on the target token (TrtT) for the extracted cases of explicitation, see Figure 1. The longest pauses are observed for the connectives at sentence start. This may indicate processes of translation finalisation of the previous sentence or reading and comprehension activity of the next sentence or phrase. We also observe longer pauses before the production of *und*, which is the most ambiguous connective here (expresses relations of expansion, comparison or time)[2]. This ambiguity causes longer pauses, as activation and selection of linguistic equivalents for more ambiguous items is more challenging. Interestingly, no or very short pauses are observed before the production of the connective *aber*. Explicitation of this connective may require less processing effort because it commonly signals the relation of contrast, a complex relation, and according to the existing studies (see Hoek et al., 2017) is more frequently made explicit as compared to simple relations. At the same time, the total reading times of the explicitation cases with *aber* and *und* are similar.

(3) *Some of the most vulnerable countries of the world have contributed the least to climate change, but are bearing the brunt of it. Einige der Länder, die den Klimawandel am härtesten zu spüren bekommen, haben nur sehr wenig dazu beigetragen.*

Next, we extracted cases of implicitation, i.e. when a connective in the source (marked as CC) is left out, see Query 2 in Table 2 above. The query extracted 11 cases with the connectives *and* (9) and *but* (2). However, manual validation revealed that the query results contained noise does and only one case of implicitation, as illustrated in example (3), where the connective *but* was left out in the German translation.

4.2 Specific connectives

Then, we extracted all cases of translations of the discourse connective *but* (Query 3 in Table 2 above). The results of the query show that our data contains translations with *aber, doch, jedoch* and *obwohl*, as well as implicitation (the connective was left out). While we consider translations with *aber* as an equivalent, translations with *doch, jedoch, obwohl* are explicitation cases, as these connectives trigger one type of relations only and hence, convey a stronger signal than *but*[3]. Production pauses and the total reading time in the source (*but*) and the target tokens (*aber, doch, jedoch, obwohl*), as well as the probability of translations are visualised in Figure 2. As expected, implicita-

[2] see Connective-Lex, the web-based multilingual lexical resource (Stede et al., 2019).

[3] The ambiguity of was verified with the help of Connective-Lex.

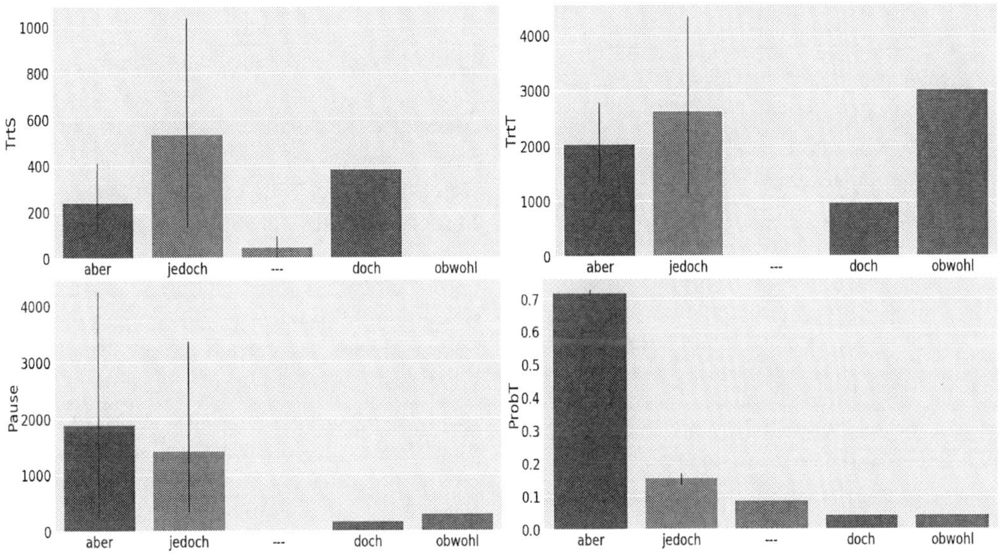

Figure 2: Total reading time, typing pauses and probability of translations of *but*

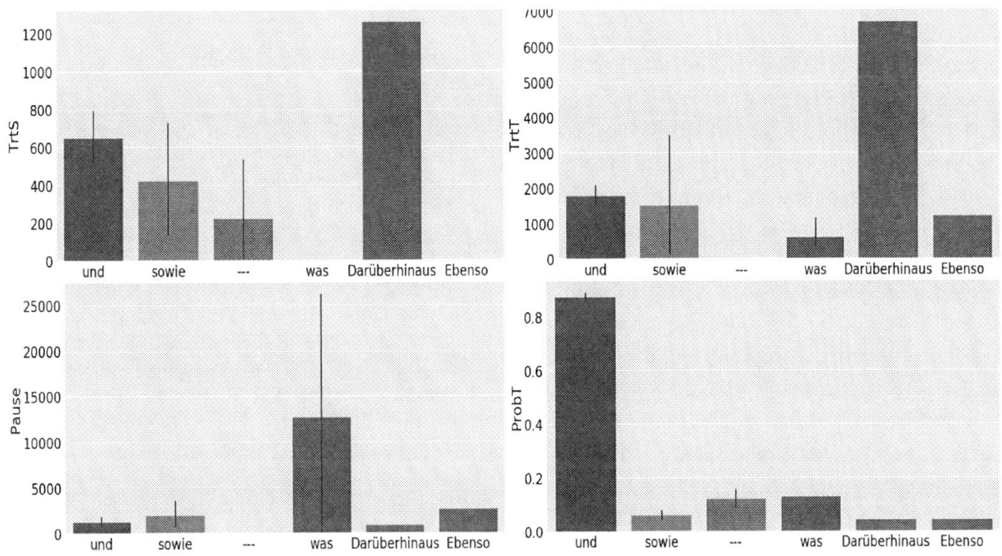

Figure 3: Total reading time, typing pauses and probability of translations of *and*

tion requires the lest effort, which is reflected in no pauses and short reading time. However, for the equivalence translation with *aber*, we observe the longest production pauses, which is against our expectations. For explicitation with *jedoch*, we observe longer pauses and longer reading times. Generally, this discourse connective is less frequent in the data and may need additional time for mental activation. Explicitation with *obwohl* has the longest reading time in the target and no reading time on the source. Both *obwohl* and *doch* have the shortest pauses. Given the source connective *but*, the connective *aber* has the highest translation probability, followed by *jedoch*, omission, *doch* and *obwohl*. The graphs reveal that higher translation probability generally causes longer production pauses.

Production pauses and the total reading time of the source *and* and the target tokens (*und, sowie, was, Darüberhinaus, Ebenso*), as well as omissions were extracted with Query 4 in Table 2 and are visualised in Figure 3.

The longest production pause is observed for *was*, which is not a connective but rather a pronoun referring to the previous clause, see example (4).

(4) *Incentives must be offered to encourage developing countries to go the extra green mile and implement clean technologies, and could also help minimise...*
Es werden daher Anreize angeboten, Entwicklungsländer zu fördern, um ihnen zusätzlich grüne Standards zu ermöglichen und saubere Technologien zu implementieren, was auch zur Minimierung...

This case is also indicated by low reading time on the target (and no reading time on the source). Similarly to translations of *but*, no pause and the shortest reading time are observed when *and* is left out, confirming that implicitation does not require a high cognitive effort. This indicates that little/no cognitive effort is required for implicitation of comparison and expansion relations triggered by *but* and *and*. Equivalence translation is featured by a very short pause (different to what we observed in the case of *but*), but high reading time. Interestingly, there is an opposite tendency here in terms of the source vs. target reading time: in equivalence translation of *but*, it was shorter on the source (also generally common in the process of translation), whereas for *and* translated as *und*, it is longer on the source. This could be due to the greater ambiguity of *and*, if compared to *but*. The highest reading time, but short pauses, are reported for the explicitation with *Darüberhinaus*. The longest pause is observed for explicitation with *was*. The equivalent connective *und* has the highest translation probability given the source *and*. Here, translation probability does not necessarily causes longer pauses and hence greater cognitive load, which is different to the cases with *but*.

5 Summary and Discussion

We attempted to analyse explicitation and implicitaion phenomena of discourse connectives in English-German translations using the parallel data from the CRITT TPR-DB. Our results show that while implicitation requires low cognitive effort, it is not necessarily so for an equivalent translation. This may depend on the connective as indicated by the differences in pauses observed. This may also be dependent on the strength of its signal and the type of relation this connective conveys. Explicitation generally causes a higher effort in the analysed cases, which are however quite few. In the future, we would like to analyse more instances of explicitation and implicitation for more connectives and include data originating from different genres, as there could be variation in processing discourse connectives across different contexts. Moreover, we also intend to analyse differences in the cognitive processing of connectives depending on the processes of translation – if a translation was produced from scratch or if it was post-edited from a machine-translated output. This will provide some insights on how human translators are impacted by discourse-related issues in machine-translated texts. Moreover, translation process data provides explanations about problems human translators face. These may correlate with the difficulties in machine translation. A better understanding of problems in human translation may also help to improve machine translation.

References

Mikel Artetxe, Gorka Labaka, and Eneko Agirre. 2020. Translation artifacts in cross-lingual transfer learning. In *Proceedings of the 2020 Conference on Empirical Methods in Natural Language Processing (EMNLP)*, pages 7674–7684, Online. Association for Computational Linguistics.

Fatemeh Torabi Asr and Vera Demberg. 2012. Measuring the strength of linguistic cues for discourse relations. In *Proceedings of the Workshop on Advances in Discourse Analysis and its Computational Aspects*, pages 33–42, Mumbai, India. The COLING 2012 Organizing Committee.

Mona Baker. 1993. Corpus linguistics and translation studies: Implications and applications. In G. Francis Baker M. and E. Tognini-Bonelli, editors, *Text and Technology: in Honour of John Sinclair*, pages 233–250. Benjamins, Amsterdam.

Shoshana Blum-Kulka. 1986. Shifts of Cohesion and Coherence in Translation. In Juliane House and Shoshana Blum-Kulka, editors, *Interlingual and intercultural communication*, pages 17–35. Gunter Narr, Tübingen.

Alice Blumenthal-Dramé. 2021. The online processing of causal and concessive relations: Comparing native speakers of English and German. *Discourse Processes*, 0(0):1–20.

Michael Carl. 2021. Micro units and the first translational response universal. In Michael Carl, editor, *Explorations in Empirical Translation Process Research*, Machine Translation: Technologies and Applications, pages 233–257. Springer.

Michael Carl, Silke Gutermuth, and Silvia Hansen-Schirra. 2015. Post-editing machine translation: Efficiency, strategies, and revision processes in professional translation settings. In *Psycholinguistic and Cognitive Inquiries into Translation and Interpreting*, volume 115 of *Benjamins Translation Library*. John Benjamins.

Michael Carl and Moritz Schaeffer. 2017. Sketch of a noisy channel model for the translation process. In Silvia Hansen-Schirra, Oliver Czulo, and Sascha Hofmann, editors, *Empirical Modelling of Translation and Interpreting*, volume 7 of *Translation and Multilingual Natural Language Processing*, pages 71–116. Language Science Press, Berlin.

Michael Carl, Moritz Schaeffer, and Srinivas Bangalore. 2016. The CRITT translation process research database. In Michael Carl, Srinivas Bangalore, and Moritz Schaeffer, editors, *New Directions in Empirical Translation Process Research*, New Frontiers in Translation Studies, pages 13–54. Springer Science+Business Media, Germany.

Ludivine Crible. 2020. Weak and strong discourse markers in speech, chat and writing: Do signals compensate for ambiguity in explicit relations? *Discourse Processes*, 57(9):793–807.

Koel Dutta Chowdhury, Cristina España-Bonet, and Josef van Genabith. 2020. Understanding translationese in multi-view embedding spaces. In *Proceedings of the 28th International Conference on Computational Linguistics*, pages 6056–6062, Barcelona, Spain (Online). International Committee on Computational Linguistics.

Martin Gellerstam. 1986. Translationese in Swedish novels translated from English. In L. Wollin and H. Lindquist, editors, *Translation Studies in Scandinavia*, pages 88–95. CWK Gleerup, Lund.

Yvette Graham, Barry Haddow, and Philipp Koehn. 2020. Statistical power and translationese in machine translation evaluation. In *Proceedings of the 2020 Conference on Empirical Methods in Natural Language Processing (EMNLP)*, pages 72–81, Online. Association for Computational Linguistics.

Jet Hoek, Jacqueline Evers-Vermeul, and Ted J.M. Sanders. 2015. The role of expectedness in the implicitation and explicitation of discourse relations. In *Proceedings of the Second Workshop on Discourse in Machine Translation*, pages 41–46, Lisbon, Portugal. Association for Computational Linguistics.

Jet Hoek, Sandrine Zufferey, Jacqueline Evers-Vermeul, and Ted J.M. Sanders. 2017. Cognitive complexity and the linguistic marking of coherence relations: A parallel corpus study. *Journal of Pragmatics*, 121:113–131.

Kinga Klaudy and Krisztina Károly. 2005. Implicitation in translation: Empirical evidence for operational asymmetry in translation. *Across Languages and Cultures*, 6:13–28.

M. Kumpulainen. 2015. On the operationalisation of 'pauses' in translation process research. *The International Journal for Translation & Interpreting Research*, 7:47–58.

I. Lacruz and GM. Shreve. 2014. Pauses and cognitive effort in post-editing. In O'Brien S., L. Balling, M. Carl, M. Simard, and L. Specia, editors, *Post-editing: processes, technology and applications*, pages 246–272. Cambridge Scholars Publishing, Newcastle upon Tyne.

Kirsten Malmkjær. 2011. Translation universals. In Kirsten Malmkjær and Kevin Windle, editors, *The Oxford handbook of translation studies*, pages 83–93. Oxford University Press, Oxford.

Thomas Meyer and Bonnie Webber. 2013. Implicitation of discourse connectives in (machine) translation. In *Proceedings of the Workshop on Discourse in Machine Translation*, pages 19–26, Sofia, Bulgaria. Association for Computational Linguistics.

Sharon O'Brien. 2006. Pauses as indicators of cognitive effort in post-editing machine translation output:. *Across Languages and Cultures*, 7(1):1 – 21.

Maeve Olohan and Mona Baker. 2000. Reporting that in translated English: Evidence for subconscious processes of explicitation? *Across Languages and Cultures*, 1:141–158.

Joost Schilperoord. 1996. The distribution of pause time in written text production. In Gert Rijlaarsdam, Huub van den Bergh, and Michel Couzijn, editors, *Theories, models and methodology in writing research*, pages 21–35. Amsterdam University Press.

Weijia Shi, Muhao Chen, Yingtao Tian, and Kai-Wei Chang. 2019. Learning bilingual word embeddings using lexical definitions. In *Proceedings of the 4th Workshop on Representation Learning for NLP (RepL4NLP-2019)*, pages 142–147, Florence, Italy. Association for Computational Linguistics.

Manfred Stede, Tatjana Scheffler, and Amália Mendes. 2019. Connective-lex: A web-based multilingual lexical resource for connectives. *Discours*, 24.

Gideon Toury. 1995. *Descriptive Translation Studies – and Beyond*. John Benjamins, Amsterdam.

Sandrine Zufferey and Bruno Cartoni. 2014. A multifactorial analysis of explicitation in translation. *Target*, 26(3):361–384.

Label distributions help implicit discourse relation classification

Frances Yung and **Kaveri Anuranjana** and **Merel Scholman** and **Vera Demberg**
Language Science and Technology, Saarland University
{frances, kaveri, m.c.j.scholman, vera}@coli.uni-saarland.de

Abstract

Implicit discourse relations can convey more than one relation sense, but much of the research on discourse relations has focused on single relation senses. Recently, DiscoGeM, a novel English multi-domain corpus, which contains 10 crowd-sourced labels per relational instance, has become available. In this paper, we analyse the co-occurrences of relations in DiscoGeM and show that they are systematic and characteristic of text genre. We then test whether information on multi-label distributions in the data can help implicit relation classifiers. Our results show that incorporating multiple labels in parser training can improve its performance, and yield label distributions which are more similar to human label distributions, compared to a parser that is trained on just a single most frequent label per instance.

1 Introduction

Much of the research on the discourse relations (DR) assumes (implicitly or explicitly) that only one relation can hold between two spans of text, particularly in the computational field. However, recent work has shown that discourse relations, and implicit relations in particular, can allow for multiple interpretations (e.g., Rohde et al., 2016; Scholman and Demberg, 2017). Prior work has also shown that certain relation senses tend to co-occur in newspaper text, such as ARG2-AS-DETAIL with REASON and CONTRAST with CONCESSION (Demberg et al., 2019). The current study investigates whether the co-occurrence of implicit relation senses depends on text genre.

We furthermore explore whether the performance of a state-of-the-art discourse relation classifier can be improved by training it on the distribution of human-annotated labels, as opposed to training it on only the top label.

The contributions of the current paper are twofold: (1) We analyse the specific patterns of DR co-occurrences in different genres, showing that the distribution of sense co-occurrences are dependent on genre. (2) We train an implicit DR classifier on distributionally upsampled DR labels for each relation instance. This approach leads to better performance according to a soft evaluation metric (cross entropy), demonstrating that the natural distribution of human interpretations can be captured better when training on the distribution of labels.

2 Previous work

2.1 Co-occurring discourse relations

The assumption that a pair of relational arguments can convey only one single relation sense has led to discourse-annotated resources typically containing one annotated sense per instance. However, recent studies have shown that many relation instances can express multiple senses (e.g., Rohde et al., 2016), and that certain senses co-occur frequently, because their meanings are similar or compatible (e.g., Demberg et al., 2019).

For example, Demberg et al. (2019) showed that newspaper texts annotated as part of both the PDTB (Prasad et al., 2008) and the RST-DT (Carlson et al., 2003) showed consistent patterns of disagreement: CONTRAST and CONCESSION were confused frequently with each other (cf. Robaldo and Miltsakaki, 2014), which can be attributed to the relation senses being similar and difficult to distinguish. Further, the data showed disagreement on INSTANTIATION, LEVEL-OF-DETAIL and REASON relations (cf. Scholman and Demberg, 2017). The confusion between INSTANTIATION and LEVEL-OF-DETAIL relations can be attributed to the relation senses being similar in meaning. The co-occurrence of these senses and REASON is because these relations tend to be multi-interpretable. In the current paper, we extend this line of work by examining whether and how the co-occurrence of relation types differs between genres.

Proceedings of 3rd Workshop on Computational Approaches to Discourse, pages 48–53
October 16 – 17, 2022. ©2022 International Conference on Computational Linguistics

2.2 Multilabel annotation

An instance of a discourse relation can be annotated with multiple labels under two scenarios. In the first scenario, one annotator (or multiple) identifies multiple co-occurring senses and annotates all identified senses. In the second scenario, each annotator only identifies one discourse sense depending on their perspective. The annotators may agree or disagree with each others.

In the current work, we include data from two corpora: the Penn Discourse Treebank 3.0 (PDTB, Webber et al., 2019) and the DiscoGeM corpus (Scholman et al., 2022). Multilabel relations annotated in the PDTB belong to the first scenario. However, the annotation does not necessarily specify all co-occurring senses (Prasad et al., 2007). In practice, only about 5% of the relations received multiple labels.

The multilabel annotations in DiscoGeM belong to the second scenario. Annotators were asked to identify the strongest relation sense they inferred, but this interpretation could vary between annotators. Every relation instance was annotated by ten participants, thus multiple perspectives were included in the relation sense annotation (that is, the different annotations for one instance were aggregated into one multilabel annotation). As in the PDTB annotation, it is not guaranteed that the multilabels include all co-occurring senses; in the extreme case, the same prominent sense could have been chosen by all workers while the other co-occurring sense does not appear in the multilabel.

2.3 Multilabel evaluation

Two forms of evaluation have been used in the context of multilabel data: (i) traditional *hard evaluation metrics* such as accuracy or F1 can be used, but these ignore the information provided by the distribution of senses; (ii) *soft evaluation metrics* can be applied in scenarios where it is assumed that the instances do not involve a single true label; these leverage the information provided by distributions, and seem best suited to our task.

Uma et al. (2021) considered a variety of soft evaluation approaches, including cross entropy (Peterson et al., 2019), Jensen-Shannen divergence (Lin, 1991), and entropy similarity and correlation. Their analyses of these metrics' results on six datasets shows that the relative performance of training methods is critically affected by the chosen evaluation. They recommend to use cross-entropy to compare the output of a system to a soft label; we follow this recommendation in the current work. Cross entropy captures how confident the model is in its top prediction compared to humans and the reasonableness of its distribution over alternative categories.

3 Data

We include data from the PDTB 3.0 (Webber et al., 2019) and the DiscoGeM corpus (Scholman et al., 2022).

PDTB The PDTB 3.0 is a news text corpus containing articles from the Wall Street Journal. The corpus contains 15,544 inter-sentential (between sentences) and 6,188 intra-sentential (within sentences) implicit relations. We follow the split suggested by Ji and Eisenstein (2015): sections 2-20, 0-1, and 21-22 are used as training, validation, and test sets.

DiscoGeM DiscoGeM is a crowdsourced mixed-genre corpus of 6,505 inter-sentential implicit relations, containing text from Europarl (prepared spoken text, argumentative genre), literature (narrative genre), and Wikipedia (informative genre) (see Scholman et al., 2022, for more details on the genres and data selection process). DiscoGeM contains texts from both original English sources as well as translated English.

The annotations were crowdsourced using a connective insertion task, that allowed the authors to extract PDTB 3.0 labels. Every instance received annotations from 10 crowdworkers to represent the multiple interpretation of the discourse relation. The Cohen's Kappa between the multiple labels annotated by the crowdworkers and trained annotators was 0.79 (see original paper for further details.) The labels used in the current study are a single majority vote label (randomly sampled in case two senses received an equal number of votes) and a soft distribution label based on the raw votes.

The DiscoGeM data was split[1] into 70% for train, 20% for test, and 10% for dev for the implicit relation classification reported in Section 5 and for future studies training and testing on DiscoGeM. In splitting the data, we first set aside texts for testing only (i.e., unseen texts). These texts consist of 26 out of 197 turns of speech in the Europarl genre,

[1]The splits can be found in DiscoGeM's online repository: `https://github.com/merelscholman/DiscoGeM`.

2 out of 20 books in the Novels genre, and 4 out of 69 Wikipedia texts. They are balanced between original English and translated English. For the remainder of the data, we ensured that each text[2] is split proportionally into train, dev and test sets. The dev and test portions are always consecutive, such that the training portions have minimal gaps, but either one comes first randomly and is randomly picked from different locations of the article. The distribution of the relation types in the training data we used is shown in Table 3.

4 Analysis of relation co-occurrence

We examine what types of DRs are often interpreted by the crowdworkers at the same time. For each annotated instance in DiscoGeM, we select the TOP1 label as the label that received the majority vote (randomly sampled in case of a tie). The TOP2 label is the label that received the second highest vote. In case where there's less than 30% agreement on the TOP2 label, we consider TOP1 to be a single label (i.e., the TOP2 label = ALONE). This allows us to focus the analysis on co-occurrences of generally accepted interpretations.

From the distributions of the TOP1 $\sim$ TOP2 pairs of the entire corpus, we extract the marginal probabilities $P(Top1)$ and $P(Top2)$, as well as expected joint probabilities $P_{exp}(Top1, Top2)$. We compare the observed joint probabilities $P(Top1, Top2)$ per genre by normalized pointwise mutual information (NPMI), as defined below:

$$NPMI(Top1; Top2) = \frac{PMI(Top1; Top2)}{-\log P_{exp}(Top1, Top2)}$$

Figure 1 shows the NPMI of each unique pair of DRs for the most frequent level-2 relation types.[3] A value of 1.0 means the relations always occur together, -1.0 means they never occur together, and 0.0 means that they co-occur as much as would be expected to happen by chance.

The results confirm the overall co-occurrence patterns established in previous work: CONTRAST and CONCESSION co-occur frequently, and INSTANTIATION, LEVEL-OF-DETAIL and REASON also co-occur in every genre. Interestingly, these

Europarl	CNJ	RES	REA	DET	INS	CNC	CNT	PRE
CNJ		.184	.063	.053	.010	.008	-.196	-.209
RES	.214		-.061	.018	.066	.175	-.025	-.172
REA	.024	-.033		.180	.103	.072	.113	-.185
DET	.057	.035	.042		.262	-.111	-.114	-.381
INS	.001	-.072	.093	.230		-.004	.000	.000
CNC	.029	.097	.001	-.118	.025		.217	.000
CNT	-.320	.005	-.047	.000	-.021	.235		.000
PRE	-.245	-.104	.000	.000	.000	-.176	-.062	
ALN	-.097	.234	.008	-.016	.033	.025	-.087	-.800

Novel	CNJ	RES	REA	DET	INS	CNC	CNT	PRE
CNJ		-.045	.006	.198	-.087	-.093	.018	.192
RES	.011		-.097	-.042	-.129	-.064	-.080	.333
REA	-.042	-.080		.171	.056	-.134	.000	-.048
DET	.144	-.172	.198		.227	-.063	-.025	-.132
INS	-.063	-.162	-.054	.153		-.110	.000	-.076
CNC	-.086	.019	.000	-.131	.000		.124	.054
CNT	.060	-.063	.032	.083	-.032	.141		-.079
PRE	.109	.246	.000	-.164	-.025	.087	.000	
ALN	.008	-.128	.085	.007	-.141	-.031	.047	.175

Wikipedia	CNJ	RES	REA	DET	INS	CNC	CNT	PRE
CNJ		.097	.000	.257	.091	-.185	.197	.208
RES	.153		.000	.004	-.017	-.137	.000	.196
REA	.000	.000		-.148	.000	.000	.000	.000
DET	.209	-.245	.000		.371	.000	.000	.000
INS	.130	.000	.000	.306		.101	.157	.000
CNC	-.021	-.096	.000	.000	.000		.302	.122
CNT	.103	-.071	.000	.004	.000	.385		.000
PRE	.186	.108	.000	-.140	.000	.220	.120	
ALN	.337	-.291	-.740	-.055	-.011	-.084	.059	-.060

Figure 1: NPMI per genre of co-occurrences of the most frequent relation senses. The x-axis represents the TOP1 label; the y-axis the TOP2 label.

co-occurrences are more likely when INSTANTIATION or LEVEL-OF-DETAIL is the TOP1 label, and not REASON. This indicates that INSTANTIATIONS and LEVEL-OF-DETAIL relations can often also convey an argumentative relation, but this is less likely vice versa.

There are also a number of interesting divergences between genres. For example, relations in the Wikipedia genre are more likely to co-occur with CONJUNCTIONS than relations in other genres; CONJUNCTIONS are also more likely to occur alone in Wikipedia. This is likely due to the expository nature of Wikipedia texts. Further, we can see differences in the patterns of RESULT and PRECEDENCE relations. These are likely to co-occur in novels in particular, as well as Wikipedia to some degree, but not in Europarl data. Rather, in Europarl, RESULT relations occur as a single label (ALN) more frequently compared to the other genres. This matches the argumentative nature of the political genre.

We can conclude from this analysis that there are not only differences in the relation distributions

[2] Europarl: turn of speech; Novels: paragraphs; Wiki: articles.

[3] CNJ: CONJUNCTION; RES: RESULT; REA: REASON; DET: LEVEL-OF-DETAIL; INS: INSTANTIATION; CNC: CONCESSION; CNT: CONTRAST; PRE: PRECEDENCE; ALN: alone

between genres, but there are also differences in the distribution of relation co-occurrences between genres. Such fine-grained differences might impact parsers. In the remainder of this paper, we will study whether incorporating multiple labels in parser training, instead of only the TOP1 label can improve performance.

5 Implicit Relation Classification

5.1 Model

We implemented the BMGF-RoBERTa model (Liu et al., 2021), which is the current state-of-the-art model for 11-way implicit relation classification on the PDTB 2.0 corpus. The model combines three modules – contextualized word representations, bilateral text span multi-perspective matching and a global gated multi-head attention module. Liu et al. (2021) reported an accuracy of 58.13% on the PDTB 2.0 (11-way).

As discussed in Section 4, the distribution of DRs varies across genres. To capture this information, we prepend a genre token to the input. This token makes the model aware of the genre while learning DR prediction from the text. We also experimented with adding the genre token to the dense layers, but adding it to the input gave better results.

We train the model for 50 epochs on the combined datasets of PDTB 3.0 and DiscoGeM (see Section 3 for the splits) based on the code implemented by Liu et al. (2021).[4] For the results, we select the epoch with the highest accuracy on the combined test set (PDTB+DiscoGeM) and report the accuracy and F1 scores on the individual test sets from that epoch.

5.2 Incorporating multiple labels in training

Peterson et al. (2019) demonstrate that models generally trained on a single label task generalize poorly on out-of-domain data because the distributions learnt across the labels do not reflect human uncertainty. We incorporate information on label co-occurances as well as human uncertainty in predicting DRs by proportionally upsampling labels from the DiscoGeM human annotations. We implement three models to study the effect of incorporating multiple labels in training:

(i) Single label model (**single**): The model is trained on the instances in the dataset using only the majority votes.

(ii) Multi-label model (**multi.**): The model is trained on duplicated instances; the repetition is proportional to the distribution of relation senses provided by the crowdworkers (labels with less than 20% votes were excluded to eliminate noisy samples).

(iii) Uncertainty model (**uncert.**): This setting is similar to multi., but all the repetitions are instances of the majority label (labels with less than 20% votes were excluded).

Consider an instance that received the following annotations from 10 crowdworkers: 5×A, 3×B, 1×C, and 1×D. In the single label model, this instance is included once in training and is classified as A. In the multi-label model, this instance is included 8 times; 5 times it is classified as A and 3 times as B. In the uncert. model, the instance is also included 8 times, but always classified as A.

The uncert. model thus takes into account the uncertainty of human annotation because instances with lower agreement are represented less in the training data. The multi-label model considers both uncertainty and sense co-occurrence, while the single model considers neither.

To keep the ratio of DiscoGeM to PDTB data as in the the single label condition, multi. and uncert. models are also upsampled. For the multi. model, if a second label is present, we treat the label distribution as a 50-50 split between the two labels. Otherwise the distribution consists only of the one label with a 100% weight. We upsample the PDTB instances by a factor of 6 (i.e., every PDTB instance is included six times in training), which is roughly the same factor by which the DiscoGem corpus was upsampled on average after excluding labels with less than 20% of the votes. For the uncert. model, we upsample only the majority label 6 times for all instances.

5.3 Results

The results are presented in Table 1; we report each metric averaged across 5 runs to account for variation in the results. Let us first consider the results on the DiscoGeM corpus – both as a complete dataset as well as per genre. When evaluated against a single gold label, the performance of the model trained on the distribution of labels (multi) is on par with the model trained just on a single

[4]The hyperparameters are identical to Liu et al. (2021) but batch size is 64.

label. However, the multi model reaches a better performance when evaluated against the distribution of human labels, compared to the single model, as shown in Table 2. Additionally, the certain-label model is substantially under-performing in both evaluation settings. This means that the improvement from training on the distribution of labels indeed comes from the information of how often each label is chosen and which labels co-occur with each other, and not simply from down-sampling difficult instances.

	DG-all	EP	Novel	Wiki	PDTB 3.0
single	48.66 (0.54)	53.25 (1.20)	45.31 (0.34)	**45.58 (2.76)**	**55.28 (1.04)**
	22.33 (1.37)	**25.88 (3.47)**	23.10 (1.71)	24.02 (2.90)	37.18 (1.91)
multi.	**49.91 (0.64)**	**54.45 (0.47)**	**47.13 (0.78)**	44.34 (2.08)	54.82 (0.73)
	23.66 (1.19)	25.44 (3.27)	**25.56 (1.07)**	**25.58 (3.91)**	**38.07 (2.25)**
uncert.	48.43 (0.54)	53.32 (1.34)	44.95 (0.85)	44.65 (4.23)	54.70 (0.61)
	21.62 (1.69)	22.08 (2.92)	23.10 (2.05)	24.65 (0.88)	32.48 (1.97)

Table 1: 11-way accuracy and macro F1 (in grey) of the single, multi. and uncert. models, evaluated against the single (majority) label. We report mean and (standard deviation) based on five runs.

	DG-all	EP	Novel	Wiki	PDTB 3.0
single	1.86 (.03)	1.79 (.02)	1.87 (.04)	2.08 (.04)	1.48 (.04)
multi.	**1.79 (.03)**	**1.73 (.02)**	**1.8 (.05)**	**2.03 (.06)**	**1.36 (.02)**
uncert.	1.83 (.05)	1.77 (.07)	1.84 (.05)	2.01 (.06)	1.48 (.02)

Table 2: Cross entropy (mean and standard deviation) of the single, multi and uncert. models, evaluated against all labels provided by the DiscoGeM crowdworkers. Smaller numbers are better.

	DG-all	EP	Novel	Wiki	PDTB 3.0
Conjunction	27.54	23.87	27.26	43.52	20.96
	53.36	51.32	51.37	62.11	52.76
Cause	33.75	43.83	28.20	18.50	26.50
	57.42	65.75	48.31	16.27	62.89
Level-of-detail	17.58	17.33	17.95	16.86	14.92
	40.84	41.31	43.07	27.34	38.93
Asynchronous	7.73	1.18	13.49	7.76	5.79
	52.91	20.20	56.40	33.50	56.70
Instantiation	4.45	5.05	3.51	6.3	6.69
	19.73	25.80	7.45	21.50	60.80
Concession	5.11	6.23	4.43	3.75	6.83
	20.19	13.6	24.8	18.3	46.00
train size	26287	11030	12511	2746	102306

Table 3: Label distribution (%, white rows) of the training data and averaged F1 (in grey) of the multi. model for the most frequent relation types. The last row shows the size of the upsampled training data.

Table 3 presents the distributions of the six relation types that most frequently occur in the training data, along with the per-class F1 score of the multi. model (i.e. after upsampling). These results show that the model's performance follows a similar pattern as the distribution per relation sense. For example, the performance on CAUSE relations is particularly high in the EP genre, likely because causal relations are abundant in the EP training data. The model shows divergent results for the LEVEL-OF-DETAIL (DET) relations: performance is particularly poor on Wiki data, even though the distribution is similar across genres. This can be explained by the co-occurrence patterns presented in Section 4. As seen in Figure 1, DET often co-occurs with CONJUNCTIONS (CNJ) in Wiki, and so the training data contains many instances annotated with DET and CNJ at the same time. Given the frequent distribution of CNJ in Wiki, the parser is likely to classify many of these instances as CNJ. For instances where DET is the majority label, the prediction of CNJ is credited by cross-entropy evaluation but penalized by the F1 score. This also explains the lower than expected performance of the CAUSE relations in the novel genre, where they frequently co-occur with ASYNCHRONOUS.

In sum, these results show that the parser is affected by genre distributions, and that when the parser diverges from the majority label, it can actually predict a related label that the annotation often co-occurs with. This indicates that our proposal of adding genre information and including multiple annotation in the training data was successful.

6 Discussion and Conclusion

We presented a simple, yet effective approach to take into account information on multi-label distributions in implicit relation classifiers. Our results show that adding multi-label information leads to results that are on par with single label models when using a hard evaluation metric. The multi-label model performs even better than single label models when using a soft evaluation metric. This means that the multi-label model generates labels that are more reasonable given the distributions of labels provided by humans. This was the case even for the PDTB test set, despite the PDTB being designed as a primarily single label dataset.

In future work, we also plan to study the impact of co-training with a large corpus such as the PDTB on the DiscoGeM genres. Furthermore, will explore methods of incorporating human uncertainty in discourse relation classification with a specific focus on out-of-domain data.

Acknowledgments

FY and KA are supported by the German Research Foundation (DFG) under Grant SFB 1102 ("Information Density and Linguistic Encoding", Project-ID 232722074). MS and VD are supported by the European Research Council (ERC) under the European Union's Horizon 2020 Research and Innovation Programme, Grant 948878 ("Individualized Interaction in Discourse").

References

Lynn Carlson, Daniel Marcu, and Mary Ellen Okurowski. 2003. Building a discourse-tagged corpus in the framework of rhetorical structure theory. In *Current and new directions in discourse and dialogue*, pages 85–112. Springer.

Vera Demberg, Merel CJ Scholman, and Fatemeh Torabi Asr. 2019. How compatible are our discourse annotation frameworks? insights from mapping rst-dt and pdtb annotations. *Dialogue & Discourse*, 10(1):87–135.

Yangfeng Ji and Jacob Eisenstein. 2015. One vector is not enough: Entity-augmented distributed semantics for discourse relations. *Transactions of the Association for Computational Linguistics*, 3:329–344.

Jianhua Lin. 1991. Divergence measures based on the Shannon entropy. *IEEE Transactions on Information theory*, 37(1):145–151.

Xin Liu, Jiefu Ou, Yangqiu Song, and Xin Jiang. 2021. On the importance of word and sentence representation learning in implicit discourse relation classification. In *Proceedings of the Twenty-Ninth International Conference on International Joint Conferences on Artificial Intelligence*, pages 3830–3836.

Joshua C Peterson, Ruairidh M Battleday, Thomas L Griffiths, and Olga Russakovsky. 2019. Human uncertainty makes classification more robust. In *Proceedings of the IEEE/CVF International Conference on Computer Vision*, pages 9617–9626.

Rashmi Prasad, Nikhil Dinesh, Alan Lee, Eleni Miltsakaki, Livio Robaldo, Aravind Joshi, and Bonnie Webber. 2008. The Penn Discourse TreeBank 2.0. In *Proceedings of the Sixth International Conference on Language Resources and Evaluation (LREC'08)*, Marrakech, Morocco. European Language Resources Association (ELRA).

Rashmi Prasad, Eleni Miltsakaki, Nikhil Dinesh, Alan Lee, Aravind Joshi, Robaldo Robaldo, and Bonnie Webber. 2007. The penn discourse treebank 2.0 annotation manual. *Philadelphia, University of Pennsylvania*.

Livio Robaldo and Eleni Miltsakaki. 2014. Corpus-driven semantics of concession: Where do expectations come from? *Dialogue & Discourse*, 5(1):1–36.

Hannah Rohde, Anna Dickinson, Nathan Schneider, Christopher NL Clark, Annie Louis, and Bonnie Webber. 2016. Filling in the blanks in understanding discourse adverbials: Consistency, conflict, and context-dependence in a crowdsourced elicitation task. In *Proceedings of the 10th Linguistic Annotation Workshop held in conjunction with ACL 2016 (LAW-X 2016)*, pages 49–58.

M C J Scholman and Vera Demberg. 2017. Examples and specifications that prove a point: Identifying elaborative and argumentative discourse relations. *Dialogue & Discourse*, 8(2):56–83.

Merel C. J. Scholman, Tianai Dong, Frances Yung, and Vera Demberg. 2022. Discogem: A crowdsourced corpus of genre-mixed implicit discourse relations. In *Proceedings of the Thirteenth International Conference on Language Resources and Evaluation (LREC'22)*, Marseille, France. European Language Resources Association (ELRA).

Alexandra N Uma, Tommaso Fornaciari, Dirk Hovy, Silviu Paun, Barbara Plank, and Massimo Poesio. 2021. Learning from disagreement: A survey. *Journal of Artificial Intelligence Research*, 72:1385–1470.

Bonnie Webber, Rashmi Prasad, Alan Lee, and Aravind Joshi. 2019. *The Penn Discourse Treebank 3.0 annotation manual*. Philadelphia, University of Pennsylvania.

The Keystone Role Played by Questions in Debate

Zlata Kikteva[1], **Kamila Gorska**[2], **Wassiliki Siskou**[1,3]
Annette Hautli-Janisz[1], **Chris Reed**[2]
[1]University of Passau, Germany
[2]University of Dundee, UK
[3]University of Konstanz, Germany

Abstract

Building on the recent results of a study into the roles that are played by questions in argumentative dialogue (Hautli-Janisz et al., 2022a), we expand the analysis to investigate a newly released corpus that constitutes the largest extant corpus of closely annotated debate. Questions play a critical role in driving dialogical discourse forward; in combative or critical discursive environments, they not only provide a range of discourse management techniques, they also scaffold the semantic structure of the positions that interlocutors develop. The boundaries, however, between providing substantive answers to questions, merely responding to questions, and evading questions entirely, are fuzzy and the way in which answers, responses and evasions affect the subsequent development of dialogue and argumentation structure are poorly understood. In this paper, we explore how questions have ramifications on the large-scale structure of a debate using as our substrate the BBC television programme *Question Time*, the foremost topical debate show in the UK. Analysis of the data demonstrates not only that questioning plays a particularly prominent role in such debate, but also that its repercussions can reverberate through a discourse.

1 Introduction

Whether employed to garner votes, determine policy, air grievances or test theories, debates rely upon questioning; questions provide the driving force, a rhythmic sparking of the engine of debate. They do not merely provide impetus for a moment or a turn, however: they can have far-reaching ramifications, scaffolding large structures of subsequent discursive interaction. We intuitively recognise this keystone role of questions, when, for example, we criticise politicians for evading questions, or are frustrated when our own are ignored. (The US 2016 presidential debates offer a good example, wherein Clinton was roundly criticised by the press at both ends of the political spectrum for failing to give direct answers to the questions she was asked). Our intuitions, however, have heretofore not been matched by a theoretical understanding. How do different types of questions lead to different interactional and argumentative structures? What patterns of ramifications do different classes of reactions to those questions have? How can questions be used strategically to open up and limit the space of information and outcome?

For the purpose of exploring these questions in naturally occurring argumentation at scale, we investigate a new dataset, QT30 (Hautli-Janisz et al., 2022b), comprising analysis of thirty episodes of broadcast topical debate from the UK BBC television programme *Question Time*. This is three times the size of the previously largest dataset and offers a rich environment in which to test the theories from Hautli-Janisz et al. (2022a). By comparing the analysis of QT30 with that of the earlier datasets, we can establish a robust grounding for our conclusions about the role that *information-seeking, assertive* and *rhetorical questions* play across domains of argumentation. We also show that the *response space* across these three question types remains consistent, i.e., whether questions are ignored, reacted to, responded to, or in fact answered.

2 Related work

Categorising the function of questions has been a notoriously tricky issue, not only in theoretical but also in computational approaches to discourse. The field is therefore confronted with "a trade-off between usefulness and ease or consistency of coding" (Carletta et al., 1997, p. 15). The majority of approaches represent and model information-seeking (or so-called 'canonical') questions, as for instance in FriendsQA (Yang and Choi, 2019). In the MapTask coding scheme (Carletta et al., 1997), rhetorical questions do not form a discrete category. The Switchboard corpus (Calhoun et al., 2010) en-

Proceedings of 3rd Workshop on Computational Approaches to Discourse, pages 54–63
October 16 – 17, 2022.

codes information-seeking questions according to their syntactic property (e.g. yes-no-questions, wh-questions), non-information seeking questions are summed up in the category 'rhetorical questions'. Stivers and Enfield (2010) propose seven different 'social actions' of questions, among them 'Request for Information', 'Outloud' ("delivered to no one in particular"), and 'Rhetorical Question' ("Questions that may seek a response but do not seek an answer").

In terms of characterising the response space, Stivers and Enfield (2010) use the four categories of 'Non-response', 'Non-answer response', 'Answer', and 'Can't determine' (p. 2624) for spontaneous, naturally occurring conversation, showing some overlap with the six-way distinction of Berninger and Garvey (1981) with 'Possible answers', 'Indirect answers', 'Confessions of Ignorance', 'Clarification requests', 'Evasive replies' and 'Miscellaneous' (targeted at nursery school child conversation). Łupkowski and Ginzburg (2016) propose a taxonomy for query responses, bearing some resemblance to Berninger and Garvey (1981). For the task-based interactions in MapTask, the BEE corpora and informal conversations in the BNC corpus, Ginzburg et al. (2019) propose a two-way distinction of responses into 'Answers' and 'Non-answers', with more fine-grained categories subsumed under them.

Our goal in this paper is to combine the strengths of these approaches whilst maintaining a simplicity in taxonomy that enables us to focus specifically upon the impact of questions in argumentative discourse. For our investigation, we pair structures of question-answering with an analysis of how argumentation is invoked or 'anchored' in dialogue. It is only in this combination that we are able to derive insights into how these two realms of structures impact surrounding discourse. The only framework that allows us to investigate both realms of discourse in parallel is Inference Anchoring Theory (IAT) (Budzynska et al., 2014, 2016), a pragmatically-driven account of dialogical argumentation.

3 Inference Anchoring Theory and the question/response space

The central motivation of Inference Anchoring Theory (IAT) (Budzynska et al., 2014, 2016) is to provide a theoretical framework for analysing dialogical argumentation. As such, IAT sets out to answer the question of where argumentation *comes from* in dialogical interaction and acts as a theory-neutral scaffolding that integrates different communicative structures, namely *dialogue structure*, *argument structure* (including inference understood in the logical manner) and *illocutionary forces* such as asserting, suggesting or promising, to anchor argument structure in dialogue structure. One of the primary loci of argumentation is precisely in the asking of, and responding to, questions of particular sorts, and it is upon these questions that we focus here, rather than questions of clarification (Purver et al., 2001, 2003); of recovery from non-understanding (Bohus and Rudnicky, 2005); or in many cases of personal information (Sakai et al., 2018), inter alia. An example of how questions can lead to argumentative structure is shown in (1) in which Question Time moderator Fiona Bruce uses questions as a tool that allows her to forward and control the debate:

(1) a. Fiona Bruce [00:48:45] *[...] Nadhim, should the UK be doing more to help find a long lasting solution? Because who knows how long this particular ceasefire will last.*

b. Nadhim Zahawi [00:49:05] *The simple answer is yes, and we have been doing. The Foreign Secretary Dominic Raab and the US Secretary of State Antony Blinken have worked tirelessly, one, to deescalate the situation... Obviously President Biden has made a huge difference, as has our Prime Minister to urge both sides...*

c. Fiona Bruce [00:49:30] *But there is no peace process at the moment. Is there anything the UK can do with the international community to try and foster a situation where that can start again?*

In (1-a) Fiona Bruce asks one of the panel members a question about a long-lasting resolution of the Israeli–Palestinian conflict. She then supports her question by expressing her concerns regarding the current ceasefire (*'Because who knows how long this particular ceasefire will last'*). Panel member Nadhim Zahawi answers Fiona Bruce's question directly with 'yes' in (1-b) and further elaborates his answer with *'we have been doing [more]'*. He then proceeds to support his claim by mentioning previous work on the de-escalation of the conflict by Foreign Secretary Dominic Raab and the US Secretary of State Antony Blinken as well as President Biden and the UK Prime Minister. However, by mentioning the past work of the UK and US politicians, he avoids going into detail regarding the future steps of the UK in the conflict. In (1-c) Fiona Bruce picks up on that and steers the conversation back to the current Israeli–Palestinian conflict by stating that 'there is no peace process at the moment'. She then uses this as a reason to ask Nadhim Zahawi another and more specific question on whether the UK can play a role in restarting the peace talks, pressing him to give a more relevant answer. This second question leads to further discussion, which is not illustrated in this example.

In the following we go through the components of analysis that are needed to investigate the role of questions in argumentative dialogue.

3.1 Propositional relations

Argumentative structures are relations between propositions; core IAT assumes three different relations that are designed to capture argumentative structure in dialogue:

Inference (Support, 'Default Inference', RA, green node) Holds between propositions when one (or more) proposition is used to provide a reason to accept another proposition.

Conflict (Attack, 'Default Conflict', CA, red node) Holds between two propositions when one proposition is used to provide an incompatible alternative to another proposition.

Rephrase (Rephrase, 'Default Rephrase', MA, orange node) Holds between two propositions when one proposition is used to rephrase, refine or generalise another proposition. Rephrases also hold between questions and answers.

3.2 Illocutionary acts of questioning

Illocutionary relations anchor propositions in locutions and capture the communicative intent of the speaker in uttering a locution or a pair of locutions. We instantiate illocutionary relations with the concept of illocutionary forces of Searle (1969) and Searle and Vanderveken (1985), however we use a simplified version in which there are no commissives or expressives and just two simple types of directives (questions and challenges). For QT30, we use a set of nine illocutionary connections that either anchor propositions in locutions (as with 'Asserting') or propositional relations in the dialogical structure (as with 'Arguing', 'Disagreeing' and 'Restating' in the case of 'Default Inference', 'Default Conflict' and 'Default Rephrase', respectively). The subset we require for the purposes of this paper are summarised briefly below.

- **Assertive Questioning** Speaker S communicates information and at the same time asks for confirmation/rejection from their interlocutor.
- **Pure Questioning** Speaker S is seeking information or asking for the opinion of their interlocutors.
- **Rhetorical Questioning** Speaker S is expressing an opinion in the form of an interrogative.
- **Restating** Speaker S rephrases a previous claim. Anchors a 'Default Rephrase'.
- **Default Illocuting** Used to anchor a a 'Default Rephrase' which captures an answer to a question, i.e., the answer instantiates (parts of) the question.

The graph on the right-hand side of Figure 1 provides the IAT analysis for Example (1), produced with OVA+ (Online Visualisation of Argument – http://ova.arg.tech/), an open-source online interface for the analysis of argumentation in dialogues (Janier et al., 2014). OVA+ allows for a representation of the argumentative structure of a text as a directed graph.[1] For zooming out of the discourse and getting a 'bird's-eye view' of an entire debate, there are visualisation tools that form a part of the Argument Web (Reed et al., 2017): the left-hand side of Figure 1, for example, is produced using *ArgNav* (argnav.arg.tech/).

The graph on the right-hand side of Figure (1) shows the different components of analysis for Example (1). In this graph, the right side shows the dialogical structure (blue boxes on the right), the left shows the propositional structure (blue boxes on the left). They are connected with the illocutionary acts (yellow) in the middle. Argument relations are between propositions on the left.

The exchange starts with Fiona Bruce questioning Nadhim Zahawi regarding the UK's further

[1]The IAT annotation guidelines are here: http://www.arg.tech/f/IATannotationguidelines.pdf.

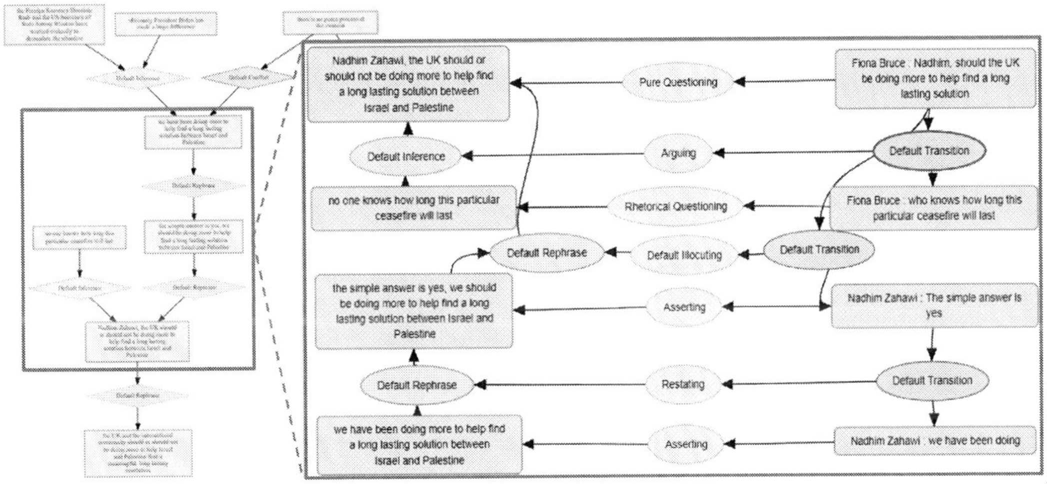

Figure 1: The IAT diagram of Example (1) (`https://www.aifdb.org/argview/21415`) on the right features locutions (blue nodes on the right-hand side), propositions (blue nodes on the left-hand side), illocutionary relations (yellow nodes in the middle), dialogical relations (purple nodes on the right) and propositional relations – 'Default Inference' (green) and 'Default Rephrase' (orange). The diagram on the left features propositions only and the argument relations between them. It captures the larger argumentative exchange of which Example (1) is part of.

help in de-escalation of the Israeli–Palestinian conflict (*'Should the UK be doing more to help find a long-lasting solution?'* – 'Pure Questioning') and then by way of a rhetorical question she brings up her concerns regarding the longevity of the current ceasefire (*'Who knows how long this particular ceasefire will last?'* – 'Rhetorical Questioning'). Nadhim Zahawi then answers her initial question in (1-b) with *'the simple answer is yes'*. The relation between propositions is 'Default Rephrase' which is anchored via 'Default Illocuting', indicating that this is an answer to a question. He then proceeds to explain his answer with *'we have been doing [more]'*. Discourse moves like that are analysed as rephrases, which are indicated with 'Default Rephrase' between two propositions and anchored in the dialogical structure on the right with 'Restating'. The graph on the left-hand side of Figure 1 shows the complete exchange between Fiona Bruce and Nadhim Zahawi from the Example (1), but only in terms of the argumentative structure. It illustrates how one question starts an elaborate conversation with intricate argumentative structures including those of inferences, rephrases and conflicts.

3.3 The response space

The context succeeding a question is generally called 'the response space', with a number of coding schemes having worked on a partition or characterisation of that space. As mentioned before, IAT pursues an approach of underspecification – in the case of responses this means that we differentiate only four types of responses:

- **Ignored** Similar to the 'Ignore' type of query response in Ginzburg et al. (2019) and the Non-response category in Stivers and Enfield (2010) where the "person did nothing in response" (p. 2624) we can identify discourse moves that entirely ignore the question and relate to discourse material before the question.

- **Reactions** The question is not ignored – it is reacted to, but is 'left hanging in the air' and the reaction rather contributes to the ongoing discourse. Reactions are identified in IAT through the existence of an outgoing 'Default Transition' (TA – purple transition between blue boxes on the left in Figure 1) from the question locution to the succeeding locution. There is no propositional relation between the proposition succeeding the question and the question itself.

- **Responses** are understood to be discourse moves directly related to a question without answering it. This is the case for rhetorical and assertive questions which can be responded to, but not answered. 'Responses' in IAT are captured via a 'Default Transition' following the question and anchoring an illocutionary structure (YA – yellow relations), e.g., due to the fact that there is an argumentative relation between the question and the succeeding proposition.

- **Answers** Discourse moves that provide answers to a question by delivering propositional information that instantiates the lambda expression (in the case of a wh-question) or resolves the disjunction (in the case of a polar and alternative question). In IAT answers are captured via a Default Rephrase between answer and question which is anchored via Default Illocuting in the transition between them.

4 Data

The combined dataset underlying our investigation consists of thirty six corpora in four argumentative genres: election debate, moral debate, public deliberation and topical debate. All corpora are annotated with full IAT. In total, our dataset consists of 414,726 words (tokens), and 51,993 illocutionary structures.

For the 'Election Debate' genre, we use the US2016tv[2] corpus (Visser et al., 2020), which includes the transcripts of all televised debates in the US 2016 Presidential Election. The 'Election Debate' dataset has 39,694 words, and 6,570 illocutionary structures and an inter-annotator agreement of Cohen's $\kappa = 0.61$ (substantial agreement) (Visser et al., 2020).

For the genre 'Moral Debate', we include two sub-corpora. MM2012[3], a collection of transcripts of BBC Radio 4's 'The Moral Maze', a series of debates about moral dilemmas and BBC2017[4], which consists of a special issue of 'The Moral Maze' and a related TV debate about the morality of abortion.The 'Moral Debate' dataset has 60,273 words, and 5,488 illocutionary structures.

For 'Public Deliberation', we include three subcorpora. USCD2011[5] consists of several transcripts of public meetings and hearings from departments of transportation (DOTs) across the USA (Lawrence et al., 2017), (Konat et al., 2016). DEDD2019[6] is a set of two experimental 4-party deliberations on whether or not to allow fracking in Germany. UKDD2019[7] is a public deliberation organised by the Royal Society of Edinburgh in the context of an inquiry about the future of energy in Scotland. The 'Public Deliberation' dataset has 34,759 words and 3,931 illocutionary structures.

The corpora in the genres 'Public Deliberation', 'Moral Debate' and 'Election Debate' were annotated by small teams of two to ten analysts. These three genres provide background and context for our main study which focuses upon the genre of 'Topical Debate', for which we use the QT30 corpus (Hautli-Janisz et al., 2022b).[8] This unique dataset includes transcripts of 30 episodes aired between June 2020 and November 2021 of BBC's Question Time, one of the most viewed political talk shows in the UK. The corpus consists of more than 29 hours of transcribed broadcast debate and comprises 280,000 words and 36,004 illocutionary structures by more than 400 participants, making it the largest corpus of analysed broadcast topical debate published to date. The annotation was conducted by 38 students of linguistics, philosophy, literature and computer science across Europe. Inter-annotator agreement for QT30 is at a Combined Argument Similarity Score (CASS) (Duthie et al., 2016) of 0.56, signaling moderate agreement.

Table 1 shows that in terms of the total number of illocutionary structures, the 'Topical Debate' corpus is the largest dataset and almost five times the size of the 'Election Debate' corpus. 'Asserting' is consistently the most frequent illocutionary connection across the four argumentative genres, making up almost 60% of all illocutionary connections, followed by 'Arguing' with around 20%. The total number of questions of all types in the QT30 corpus is comparable to the number of questions across the other corpora, i.e. 4.71% and 4.75% respectively. This number is slightly lower than the number of questions in the Switchboard corpus (8%) (Jurafsky et al., 1997), but higher than in the Penn Discourse Treebank 3.0, where questions make up only 0.2% of all explicit and implicit discourse relations (Webber et al., 2017). In the following, we discuss question-answering and argumentative structures in more detail.

[2] http://corpora.aifdb.org/US2016tv

[3] http://corpora.aifdb.org/mm2012

[4] http://corpora.aifdb.org/BBCaaaTV5RADIO

[5] http://corpora.aifdb.org/cd

[6] http://corpora.aifdb.org/DEDD2019

[7] http://corpora.aifdb.org/UKDD2019

[8] http://corpora.aifdb.org/qt30

	Election Debate	Moral Debate	Public Deliberation	Topical Debate	Total
Sum Non-questioning	6289 (95.72%)	5243 (95.54%)	3760 (95.65%)	32506 (94.66%)	47798 (95.28%)
Asserting	4218 (64.20%)	2953 (53.81%)	2245 (57.11%)	19224 (55.98%)	28640 (57.09%)
Arguing	1523 (23.18%)	1280 (23.32%)	879 (22.36%)	5497 (16.01%)	9179 (18.30%)
Agreeing	36 (0.55%)	180 (3.28%)	65 (1.65%)	346 (1.01%)	627 (1.25%)
Disagreeing	153 (2.33%)	368 (6.71%)	151 (3.84%)	1259 (3.67%)	1931 (3.85%)
Restating	243 (3.70%)	189 (3.44%)	376 (9.56%)	4082 (11.88%)	4890 (9.75%)
Default Illocuting	93 (1.42%)	243 (4.43%)	35 (0.89%)	1969 (5.73%)	2340 (4.66%)
Challenging	23(0.35%)	30 (0.55%)	9 (0.23%)	129 (0.38%)	191 (0.38%)
Sum Questioning	281 (4.28%)	245 (5.01%)	171 (4.35%)	1671 (4.71%)	2368 (4.72%)
Pure Questioning	166 (2.53%)	113 (2.06%)	52 (1.32%)	1201 (3.50%)	1532 (3.05%)
Rhetorical Questioning	30 (0.46%)	39 (0.71%)	20 (0.51%)	224 (0.65%)	313 (0.62%)
Assertive Questioning	85 (1.29%)	93 (1.69%)	99 (2.52%)	246 (0.72%)	523 (1.04%)
Total	6570	5488	3931	34177	50166

Table 1: Distribution of illocutionary structures across genres of argumentative discourse.

5 The role of questions in broadcast topical debate

5.1 Types of questioning

'Pure Questioning' makes up 3.5% of illocutionary structures in the QT30 corpus ('Topical Debate'), in comparison to 2.07% across previous corpora. Assertive questions are substantially more unusual in QT30 by comparison to the other corpora - 0.72% in QT30 vs aggregated 1.83%, constituting barely a third of the frequency. The proportion of pure (information-seeking) questions makes up the majority across the total number of questions of all types in both corpora, but to a marked extent in QT30 – 72% in the QT30 corpus, and 44% across other corpora. This increase in instances of 'Pure Questioning' is expected due to the nature of a topical debate, in which explanations are sought after by the audience members. In addition to that, on multiple occasions, the moderator is forced to rephrase the questions in order to urge panel members to react to those they have previously attempted to avoid.

	Topical Debate
Pure Questioning	**1201**
~**Ignored** (no outgoing TA)	**135**
~**with Reactions** (existence of outgoing TA)	**1066**
~~**with Responses** (anchor a YA)	**679**
~~**with Answers** (the content is MA)	**468**
Same speaker	53
Different speaker	406
Same and different speakers	9
Assertive Questioning	**246**
~**Ignored** (no outgoing TA)	**43**
~**with Reactions** (existence of outgoing TA)	**203**
~~**with Responses** (anchor a YA)	**132**
~~**with Answers** (the content is MA)	**34**
Same speaker	7
Different speaker	27
Same and different speakers	0
Rhetorical Questioning	**224**
~**Ignored** (no outgoing TA)	**24**
~**with Reactions** (existence of outgoing TA)	**200**
~~**with Responses** (anchor a YA)	**111**
~~**with Answers** (the content is MA)	**29**
Same speaker	24
Different speaker	5
Same and different speakers	0
Questions of all types	**1671**
~**Ignored** (no outgoing TA)	**202**
~**with Reactions** (existence of outgoing TA)	**1469**
~~**with Responses** (anchor a YA)	**922**
~~**with Answers** (the content is MA)	**531**
Same speaker	84
Different speaker	438
Same and different speakers	9

Table 2: Analysis of Question-Response patterns (individual question types)

5.2 The response space

Table 2 shows that questions (of any type) are rarely left ignored, with 83%-89% eliciting some type of reaction, over half of which are responses, with around 58% of all responses being answers. If we compare question types based on their response pattern, 'Pure Questioning' is distinct in that it has the highest frequency of answers: 39% of 'Pure Questioning' are answered while the other two question types, 'Assertive Questioning' and 'Rhetorical Questioning', are answered 14% and 13% of the time, respectively. These observations are exactly as our intuitions would suggest: assertive and rhetorical questions by their very nature do not typically invite an answer, as part of the role they play is to convey information or provide an opinion. In terms of speaker patterns, a large proportion of pure and assertive questions are answered by a different speaker (87% and 79% respectively), in contrast to rhetorical questions where 83% were answered by

	Topical Debate
Inferences	**5675**
Premise is a question	**104**
Pure Questioning	35
Assertive Questioning	22
Rhetorical Questioning	47
Conclusion is a question	**235**
Pure Questioning	106
Assertive Questioning	63
Rhetorical Questioning	66
As immediate response to questions	**132**
Pure Questioning	48
Assertive Questioning	36
Rhetorical Questioning	48
As eventual response to questions	**627**
Pure Questioning	477
Assertive Questioning	70
Rhetorical Questioning	80
Conflicts	**1240**
Antecedent is a question	**31**
Pure Questioning	4
Assertive Questioning	17
Rhetorical Questioning	10
Consequent is a question	**52**
Pure Questioning	17
Assertive Questioning	24
Rhetorical Questioning	10
As immediate response to questions	**44**
Pure Questioning	12
Assertive Questioning	22
Rhetorical Questioning	10
As eventual response to questions	**158**
Pure Questioning	107
Assertive Questioning	27
Rhetorical Questioning	24

Table 3: Analysis of Question-Argument patterns

the same speaker. This is to be expected as rhetorical questions typically do not seek an answer from another interlocutor, being used rather as rhetorical tools, with the speaker asking and answering their own question as a way of bringing their point forward.

5.3 The argumentative impact of questions

Our analysis in Table 3 is divided into the two sides of the argumentative coin: inference (support) and conflict (attack). For each, we look first at the overall frequencies of the antecedent and consequent (for inferences, the premise, and conclusion) and the proportion of them that are realised by questions ('the premise/conclusion/antecedent/consequent is a question'). This allows us to answer the question of whether (particular types of) questions are stereotypically associated with particular local roles in argumentative structures.

In the next step, we look at cases where inferences and conflicts are direct responses to questions ('As immediate response to'), i.e., their length of the chain of dialogical or argumentative structures between the question and an inference or conflict that follows it is exactly one. We then also identify how often inferences and conflicts occur in response to a question at any number of dialogically relevant steps later ('As eventual response to'); i.e. where the chain is of length greater than one. At each step in the chain, there must, in the IAT analysis, be both dialogical relevance (i.e. a chain of TAs and locutions from the locution constituting the initial question) and propositional relevance (i.e. a chain of inferences, RAs, conflicts, CAs and/or rephrases, MAs from the propositional content of the initial question).

Table 3 indicates that questions are used as elements of both inferences and conflicts in about 3.1% of all of the structures. More specifically, questions are encountered as either antecedents or consequents in 3.3% of all conflicts in the topical debate data, which is slightly more frequently than questions used as either a premise or conclusion in inferences (3%). In the case of inferences, questions of all types are two times more frequent in a role of a conclusion rather than a premise with 2.1% and 0.9% respectively.

Closer inspection reveals particular roles that questions of different types play in the debate. 'Pure Questioning' make up almost half of all questions used as the conclusion in the inferential structures with the rest fairly equally split between assertive questions and rhetorical ones. This kind of use of pure questions is illustrated in Example (1-a) where Fiona Bruce uses her concern regarding the current ceasefire as a reason to inquire about UK's further involvement in the peace talks. We hypothesize that speakers often give a reason as to why they are asking a particular question in order to justify it. A need for justification might be stronger in the case of 'Pure Questioning' since the speakers ask those questions with an intention of getting answers.

With respect to premises expressed by questions, it is most often 'Rhetorical Questioning' (45%) that is used (compared to 34% for 'Pure Questioning' and 21% for 'Assertive Questioning'). As already discussed in Section 5.2, this type of question is often employed in a manner that allows speakers to make certain points or put forward ideas. The use of rhetorical questions as premises further supports this theory: questions are used as a sophisticated linguistic means to express an opinion and to draw conclusions.

In terms of conflict, 'Assertive Questioning' is most commonly encountered in both antecedents and consequents (55% and 46% respectively). This suggests that when using assertive questions in the role of an antecedent (the source of a conflict), speakers tend to soften their disagreement via the use of assertive questions instead of expressing their position via an assertion. Frequent use of assertive questions as the consequent (the target) of conflict implies that this type of question provokes more disagreement than other types.

The number of inferences and conflicts used in responses (either immediate or eventual) to questions of all types indicates their particular role in the development of complex argumentative structures. Almost 7% of all inferential constructions are elicited by questions; in the case of conflicts, the number is slightly higher at 8%. These percentages are more indicative when put into perspective by the fact that questions make up less than 5% of all illocutionary structures.

'Pure Questioning' is by far the most common type of question making up around 72% of questions of all types. Surprisingly, it does not elicit a higher share of immediate responses than 'Assertive Questioning' or 'Rhetorical Questioning, neither for inferences nor conflicts. Only between 27% and 36% of all immediate responses were directed at pure questions. 'Assertive Questioning' on the other hand elicits the most immediate responses which are conflicts (making up 50% of responses). This supports previous observations regarding the role assertive questions play in provoking disagreement.

About 5.5% of inferences and 6.3% of conflicts are elements in chains of responses to questions. It is 'Pure Questioning' that elicits the majority of responses, with 76% and 82% in case of inferences and conflicts, respectively. This illustrates how pure questions are more than just information-seeking instruments. They trigger extended discussions that can be traced through a number of argumentative moves including those of inference and conflict. The diagram on the left in Figure 1 illustrates how one question can elicit a chain of responses including two linked arguments and a conflict followed up by another inference.

6 Conclusion

Our analysis here extends upon and refines the findings reported in Hautli-Janisz et al. (2022a), which illustrates the strategic role questions play in formulating various argumentative structures across genres of debate. For the first time, we are able to inspect the role of questions at scale, in the largest annotated corpus of dialogical argumentation, QT30 (Hautli-Janisz et al., 2022b). The results reported here scale up previous work in two distinct ways. First of all, there is explicit annotation of relationships diachronically through each hour, allowing tracking of ramifications and consequences of questions long after they have been uttered. Secondly, we also scale up the robustness of analysis by considering more debates – thereby covering more speakers (so we are at less risk of merely picking up on speaker idiosyncrasy), and more themes (so we are less at risk of merely picking up on thematic specificity). Some of the observations presented in the analysis are to be expected – that pure questions elicit more answers and that rhetorical questions are usually answered by the same speaker. Some are a little less straightforward – that assertive questions and rhetorical questions often present material that is used to support further argumentation, whereas the contents of pure questions typically end up being the conclusions of arguments. That assertive and rhetorical questions are used to provide an evidential basis for further reasoning further supports the hypothesis that such illocutions provide a rhetorical means to lower the interpersonal cost of making an assertion – a gambit to reduce dialogical risk. Sometimes, though, this gambit fails, as suggested by the fact that assertive questions in particular very often lie at the heart of conflict. The most striking new insight from this analysis is that across both inferential and conflict structures by which argumentation is driven forward, almost a quarter are triggered, either immediately or eventually, by questioning.

Questions are important to debate and reasoning: from journalistic punditry, from personal experience, from scholarly study across philosophy of science to rhetoric, from practical political training; wherever humans debate, the role of questions and question-answering is placed front and centre. This work, however, is the first time that it has become possible to quantify that role, and pin down exactly how it is, and to what extent, questions are keystone in the development of reasoning in debate.

Acknowledgements

The work reported on in this paper was funded by the Deutsche Forschungsgemeinschaft (DFG – German Research Foundation) under Germany's Excellence Strategy – EXC-2035/1 – 390681379, the VolkswagenStiftung under grant Az. 98544 'Deliberation Laboratory'.

References

Ginger Berninger and Catherine Garvey. 1981. Relevant replies to questions: Answers versus evasions. *Journal of Psycholinguistic Research*, 10:403–420.

Dan Bohus and Alexander I. Rudnicky. 2005. Sorry and I didn't catch that! - an investigation of non-understanding errors and recovery strategies. In *Proceedings of the 6th SIGdial Workshop on Discourse and Dialogue*, pages 128–143, Lisbon, Portugal. Special Interest Group on Discourse and Dialogue (SIGdial).

Katarzyna Budzynska, Mathilde Janier, Juyeon Kang, Chris Reed, Patrick Saint-Dizier, Manfred Stede, and Olena Yaskorska. 2014. Towards argument mining from dialogue. In *Proceedings of the Fifth International Conference on Computational Models of Argument (COMMA 2014)*, pages 185–196. IOS Press.

Katarzyna Budzynska, Mathilde Janier, Chris Reed, and Patrick Saint Dizier. 2016. Theoretical foundations for illocutionary structure parsing. *Argument & Computation*, 7(1):91–108.

Sasha Calhoun, Jean Carletta, Jason M. Brenier, Neil Mayo, Dan Jurafsky, Mark Steedman, and David Beaver. 2010. The nxt-format switchboard corpus: a rich resource for investigating the syntax, semantics, pragmatics and prosody of dialogue. *Language Resources and Evaluation*, 44(4):387–419.

Jean Carletta, Amy Isard, Stephen Isard, Jacqueline C. Kowtko, Gwyneth Doherty-Sneddon, and Anne H. Anderson. 1997. The reliability of a dialogue structure coding scheme. *Computational Linguistics*, 23(1):13–31.

Rory Duthie, John Lawrence, Katarzyna Budzynska, and Chris Reed. 2016. The CASS technique for evaluating the performance of argument mining. In *Proceedings of the Third Workshop on Argument Mining (ArgMining2016)*, pages 40–49, Berlin, Germany. Association for Computational Linguistics.

Jonathan Ginzburg, Zulipiye Yusupujiang, Chuyuan Li, Kexin Ren, and Pawel Lupkowski. 2019. Characterizing the response space of questions: a corpus study for English and Polish. In *Proceedings of the 20th Annual SIGdial Meeting on Discourse and Dialogue*, pages 320–330.

Annette Hautli-Janisz, Katarzyna Budzynska, Conor McKillop, Brian Plüss, Valentin Gold, and Chris Reed. 2022a. Questions in argumentative dialogue. *Journal of Pragmatics*, 188:56–79.

Annette Hautli-Janisz, Zlata Kikteva, Wassiliki Siskou, Kamila Gorska, and Chris Reed. 2022b. QT30: A corpus of argument and conflict in broadcast debate. In *Proceedings of the Thirteenth International Conference on Language Resources and Evaluation (LREC 2022)*. European Language Resources Association (ELRA).

Mathilde Janier, John Lawrence, and Chris Reed. 2014. OVA+: An argument analysis interface. In *Computational Models of Argument: Proceedings of COMMA*, volume 266, pages 463–464.

Daniel Jurafsky, Elizabeth Shriberg, and Debra Biasca. 1997. Switchboard swbd-damsl shallow-discourse-function annotation – coders manual, draft 13. Technical report, University of Colorado Institute of Cognitive Science.

Barbara Konat, John Lawrence, Joonsuk Park, Katarzyna Budzynska, and Chris Reed. 2016. A corpus of argument networks: Using graph properties to analyse divisive issues. In *Proceedings of the Tenth International Conference on Language Resources and Evaluation (LREC'16)*, pages 3899–3906, Portorož, Slovenia. European Language Resources Association (ELRA).

John Lawrence, Mark Snaith, Barbara Konat, Katarzyna Budzynska, and Chris Reed. 2017. Debating technology for dialogical argument: Sensemaking, engagement, and analytics. *ACM Trans. Internet Technol.*, 17(3):24:1–24:23.

Matthew Purver, Jonathan Ginzburg, and Patrick Healey. 2001. On the means for clarification in dialogue. In *Proceedings of the Second SIGdial Workshop on Discourse and Dialogue*.

Matthew Purver, Patrick G.T. Healey, James King, Jonathan Ginzburg, and Greg J. Mills. 2003. Answering clarification questions. In *Proceedings of the Fourth SIGdial Workshop of Discourse and Dialogue*, pages 23–33.

Chris Reed, Katarzyna Budzynska, Rory Duthie, Mathilde Janier, Barbara Konat, John Lawrence, Alison Pease, and Mark Snaith. 2017. The argument web: An online ecosystem of tools, systems and services for argumentation. *Philosophy & Technology*, 30(2):137–160.

Kazuki Sakai, Ryuichiro Higashinaka, Yuichiro Yoshikawa, Hiroshi Ishiguro, and Junji Tomita. 2018. Introduction method for argumentative dialogue using paired question-answering interchange about personality. In *Proceedings of the 19th Annual SIGdial Meeting on Discourse and Dialogue*, pages 70–79, Melbourne, Australia. Association for Computational Linguistics.

John Searle. 1969. *Speech acts: An essay in the philosophy of language*. Cambridge: Cambridge University Press.

John Searle and Daniel Vanderveken. 1985. *Foundations of Illocutionary Logic*. Cambridge: Cambridge University Press.

Tanya Stivers and N.J. Enfield. 2010. A coding scheme for question-response sequences in conversation. *Journal of Pragmatics*, 42(10):2620 – 2626. Question-Response Sequences in Conversation across Ten Languages.

Jacky Visser, Barbara Konat, Rory Duthie, Marcin Koszowy, Katarzyna Budzynska, and Chris Reed. 2020. Argumentation in the 2016 us presidential elections: annotated corpora of television debates and social media reaction. *Language Resources and Evaluation*, 54:123–154.

Bonnie Webber, Rashmi Prasad, Alan Lee, and Aravind Joshi. 2017. The Penn Discourse Treebank 3.0 annotation manual. Technical report, LDC.

Zhengzhe Yang and Jinho D. Choi. 2019. FriendsQA: Open-domain question answering on TV show transcripts. In *Proceedings of the 20th Annual SIGdial Meeting on Discourse and Dialogue*, pages 188–197, Stockholm, Sweden. Association for Computational Linguistics.

Paweł Łupkowski and Jonathan Ginzburg. 2016. Query responses. *Journal of Language Modeling*, 4:245–292.

Shallow Discourse Parsing for Open Information Extraction and Text Simplification

Christina Niklaus
Institute of Computer Science
University of St.Gallen
christina.niklaus@unisg.ch

André Freitas
Department of Computer Science
University of Manchester
Idiap Research Institute
andre.freitas@manchester.ac.uk

Siegfried Handschuh
Institute of Computer Science
University of St.Gallen
University of Passau
siegfried.handschuh@unisg.ch

Abstract

We present a discourse-aware text simplification (TS) approach that recursively splits and rephrases complex English sentences into a semantic hierarchy of simplified sentences. Using a set of linguistically principled transformation patterns, sentences are converted into a hierarchical representation in the form of core sentences and accompanying contexts that are linked via rhetorical relations. As opposed to previously proposed sentence splitting approaches, which commonly do not take into account discourse-level aspects, our TS approach preserves the semantic relationship of the decomposed constituents in the output. A comparative analysis with the annotations contained in RST-DT shows that we capture the contextual hierarchy between the split sentences with a precision of 89% and reach an average precision of 69% for the classification of the rhetorical relations that hold between them. Moreover, an integration into state-of-the-art Open Information Extraction (IE) systems reveals that when applying our TS approach as a preprocessing step, the generated relational tuples are enriched with additional meta information, resulting in a novel lightweight semantic representation for the task of Open IE.

1 Introduction

Sentences that present a complex structure can be hard to comprehend by human readers, as well as difficult to analyze by semantic applications (Mitkov and Saggion, 2018). Identifying grammatical complexities in a sentence and transforming them into simpler structures is the goal of syntactic TS. The most relevant method that is used to perform this rewriting step is *sentence splitting*: it divides a sentence into several shorter components with each of them presenting a more regular syntax that is easier to process by both humans (Siddharthan and Mandya, 2014; Ferrés et al., 2016) and machines (Štajner and Popović, 2018; Saha and Mausam, 2018).

We propose a sentence splitting approach that can be used as a preprocessing step to generate an intermediate representation. The objective is to facilitate and improve the performance of downstream tasks whose predictive quality deteriorates with sentence length and complexity (e.g., see Cetto et al. (2018); Saha and Mausam (2018); Heilman and Smith (2010); Štajner and Popović (2018)). Our approach aims to **break down a complex sentence into a set of minimal propositions**, i.e. a sequence of sound, self-contained utterances with a simple and regular structure. Each of them presents a minimal unit of coherent information and, consequently, cannot be further decomposed into meaningful propositions. However, any sound and coherent text is not simply a loose arrangement of self-contained units, but rather a logical structure of utterances that are semantically connected (Siddharthan, 2014). Consequently, when carrying out syntactic TS operations without considering discourse implications, the rewriting may easily result in a disconnected sequence of simplified sentences, making the text harder to interpret. The vast majority of existing structural TS approaches though do not take into account discourse-level aspects. Therefore, they are prone to producing a set of incoherent utterances where important contextual information is lost. Thus, to **preserve the coherence structure** of the input we propose a context-preserving TS approach. It establishes a semantic hierarchy between the split components by (1) setting up a contextual hierarchy and (2) classifying the semantic relationship that holds between them (see Figure 1).

To the best of our knowledge, this is the first time that syntactically complex sentences are *split and rephrased within the semantic context* in which they occur. Our framework differs from previously proposed approaches by using a linguistically grounded transformation stage that applies clausal and phrasal disembedding mechanisms to

Proceedings of 3rd Workshop on Computational Approaches to Discourse, pages 64–76
October 16 – 17, 2022. ©2022 International Conference on Computational Linguistics

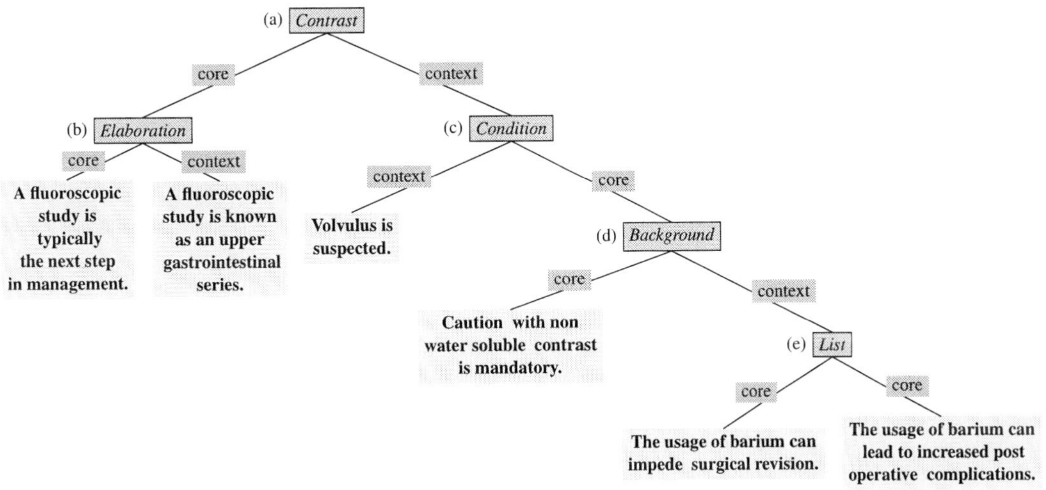

Figure 1: A complex sentence (*"A fluoroscopic study which is known as an upper gastrointestinal series is typically the next step in management, although if volvulus is suspected, caution with non water soluble contrast is mandatory as the usage of barium can impede surgical revision and lead to increased post operative complications."*) is transformed into a semantic hierarchy of simplified sentences in the form of minimal, self-contained propositions that are linked to each other via rhetorical relations. The output presents a regular, fine-grained structure that preserves the context of the input in the form of hierarchically ordered and semantically interconnected sentences.

transform sentences into shorter utterances with a more regular structure. By using a recursive top-down approach, it generates a novel *hierarchical representation* between those units, capturing both their semantic context and relations to other units in the form of rhetorical relations.[1] By taking advantage of the resulting fine-grained representation, the complexity of downstream tasks may be reduced, thus improving their performance. In addition, by incorporating the semantic context of the source sentences, our proposed representation preserves contextual information that is needed to maintain the coherence structure of the input, allowing for a proper interpretation of complex assertions.

In summary, we make the following contributions: (i) We propose a discourse-aware syntactic TS approach which transforms complex sentences into a semantic hierarchy of minimal propositions, resulting in a novel representation that puts a semantic layer on top of the simplified sentences. (ii) The proposed method is linguistically grounded and does not require any training data. (iii) As a proof of concept, we develop a reference implementation. (iv) We perform a comprehensive empirical evaluation, demonstrating that we reach state-of-the-art performance in the classification of both the hierarchical order and the semantic relationship that hold between the split sentences. (v) We show that the semantic hierarchy can be leveraged to extract relational tuples within their semantic context, resulting in a novel lightweight semantic representation for complex text data in the form of normalized and context-preserving tuples.

2 Discourse-Aware Sentence Splitting

We present DisSim, a discourse-aware TS approach that creates a semantic hierarchy of simplified sentences.[2] It takes a sentence as input and performs a recursive transformation stage that is based upon a small set of 35 hand-crafted rules.

2.1 Transformation Patterns

In the development of the transformation patterns, we followed a principled and systematic procedure, with the goal of eliciting a universal set of transformation rules. They were heuristically determined in a rule-engineering process that was carried out on the basis of an in-depth study of the literature on syntactic sentence simplification, e.g. Siddharthan (2006, 2014, 2002); Siddharthan and Mandya (2014); Evans and Orăsan (2019); Ferrés et al. (2016). Next, we performed a thorough lin-

[1] For this purpose, we make use of a subset of the classical set of RST relations defined in Mann and Thompson (1988) that we adapted from the work of Taboada and Das (2013).

[2] The source code of our framework is available under `https://github.com/Lambda-3/DiscourseSimplification` (Niklaus et al., 2019a).

guistic analysis of the syntactic phenomena that need to be tackled in the sentence splitting task.[3] The transformation patterns encode syntactic and lexical features that can be derived from a sentence's phrase structure. Each rule specifies (1) how to *split up and rephrase* the input into structurally simplified sentences and (2) how to *set up a contextual hierarchy* between the split components and how to *identify the semantic relationship* that holds between those elements.[4]

2.2 Data Model: Linked Proposition Tree

The transformation algorithm takes a complex sentence as input and recursively transforms it into a semantic hierarchy of minimal propositions. The output is represented as a linked proposition tree (LPT). Its basic structure is depicted in Figure 2. A LPT is a labeled binary tree $LPT = (V, E)$.

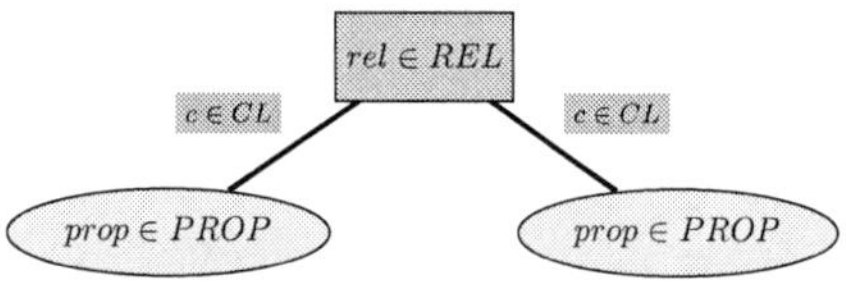

Figure 2: Basic structure of a LPT. It represents the data model of the sem. hierarchy of min. propositions.

Let $V \in \{REL, PROP\}$ be the set of nodes, where $PROP$ is the set of leaf nodes denoting the set of minimal propositions. A $prop \in PROP$ is a triple $(s, v, o) \in CT$, where $CT = \{SV, SVA, SVC, SVO, SVOO, SVOA, SVOC\}$ represents the set of clause types (Del Corro and Gemulla, 2013). Hence, $s \in S$ denotes a subject, $v \in V$ a verb and $o \in \{O, A, C, OO, OA, OA, \emptyset\}$ a direct or indirect object, adverbial or complement (or a combination thereof). Accordingly, a minimal proposition $prop \in PROP$ is a simple sentence[5] that is reduced to its clause type.[6] Thus, it represents a minimal unit of coherent information where all optional constituents are discarded, resulting in an utterance that expresses a single event consisting of a predicate and its core arguments.

Furthermore, let $REL = \{$*Contrast, List, Disjunction, Cause, Result, Temporal, Background, Condition, Elaboration, Explanation, Spatial, Attribution, Unknown*$\}$ be the set of rhetorical relations, comprising the set of inner nodes. A $rel \in REL$ represents the semantic relationship that holds between its child nodes. It reflects the semantic context of the associated propositions $prop \in PROP$. In that way, the coherence structure of the input is preserved.

Finally, let $E \in CL$, with $CL \in \{$*core, context*$\}$, be the set of constituency labels. A $c \in CL$ represents a labeled edge that connects two nodes $V \in LPT$. It enables the distinction between core information and less relevant contextual information. In that way, hierarchical structures between the split propositions $prop \in PROP$ are captured. Figure 1 shows the LPT that is generated by our TS approach on an example sentence.

2.3 Transformation Algorithm

Algorithm 1 Transform into Semantic Hierarchy

Input: complex source sentence str
Output: linked proposition tree $tree$

```
function INITIALIZE(str)
    new_leaves ← source sentence str
    new_node ← create a new parent node for new_leaves
    new_node.labels ← None
    new_node.rel ← ROOT
    linked proposition tree tree ← initialize with new_node
    return tree
end function

procedure TRAVERSETREE(tree)
    ▷ Process leaves (i.e. propositions) from left to right
    for leaf in tree.leaves do
        ▷ Check transformation rules in fixed order
        for rule in TRANSFORM_RULES do
            if match then
                ▷ (a) Sentence splitting
                simplified_propositions ← decompose leaf into a
                set of simplified propositions
                new_leaves ← convert simplified_propositions
                into leaf nodes
                ▷ (b) Constituency Type Classification
                new_node ← create a new parent node for new_leaves
                new_node.labels ← link each leaf in new_leaves to
                new_node and label each edge with the leaf's constituency
                type c ∈ CL
                ▷ (c) Rhetorical Relation Identification
                cue_phrase ← extract cue phrase from leaf.parse_tree
                new_node.rel ∈ REL ← match cue_phrase against a
                predefined set of rhetorical cue words
                ▷ Update Tree
                tree.replace(leaf, new_node)
                ▷ Recursion
                TRAVERSETREE(tree)
            end if
        end for
    end for
    return tree
end procedure
```

[3] Details on the underlying linguistic principles, supporting the systematicity and universality of the developed transformation patterns, can be found in Niklaus (2022), p. 92–97.

[4] An example of a transformation rule is provided in Table 5 in Section A. For reproducibility purposes, the full set of patterns is presented in Niklaus (2022), p. 111–141.

[5] A simple sentence comprises exactly one clause.

[6] In addition, a specified set of phrasal elements were extracted. The reader may refer to Section A for more details.

The transformation algorithm of our approach (see Algorithm 1) takes a natural language sentence as input and applies the transformation patterns to recursively transform it into a semantic hierarchy of minimal propositions, represented as an LPT.

Initialization In the initialization step (see lines 1-8 of Algorithm 1), the linked proposition tree LPT is instantiated with the source sentence. It is represented as a single leaf node that has an unlabeled edge to the root node.

Tree Traversal Next, the LPT is recursively traversed, splitting up the input in a top-down approach (9-37). Starting from the root node, the leaves are processed in depth-first order. For every leaf (11), we check if its phrasal parse tree matches one of the transformation patterns (13). The rules are applied in a fixed order that was empirically determined. The first pattern that matches the proposition's parse tree is executed (14). For instance, the first rule that matches the source sentence from Fig. 1 is the pattern shown in Table 5.

(a) Sentence Splitting In a first step, the current proposition is decomposed into a set of shorter utterances that present a more regular structure (16-17). This is achieved through disembedding clausal or phrasal components and converting them into stand-alone sentences. Accordingly, the transformation rule encodes both the split point and the rephrasing procedure for reconstructing grammatically sound sentences.[7] Each split will result in two sentences with a simpler syntax. They are represented as leaf nodes in the LPT (18-19) (see subtask (a) in Figure 3). To establish a semantic hierarchy between the split spans, two further subtasks are carried out, as described below.

(b) Constituency Type Classification To set up a contextual hierarchy between the split sentences, the transformation rule determines the constituency type $c \in CL$ of the leaf nodes that were created in the previous step (21-24). To differentiate between *core* sentences that contain the key message of the input and *contextual* sentences that provide additional information about it, the transformation pattern encodes a simple syntax-based method. Based on the assumption that subordinations commonly express background information, simplified propositions resulting from subordinate clausal or phrasal elements are classified as context sentences, while those emerging from their superordinate counterparts are labelled as core sentences. Coordinations, too, are flagged as core sentences, as they are of equal status and typically depict the main information of the input (see subtask b in Figure 3).[8]

(c) Rhetorical Relation Identification To preserve the semantic relationship between the simplified propositions, we classify the rhetorical relation $rel \in REL$ that holds between them. For this purpose, we utilize a predefined list of rhetorical cue words adapted from the work of Taboada and Das (2013).[9] To infer the type of rhetorical relation, the transformation pattern first extracts the cue phrase of the given sentence (26). It is then used as a lexical feature for classifying the semantic relationship that connects the split propositions (27-28). For example, the rule in Table 5 specifies that the phrase *"although"* is the cue word in the source sentence of Figure 1, which is mapped to a "Contrast" relationship according to the findings in Taboada and Das (2013) (see subtask c in Figure 3).

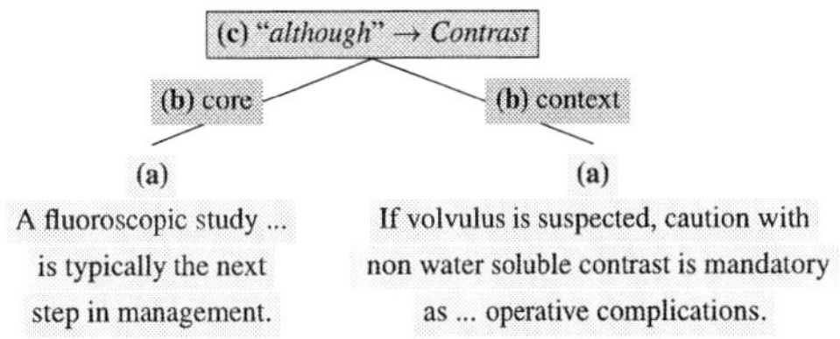

Figure 3: Semantic hierarchy after the first transformation pass. **(Subtask a)** The source sentence is split up and rephrased into a set of syntactically simplified sentences. **(Subtask b)** Then, the split sentences are connected with information about their constituency type to establish a contextual hierarchy between them. **(Subtask c)** Finally, by identifying and classifying the rhetorical relation that holds between the simplified sentences, their semantic relationship is preserved.

Recursion Next, the LPT is updated by replacing the leaf node that was processed in this run

[7]Table 4 in Section A provides an overview of the linguistic constructs that are tackled by our approach. Note that this subtask is presented in detail in Niklaus et al. (2019b). Therefore, we focus on subtasks b and c in this work.

[8]This approach relates to the concept of nuclearity in RST. In RST, each text span is specified as either a nucleus or a satellite. The *nucleus* span embodies the central piece of information and is comparable to what we denote a core sentence, whereas the role of the *satellite* is to further specify the nucleus, corresponding to a context sentence in our case.

[9]The full list of cue phrases that serve as lexical features for the identification of rhetorical relations in our approach, as well as the corresponding relations to which they are mapped, is provided in Section B.

with the newly generated subtree (30). It is composed of the simplified propositions, their semantic relationship $rel \in REL$ and constituency labels $c \in CL$. Figure 3 depicts the result of the first transformation pass on the example sentence from Figure 1. The resulting leaf nodes are then recursively simplified in a top-down fashion (32).

Termination The algorithm terminates when no more rule matches the set of simplified propositions $prop \in PROP$ in the leaf nodes. It outputs the source sentence's LPT (36), representing its semantic hierarchy of minimal semantic units. In that way, the input is transformed into a set of hierarchically ordered and semantically interconnected sentences that present a simplified syntax. Figure 1 shows the final LPT of our example sentence.

3 Evaluation

3.1 Experimental Setup

3.1.1 Automatic Metrics

We evaluate the constituency type classification and rhetorical relation identification steps by mapping the simplified sentences that were generated in the sentence splitting subtask to the Elementary Discourse Units (EDUs) of the RST-DT corpus (`https://t1p.de/n6t9`). This dataset is a collection of 385 Wall Street Journal articles annotated with rhetorical relations based on the RST framework (Mann and Thompson, 1988). For matching simplified sentences generated by our TS approach to the annotations of the RST-DT corpus, we compare each split sentence to all the EDUs of the corresponding input sentence. For each pair, we search for the longest contiguous matching subsequence. Next, based on the size of the matched sequences, a similarity score between the two input strings is calculated. Each pair whose similarity score surpasses an empirically determined threshold of 0.65 is considered a match.

Constituency Type Classification To determine whether the hierarchical relationship that is assigned by our TS framework between a pair of simplified sentences is correct, we check if the hierarchy of its contextual layers corresponds to the nuclearity of the aligned text fragments of the RST-DT. For this purpose, we make use of the nuclearity status encoded in the annotations of this dataset. In addition, we compare the performance of our TS approach with that of a set of widely used sentence-level discourse parsers on this task.

Rhetorical Relation Identification To assess the performance of the rhetorical relation identification step, we determine the distribution of the relation types allocated by our TS approach when operating on the 7,284 input sentences of the RST-DT and compare it to the distribution of the manually annotated rhetorical relations of this corpus. Moreover, we examine for each matching sentence pair whether the rhetorical relation assigned by our TS framework equates the relation that connects the corresponding EDUs in the RST-DT dataset. For this purpose, we apply the more coarse-grained classification scheme from Taboada and Das (2013), who group the full set of 78 rhetorical relations that are used in the RST-DT corpus into 19 classes of relations that share rhetorical meaning. Finally, we analyze the performance of our framework on the relation labeling task in comparison to a number of discourse parser baselines.

3.1.2 Manual Analysis

To get a deeper insight into the accuracy of the semantic hierarchy established between the split components, the automatic evaluation described above is complemented by a manual analysis. Three human judges independently of each other assessed each decomposed sentence according to the following four criteria: (i) **Limitation to core information**: Is the simplified output limited to core information of the input sentence? *(yes - no - malformed)*; (ii) **Soundness of the contextual proposition**: Does the simplified sentence express a meaningful context fact? *(yes - no)*; (iii) **Correctness of the context allocation**: Is the contextual sentence assigned to the parent sentence to which it refers? *(yes - no)*; and (iv) **Properness of the identified semantic relationship**: Is the contextual sentence linked to its parent sentence via the correct semantic relation? *(yes - no - unspecified)*. The first three categories of our analysis address the correctness of the constituency type classification task, while the latter targets the rhetorical relation identification step. The annotation task was carried out on a random sample of 100 sentences from the OIE2016 Open IE benchmark (Stanovsky and Dagan, 2016).

3.2 Results

3.2.1 Automatic Metrics

Using the matching function described in Section 3.1.1, we obtained 1,827 matched sentence pairs, i.e. 11.74% of the pairs of simplified sentences were successfully mapped to a counterpart of EDUs from the RST-DT. The relatively low number of matches can be attributed to the fact that the text spans we compare have very different features.[10] As we are primarily interested in determining whether the constituency and relation labels that are assigned by our approach are correct, we will focus on precision in the following.[11]

Constituency Type Classification In 88.88% of the matched sentence pairs, the hierarchical relationship that is allocated between a pair of simplified sentences by our reference TS implementation DISSIM corresponds to the nuclearity status of the aligned EDUs from RST-DT, i.e. in case of a nucleus-nucleus relationship in RST-DT, both output sentences from DISSIM are assigned to the same context layer, while in case of a nucleus-satellite relationship the sentence mapped to the nucleus EDU is allocated to the context layer *cl*, whereas the sentence mapped to the satellite span is assigned to the subordinate context layer *cl*+1. The majority of the cases where our TS approach assigns a hierarchical relationship that differs from the nuclearity in the RST-DT corpus can be attributed to relative clauses.

	nuclearity	relation
DPLP (Ji and Eisenstein, 2014)	71.1	61.8
Feng and Hirst (2014)	71.0	58.2
2-Stage Parser (Wang et al., 2017)	72.4	59.7
Lin et al. (2019)	**91.3**	**81.7**
SPADE (Soricut and Marcu, 2003)	56.1	44.9
HILDA (Hernault et al., 2010)	59.7	48.2
PAR-S (Joty et al., 2015)	75.2	66.1
Lin et al. (2019)	(86.4)*	(77.5)*
DISSIM	**88.9**	**69.5**

Table 1: Precision of DISSIM and the discourse parser baselines, as reported by their authors. (*) In case of automatic discourse segmentation, for Lin et al. (2019) the F_1-score is available only.

Table 1 displays the precision that the discourse parser baselines achieve on the 991 sentences of the RST-DT test set in distinguishing between nucleus and satellite spans *("nuclearity")*. For the approaches in the upper part of the table, the authors report the systems' performance when using gold EDU segmentation, while for those in the lower part the performance is indicated based on automatic segmentation, i.e. when they are fed the output of their respective discourse segmenter. Since our framework makes use of the simplified sentences that were generated in the previous step when setting up the semantic hierarchy, it is better comparable to the latter group. The figures show that in this case our approach outperforms all other systems in the constituency type classification task by a large margin of 13.7% at a minimum.[12]

Rhetorical Relation Identification Table 2 displays the frequency distribution of the 19 classes of rhetorical relations that were specified in Taboada and Das (2013). The ten most frequently occurring classes make up for 89.45% of the relations that are present in the dataset. We decided to limit ourselves to these classes in the evaluation of the rhetorical relation identification step, with two exceptions. First, we did not take into account the "Topic-change" and "Same-unit" classes. Second, we merged the two highly related classes of "Cause" and "Explanation" into a single category.

RHET. RELATION	COUNT	PERCENT.	PRECISION
Elaboration	7,675	25.65%	0.5550
Joint	7,116	23.78%	0.6673
Attribution	2,984	9.97%	0.9601
Same-unit	2,788	9.32%	—
Contrast	1,522	5.09%	0.7421
Topic-change	1,315	4.39%	—
Explanation	966	3.21%	0.7037
Cause	754	2.52%	
Temporal	964	3.22%	0.7895
Background	897	2.30%	0.4459
			avg.: 0.6948

Evaluation (2.0%), Enablement (1.8%), Comparison (1.5%), Textual organization (1.2%), Condition (1.1%), Topic-comment (0.9%), Manner-means (0.7%), Summary (0.7%), Span (0.0%)

Table 2: Frequency distribution of the 19 classes of relations from Taboada and Das (2013) and the precision of DISSIM's rhetorical relation identification step.

The right column in Table 2 displays the precision of our TS approach for each class of rhetorical relation when run over the sentences from RST-DT. The "Attribution" relation reaches by far the highest precision. The remaining relations, too, show decent scores, with a precision of around 70%. The only exception is "Background". The difficulty with this type of relationship is that it signifies a very broad category that is not signalled by discourse markers and therefore hard to detect by our approach (Taboada and Das, 2013). With an average precision of 69.5% in the relation labeling task (see Table 1), our framework again surpasses all

[10] For details, see Section C.

[11] The fraction of labels that are successfully retrieved (i.e. recall) is of minor importance in our setting. In addition, this score might be biased, since a large proportion of EDUs from RST-DT is not mapped to a counterpart of simplified propositions in our experiments. Therefore, we refrain from reporting recall scores.

[12] A very recent approach to intra-sentential sentence parsing was proposed in Lin et al. (2019), achieving an F_1-score of 86.4%. However, the authors do not report its precision.

the discourse parser baselines under consideration when using automatic discourse segmentation.[13]

When comparing the distribution of the rhetorical relations that were identified by our TS approach on the source sentences from the RST-DT (see Figure 4) to that of the manually annotated gold relations displayed in Table 2, it turns out that there is a very high similarity between the two of them. However, it must be noted that in about 20% of the cases, our TS approach is not able to identify a rhetorical relation between a pair of split sentences *("Unknown")*. For the most part, this can be attributed to sentence pairs whose relation is not explicitly stated in the underlying source sentence. As our approach is based on cue phrases, searching for discourse markers that explicitly signal rhetorical relations, it has difficulties in identifying relations that can merely be implied.

3.2.2 Manual Analysis

The results of the human evaluation are displayed in Table 3. The inter-annotator agreement was calculated using Fleiss' κ (Fleiss, 1971). The figures indicate fair to substantial agreement between the three annotators, suggesting that the evaluation scores present a reliable result.

Category	Yes	No	Malf.	Unspec.	κ
Limitation to core information	68.2%	20.0%	11.9%	—	0.39
Soundness of the contextual proposition	83.1%	16.9%	—	—	0.51
Correctness of the context allocation	93.2%	6.8%	—	—	0.41
Properness of the semantic relationship	69.8%	7.0%	—	23.2%	0.69

Table 3: Results of the manual analysis.

In more than two out of three cases, the annotators marked the propositions that were classified as core sentences by our TS approach as correct, thus approving that they have a meaningful interpretation and that their content is truly restricted to core information of the underlying source sentence. Only about 12% of the simplified sentences are malformed according to our annotations. The remaining fifth of output core sentences was judged as being misclassified, i.e. they rather contribute less relevant background data than key information of the input. Regarding the soundness of the context propositions, only about 17% of the output propositions that were classified as context sentences were labelled as being inaccurate, while as many as 83% present proper contextual propositions, expressing a meaningful context fact that is asserted by the input and can be properly interpreted. Furthermore, 93% of the context sentences are assigned to their respective parent sentence, whereas only 6% of them are misallocated, according to the annotators' labels. Finally, our evaluation revealed that our TS approach shows a decent performance for the rhetorical relation identification step, too. More than two-thirds of the sentence pairs are classified with the correct rhetorical relation, according to our manual analysis. Only 7% of them are assigned an improper relation. However, in nearly a quarter of the cases, our TS approach was not able to identify a semantic relationship between the given pair of sentences. This can be explained by the fact that for this subtask, our framework follows a rather simplistic approach that is primarily based on cue phrases. Therefore, it fails to identify a semantic relationship whenever none of the specified keywords appears in the underlying input sentence. As a result, our approach provides very precise results. Covering only a small subset of rhetorical relations it lacks in completeness, though.

4 A Lightweight Semantic Representation for Open IE

The fine-grained representation of complex sentences in the form of hierarchically ordered and semantically interconnected propositions may serve as an intermediate representation for downstream tasks. An application area that may benefit greatly from our approach as a preprocessing step is the task of Open IE (Banko et al., 2007). We thus assessed the merits of our proposed discourse-aware TS approach in supporting the extraction of relational tuples from complex assertions in downstream Open IE applications, demonstrating that the semantic hierarchy of minimal propositions benefits them in two dimensions:

(a) *The normalized subject-predicate-object syntax of the simplified sentences reduces the complexity of the relation extraction step, resulting in a simplistic canonical predicate-argument structure of the output.*

(b) *By capturing intra-sentential rhetorical structures and hierarchical relationships between the propositions, it allows for the enrichment*

[13]with the exception of Lin et al. (2019)'s parser, for which only the F_1-score is reported by the authors, though. Hence, it is not directly comparable to the other approaches whose performance is analyzed based on their precision.

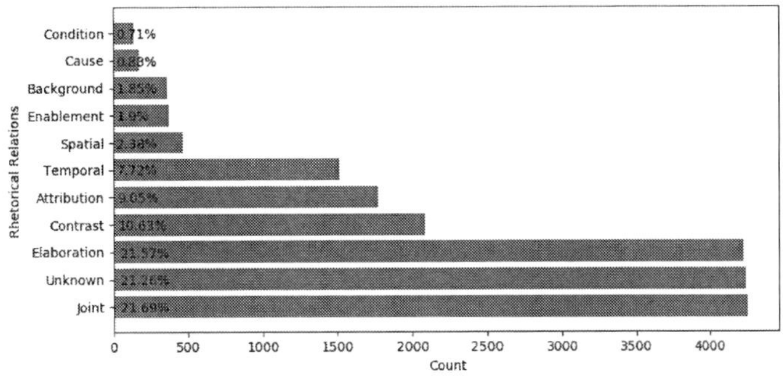

Figure 4: Distribution of the rhetorical relations identified by our TS approach on the RST-DT.

of the extracted relational tuples with additional meta information that supports their interpretability.

In that way, the shallow semantic representation of state-of-the-art Open IE systems is transformed into a canonical context-preserving representation of relational tuples.

```
(1) she;   was confirmed on;          August 6, 2009
(2) He;    nominated Sonia Sotomayor on; May 26
(3) He;    nominated Sonia Sotomayor; 2009
(4) He;    nominated 2009 on;         May 26
(5) Sonia Sotomayor;  be nominated 2009 on;  May 26
(6) He;    nominated 2009;            Sonia Sotomayor
(7) 2009; be nominated Sonia Sotomayor on;May 26
```

Figure 5: OLLIE's extractions (Mausam et al., 2012).

Extraction of Canonical Predicate-Argument Structures Representing normalized monopredicative units, the simplified sentences reduce the complexity of the relation extraction step and inherently support the extraction of canonical predicate-argument structures. Thus, a standardized output scheme is created, where each simplified sentence results in a *normalized (mostly) binary predicate-argument structure*, in which *both the predicate and the argument slots are reduced to their essential components*. In that way, the generation of overly specific predicate and argument phrases, as well as (quasi-)redundant extractions is prevented, as illustrated by the examples in Figures 5 to 7.[14]

Enrichment of the Output with Semantic Information Moreover, our TS approach enables existing Open IE systems to enrich their output with semantic information. The semantic hierarchy can be leveraged to incorporate important contextual information of the extracted relational tuples, thus extending the shallow semantic representation (in the form of isolated predicate-argument structures) of state-of-the-art Open IE systems.[15] First, the semantic hierarchy supports the specification of a hierarchical order between the extracted relational tuples, as it enables to distinguish between *different levels of context* - the lower the allotted layer, the more relevant is the information contained in it. Second, the semantic hierarchy generated by our discourse-aware TS approach can be used to enrich the output of Open IE approaches with additional meta information in terms of rhetorical relations, allowing for the representation of *semantically typed relational tuples*. Thus, the extracted relations are put into a *logical structure that preserves the semantic context of the extractions*, resulting in an output that is more informative and coherent, and thus easier to interpret. See Figure 8 for an example.

Hence, the semantic hierarchy of minimal propositions generated by our discourse-aware TS approach can be leveraged to transform the shallow semantic representation of existing Open IE systems into a novel canonical context-preserving representation of relational tuples. The proposed representation allows for a simplistic unified representation of predicate-argument structures that can easily be enriched with contextual information in terms

[14]In addition, we demonstrated that the precision and recall of state-of-the-art Open IE systems is improved by up to 346% and 52%, respectively, when taking advantage of the split propositions instead of dealing with the complex source sentences (Niklaus et al., 2019b).

[15]Previous work in the area of Open IE has mainly focused on the extraction of isolated relational tuples, ignoring the cohesive nature of texts where important contextual information is spread across clauses or sentences. Consequently, state-of-the-art Open IE approaches are prone to generating a loose arrangement of tuples that lack the expressiveness needed to infer the true meaning of complex assertions.

```
(1) he;     nominated;        Sonia Sotomayor on May 26 2009 to replace David Souter
(2) she;    was confirmed;    on August 6 2009 becoming the first Supreme Court Justice of Hispanic descent
(3) she;    was confirmed;    becoming the first Supreme Court Justice of Hispanic descent
```

Figure 6: Relations extracted by ClausIE (Del Corro and Gemulla, 2013) from the sentence: *"He nominated Sonia Sotomayor on May 26, 2009 to replace David Souter; she was confirmed on August 6, 2009, becoming the first Supreme Court Justice of Hispanic descent."*.

```
(1) #1  0  he;     nominated;      Sonia Sotomayor
(1a)            PURPOSE       to replace David Souter.
(1b)            TEMPORAL      on May 26, 2009.
(2) #2  0  she;     was confirmed;
(2a)            TEMPORAL      on August 6, 2009.
(3) #3  0  she;     was becoming;     the first
           Supreme Court Justice of Hispanic descent
```

Figure 7: Relations extracted by OLLIE and ClausIE when using our TS approach as a preprocessing step.

```
(1) A fluoroscopic study; known; as an upper gastro-
                                  intestinal series
(2) caution with non water soluble contrast; is; man-
                          datory as the usage of barium
(3) as the usage; of barium can impede;    surgical
                                revision and lead
(4)  ;   to increased;  post operative complications

(5)   #1  0  A fluoroscopic study; is; typically, the
                               next step in management
(5a)                ELABORATION   #2
(5b)                CONTRAST      #3
(6)   #2  1  This; fluoroscopic study is known;    as
               an upper gastrointestinal series
(7)   #3  0  Caution with non water soluble; is; man-
                                              datory
(7a)                CONTRAST      #1
(7b)                CONDITION     #6
(7c)                BACKGROUND    #4
(7d)                BACKGROUND    #5
(8)   #4  1  The usage of barium; can impede;surgical
                                            revision
(8a)                LIST          #5
(9)   #5  1  The usage of barium;  can lead;   to in-
                creased post operative complications
(9a)                LIST          #4
(10) #6  1  Volvulus;     is suspected;
```

Figure 8: Comparison of the tuples extracted by RnnOIE (Stanovsky et al., 2018) *with* (5 - 10) and *without* (1 - 4) using our TS approach as a preprocessing step.

of intra-sentential rhetorical structures and hierarchical relationships between the extracted tuples, resulting in a set of interrelated semantically typed tuples that preserve the coherence of the output.

5 Related Work

Discourse-level TS The vast majority of structural TS approaches do not take into account discourse-level aspects. However, two notable exceptions have to be mentioned. Siddharthan (2006) was the first to use discourse-aware cues in the simplification process. As opposed to our approach, though, where a semantic relationship is established for each simplified output sentence, only a comparatively low number of sentences is linked by such cue words. Another approach that operates on the level of discourse was proposed by Štajner and Glavaš (2017). It performs a semantically motivated content reduction by maintaining only those parts of a sentence that belong to factual event mentions. Our approach, on the contrary, aims to preserve all the information contained in the source.

Discourse Parsing The challenge of uncovering coherence structures in texts is pursued in the field of Discourse Parsing. It aims to identify discourse relations that hold between textual units in a document (Marcu, 1997). A well-established theory of text structure used in this area is RST. Here, textual coherence is explained by the existence of rhetorical relations that hold between adjacent text spans in a hierarchical structure. Approaches to detect rhetorical structure arrangements in texts range from early rule-based approaches (Marcu, 2000) to supervised data-driven models that were trained on annotated corpora such as the RST-DT (Feng and Hirst, 2014; Li et al., 2014; Lin et al., 2019).[16]

6 Conclusion

We presented a context-preserving TS approach that transforms structurally complex sentences into a hierarchical representation in the form of core sentences and accompanying contexts that are semantically linked by rhetorical relations. In our experiments, we mapped the simplified sentences from our reference implementation DISSIM to the EDUs from RST-DT and showed that we obtain a very high precision of 89% for the constituency type classification and a decent score of 69% on average for the rhetorical relation identification. In the future, we plan to improve the latter step by extending our approach to also capture implicit relationships between the decomposed sentences.

References

Michele Banko, Michael J. Cafarella, Stephen Soderland, Matt Broadhead, and Oren Etzioni. 2007. Open information extraction from the web. In *Proceedings*

[16]Section D elaborates on why it is not possible to simply use an RST parser for establishing the semantic hierarchy between the decomposed spans.

of the 20th International Joint Conference on Artifical Intelligence, pages 2670–2676, San Francisco, CA, USA. Morgan Kaufmann Publishers Inc.

Lynn Carlson and Daniel Marcu. 2001. Discourse tagging reference manual. *ISI Technical Report ISI-TR-545*, 54:56.

Matthias Cetto, Christina Niklaus, André Freitas, and Siegfried Handschuh. 2018. Graphene: Semantically-linked propositions in open information extraction. In *Proceedings of the 27th International Conference on Computational Linguistics*, pages 2300–2311, Santa Fe, New Mexico, USA. Association for Computational Linguistics.

Luciano Del Corro and Rainer Gemulla. 2013. Clausie: Clause-based open information extraction. In *Proceedings of the 22nd International Conference on World Wide Web*, WWW '13, page 355–366, New York, NY, USA. Association for Computing Machinery.

Richard Evans and Constantin Orăsan. 2019. Identifying signs of syntactic complexity for rule-based sentence simplification. *Natural Language Engineering*, 25(1):69–119.

Vanessa Wei Feng and Graeme Hirst. 2014. A linear-time bottom-up discourse parser with constraints and post-editing. In *Proceedings of the 52nd Annual Meeting of the Association for Computational Linguistics (Volume 1: Long Papers)*, pages 511–521, Baltimore, Maryland. Association for Computational Linguistics.

Daniel Ferrés, Montserrat Marimon, Horacio Saggion, and Ahmed AbuRa'ed. 2016. YATS: yet another text simplifier. In *Natural Language Processing and Information Systems - 21st International Conference on Applications of Natural Language to Information Systems, NLDB 2016, Salford, UK, June 22-24, 2016, Proceedings*, volume 9612 of *Lecture Notes in Computer Science*, pages 335–342. Springer.

J.L. Fleiss. 1971. Measuring nominal scale agreement among many raters. *Psychological Bulletin*, 76(5):378–382.

Michael Heilman and Noah A. Smith. 2010. Extracting simplified statements for factual question generation. In *Proceedings of the QG2010: The Third Workshop on Question Generation*, pages 11–20.

Hugo Hernault, Helmut Prendinger, Mitsuru Ishizuka, et al. 2010. Hilda: A discourse parser using support vector machine classification. *Dialogue & Discourse*, 1(3).

Yangfeng Ji and Jacob Eisenstein. 2014. Representation learning for text-level discourse parsing. In *Proceedings of the 52nd Annual Meeting of the Association for Computational Linguistics (Volume 1: Long Papers)*, pages 13–24, Baltimore, Maryland. Association for Computational Linguistics.

Shafiq Joty, Giuseppe Carenini, and Raymond T. Ng. 2015. CODRA: A novel discriminative framework for rhetorical analysis. *Computational Linguistics*, 41(3):385–435.

Roger Levy and Galen Andrew. 2006. Tregex and tsurgeon: tools for querying and manipulating tree data structures. In *Proceedings of the Fifth International Conference on Language Resources and Evaluation (LREC'06)*, Genoa, Italy. European Language Resources Association (ELRA).

Jiwei Li, Rumeng Li, and Eduard Hovy. 2014. Recursive deep models for discourse parsing. In *Proceedings of the 2014 Conference on Empirical Methods in Natural Language Processing (EMNLP)*, pages 2061–2069, Doha, Qatar. Association for Computational Linguistics.

Xiang Lin, Shafiq Joty, Prathyusha Jwalapuram, and M Saiful Bari. 2019. A unified linear-time framework for sentence-level discourse parsing. In *Proceedings of the 57th Annual Meeting of the Association for Computational Linguistics*, pages 4190–4200, Florence, Italy. Association for Computational Linguistics.

William C Mann and Sandra A Thompson. 1988. Rhetorical structure theory: Toward a functional theory of text organization. *Text-Interdisciplinary Journal for the Study of Discourse*, 8(3):243–281.

Daniel Marcu. 1997. The rhetorical parsing of unrestricted natural language texts. In *35th Annual Meeting of the Association for Computational Linguistics and 8th Conference of the European Chapter of the Association for Computational Linguistics*, pages 96–103, Madrid, Spain. Association for Computational Linguistics.

Daniel Marcu. 2000. The rhetorical parsing of unrestricted texts: a surface-based approach. *Computational Linguistics*, 26(3):395–448.

Mausam, Michael Schmitz, Stephen Soderland, Robert Bart, and Oren Etzioni. 2012. Open language learning for information extraction. In *Proceedings of the 2012 Joint Conference on Empirical Methods in Natural Language Processing and Computational Natural Language Learning*, pages 523–534, Jeju Island, Korea. Association for Computational Linguistics.

Ruslan Mitkov and Horacio Saggion. 2018. Text simplification.

Christina Niklaus. 2022. *From Complex Sentences to a Formal Semantic Representation using Syntactic Text Simplification and Open Information Extraction*. Springer Fachmedien Wiesbaden, Wiesbaden.

Christina Niklaus, Matthias Cetto, André Freitas, and Siegfried Handschuh. 2019a. DisSim: A discourse-aware syntactic text simplification framework for English and German. In *Proceedings of the 12th International Conference on Natural Language Generation*, pages 504–507, Tokyo, Japan. Association for Computational Linguistics.

Christina Niklaus, Matthias Cetto, André Freitas, and Siegfried Handschuh. 2019b. Transforming complex sentences into a semantic hierarchy. In *Proceedings of the 57th Annual Meeting of the Association for Computational Linguistics*, pages 3415–3427, Florence, Italy. Association for Computational Linguistics.

Swarnadeep Saha and Mausam. 2018. Open information extraction from conjunctive sentences. In *Proceedings of the 27th International Conference on Computational Linguistics*, pages 2288–2299, Santa Fe, New Mexico, USA. Association for Computational Linguistics.

Advaith Siddharthan. 2002. An architecture for a text simplification system. In *Language Engineering Conference, 2002. Proceedings*, pages 64–71. IEEE.

Advaith Siddharthan. 2006. Syntactic simplification and text cohesion. *Research on Language and Computation*, 4(1):77–109.

Advaith Siddharthan. 2014. A survey of research on text simplification. *ITL-International Journal of Applied Linguistics*, 165(2):259–298.

Advaith Siddharthan and Angrosh Mandya. 2014. Hybrid text simplification using synchronous dependency grammars with hand-written and automatically harvested rules. In *Proceedings of the 14th Conference of the European Chapter of the Association for Computational Linguistics*, pages 722–731, Gothenburg, Sweden. Association for Computational Linguistics.

Radu Soricut and Daniel Marcu. 2003. Sentence level discourse parsing using syntactic and lexical information. In *Proceedings of the 2003 Human Language Technology Conference of the North American Chapter of the Association for Computational Linguistics*, pages 228–235.

Sanja Štajner and Goran Glavaš. 2017. Leveraging event-based semantics for automated text simplification. *Expert systems with applications*, 82:383–395.

Sanja Štajner and Maja Popović. 2018. Improving machine translation of English relative clauses with automatic text simplification. In *Proceedings of the 1st Workshop on Automatic Text Adaptation (ATA)*, pages 39–48, Tilburg, the Netherlands. Association for Computational Linguistics.

Gabriel Stanovsky and Ido Dagan. 2016. Creating a large benchmark for open information extraction. In *Proceedings of the 2016 Conference on Empirical Methods in Natural Language Processing*, pages 2300–2305, Austin, Texas. Association for Computational Linguistics.

Gabriel Stanovsky, Julian Michael, Luke Zettlemoyer, and Ido Dagan. 2018. Supervised open information extraction. In *Proceedings of the 2018 Conference of the North American Chapter of the Association for Computational Linguistics: Human Language Technologies, Volume 1 (Long Papers)*, pages 885–895, New Orleans, Louisiana. Association for Computational Linguistics.

Maite Taboada and Debopam Das. 2013. Annotation upon annotation: Adding signalling information to a corpus of discourse relations. *D&D*, 4(2):249–281.

Yizhong Wang, Sujian Li, and Houfeng Wang. 2017. A two-stage parsing method for text-level discourse analysis. In *Proceedings of the 55th Annual Meeting of the Association for Computational Linguistics (Volume 2: Short Papers)*, pages 184–188, Vancouver, Canada. Association for Computational Linguistics.

A Transformation Patterns

One of the fundamental objectives of our discourse-aware TS approach is to decompose complex assertions into a set of self-contained minimal propositions. Table 4 provides an overview of the linguistic constructs that are addressed by our framework in order to achieve this goal, including the number of transformation patterns that were specified for each syntactic phenomenon. Table 5 shows an example of a transformation rule.

B Mapping of Cue Phrases to Rhetorical Relations

Table 6 lists the full set of cue phrases that serve as lexical features for the identification of rhetorical relations when establishing the semantic hierarchy between a pair of split sentences. It further shows to which rhetorical relation each of them is mapped.

In addition, *Spatial* and *Temporal* relationships are identified on the basis of named entities, while *Attribution* relations are detected using a predefined list of verbs of reported speech and cognition (Carlson and Marcu, 2001).

Furthermore, in some cases, the type of relationship that is set between two decomposed spans is selected based on syntactic information. This applies to the following rhetorical relations:

- *Purpose* (in case of adverbial clauses of purpose, lexicalized on the preposition *"to"*),
- *Elaboration* (in case of appositives, adjectival/adverbial phrases, participial phrases without an adverbial connector and relative clauses that are *not* introduced by the relative pronoun *"where"*),
- *Spatial* (in case of relative clauses commencing with the relative pronoun *"where"*) and
- *Temporal* (in case of lead noun phrases).

	CLAUSAL/PHRASAL TYPE	HIERARCHY	# RULES
	Clausal disembedding		
1	Coordinate clauses	coordinate	1
2	Adverbial clauses	subordinate	6
3a	Relative clauses (non-restrictive)	subordinate	5
3b	Relative clauses (restrictive)	subordinate	4
4	Reported speech	subordinate	4
	Phrasal disembedding		
5	Coordinate verb phrases	coordinate	1
6	Coordinate noun phrases	coordinate	2
6	Participial phrases	subordinate	4
8a	Appositions (non-restrictive)	subordinate	1
8b	Appositions (restrictive)	subordinate	1
9	Prepositional phrases	subordinate	3
10	Adjectival and adverbial phrases	subordinate	2
11	Lead NPs	subordinate	1
	Total		35

Table 4: Linguistic constructs addressed by our discourse-aware TS approach DISSIM.

```
ROOT <<: (S < (NP $.. (VP < +(VP) (SBAR <, (IN $+ ( S < (NP $.. VP )))))))
```

Table 5: Example of a transformation pattern (for decomposing adverbial clauses). They are specified in terms of Tregex patterns (Levy and Andrew, 2006). A boxed pattern represents the part of a sentence that is extracted from the input and transformed into a new stand-alone sentence. A pattern in bold is deleted from the source. The underlined part is labelled as a context sentence, while the remaining part represents core information. The italic pattern is used as a cue phrase for identifying the rhetorical relation that holds between the decomposed spans.

RHET. RELATION	CUE PHRASES
Contrast	although, but, but now, despite, even though, even when, except when, however, instead, rather, still, though, thus, until recently, while, yet
List	and, in addition, in addition to, moreover
Disjunction	or
Cause	largely because, because, since
Result	as a result, as a result of
Temporal	after, and after, next, then, before, previously
Background	as, now, once, when, with, without
Condition	if, in case, unless, until
Elaboration	more provocatively, even before, for example, further, recently, since, since now, so, so far, where, whereby, whether
Explanation	simply because, because of, indeed, so, so that

Table 6: Mapping of cue phrases to rhetorical relations.

C Evaluation

While the goal of our TS approach is to generate well-formed syntactically simplified sentences, the EDUs in the RST-DT are copied verbatim from the source, resulting in an output of varied length that is usually not grammatically sound. Moreover, in many cases, the EDUs mix multiple semantic units, whereas our approach aims to split the input into atomic components, with each of them expressing a coherent and indivisible proposition.

D Discourse Parsing

The syntactic analysis we propose for establishing the semantic hierarchy between the decomposed spans is bound to the RST discourse markers. However, it is not possible to simply use an RST parser for this task. As illustrated in Figure 9, such a parser does not return grammatically sound sentences. Instead, it segments the input into basic textual units, so-called elementary discourse units (EDUs), which are copied verbatim from the source. In order to reconstruct proper sentences, rephrasing is required. For this purpose, amongst others, referring expressions have to be identified, and phrases have to be rearranged and inflected. Moreover, the textual units resulting from the segmentation process are too coarse-grained for our purpose, since

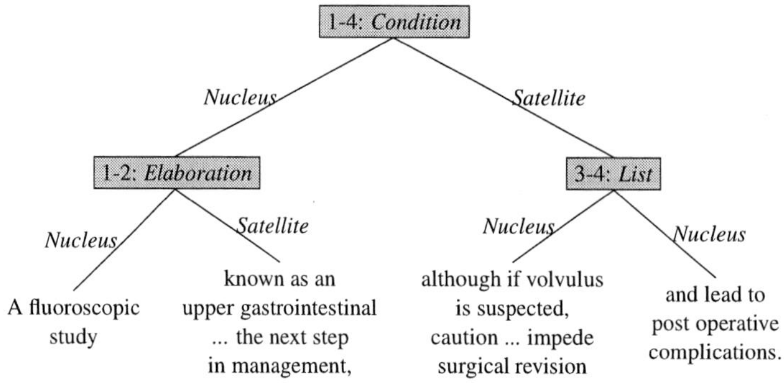

Figure 9: Rhetorical structure tree of our example sentence, generated using the RST parser proposed in Ji and Eisenstein (2014). The leaves correspond to *EDUs*, while each node is characterized by its *nuclearity* and a *rhetorical relation* between adjacent text spans.

RST parsers mostly operate on clausal level. The goal of our approach, though, is to split the input into minimal semantic units, which requires to go down to the phrasal level in order to produce a much more fine-grained output in the form of minimal propositions.

Predicting Political Orientation in News with Latent Discourse Structure to Improve Bias Understanding

Nicolas Devatine[1], **Philippe Muller**[1,3], **Chloé Braud**[2,3]
[1]IRIT, University of Toulouse
[2]IRIT, CNRS
[3]Artificial and Natural Intelligence Toulouse Institute (ANITI)

`firstname.lastname@irit.fr`

Abstract

With the growing number of information sources, the problem of media bias becomes worrying for a democratic society. This paper explores the task of predicting the political orientation of news articles, with a goal of analyzing how bias is expressed. We demonstrate that integrating rhetorical dimensions via latent structures over sub-sentential discourse units allows for large improvements, with a +7.4 points difference between the base LSTM model and its discourse-based version, and +3 points improvement over the previous BERT-based state-of-the-art model. We also argue that this gives a new relevant handle for analyzing political bias in news articles.

1 Introduction

Misinformation is a major threat on modern democracy, influencing political agendas in an arguably unfair way, through multiple sources that are more or less transparent in their orientations. Biased media can influence public opinion by selecting reported facts and angles, oriented presentation of events, with a proven impact, e.g. on electoral behaviours (DellaVigna and Kaplan, 2007) or public health (Simonov et al., 2020). The automatic identification of such biases can thus help more transparent and democratic sharing of information, and the understanding of its typical expression.

The study of bias has generated a lot of interest in political sciences with some emphasis on its linguistics aspects (Lee and Solomon, 1990; Levasseur, 2008), which also gave rise to numerous studies on automating bias detection (Hamborg et al., 2019). NLP approaches mostly rely on lexical information (Recasens et al., 2013), or syntax (Iyyer et al., 2014), with, recently, the use of pretrained language models (Baly et al., 2020) or document-level bias distribution (Chen et al., 2020).

Bias can be expressed in more subtle ways however. In the excerpts below (Figure 1), discussing the 2019 Virginia Beach mass shooting[1], we can clearly identify the difference in coverage, with specific lexical choices ("epidemic", "refuse to cover") but also different ways of presenting the event: the style is either descriptive (BBC) or more emotional (WP, Townhall) ; the writer insists on particular topics or angles (*use of silencers*, *weapon prohibition*). The choice of topics is indeed an important aspect of information manipulation (Scheufele and Tewksbury, 2007), and has also generated NLP work, still lexically focused (Card et al., 2015; Baumer et al., 2015; Field et al., 2018; Morstatter et al., 2018)

"The Virginia Beach shooter put a sound suppressor (...) so that the death shots were muffled, perhaps denying others the warning that would have allowed them to escape. It is long past time to remove the silencer that seems to suppress action on gun-control legislation, to treat mass shooting as the epidemic it is, and do everything possible to save lives.'" **(Washington Post, left-leaning)**

"The attack began shortly after 16:00 (20:00 GMT), at Virginia Beach Municipal Center, in an area which is home to a number of city government buildings. The area was put into lockdown by police and employees were evacuated. 'We just heard people yelling and screaming at people to get down,' Megan Banton, an administrative assistant in the building, told local television news station WAVY." **(BBC, center)**

"The chilling fact is that mass public killers are attracted to targets where people can't defend themselves. (...) Ninety-eight percent of US mass public shootings since 1950 have occurred in places where people weren't allowed to defend themselves. But the news media refuses to cover this fact, which illustrates the need for self-defense, not for more gun control that doesn't work." **(Townhall, right-leaning)**

Figure 1: Excerpts from articles on the 2019 Virgina Beach mass shooting from media with different political tendencies.

In contrast, we investigate the task of predicting political orientation of news articles, while trying to consider global argumentative aspects instead of local, lexical ones. This classification task consists in predicting the political leaning of an article by considering, in our case, 3 political classes (left, center, right). Since text-level discourse analysis

[1]https://www.allsides.com/blog/virginia-beach-shooting-reinvigorates-gun-debate

Proceedings of 3rd Workshop on Computational Approaches to Discourse, pages 77–85
October 16 – 17, 2022.

is still a difficult problem (Zhang et al., 2020), our architecture encodes a document while automatically inducing latent structural dependencies as in Liu and Lapata (2018), with a focus on elementary discourse units instead of sentences. We hypothesize that structural information can help identify political sides and give insights into aspects related to the argumentative nature of different media.

We evaluate our approach on news articles (Baly et al., 2020) and also perform a preliminary interpretability study. Our contributions are: (i) a model predicting political orientation of news articles, inducing a latent structure over discourse segmented texts, with state-of-the-art results ; (ii) a preliminary analysis of the impact of lexical and structural information for bias detection. Our code is available at: https://github.com/neops9/news_political_bias.

2 Related work

There are multiple ways to consider the task of classifying political ideologies, especially by varying the number and type of classes, and the level of analysis. For example, one SemEval 2019 shared task focused on identifying hyperpartisan articles (Kiesel et al., 2019). Political bias can also be characterized by locating "propaganda techniques" in texts, as in the SemEval 2020 shared task (Da San Martino et al., 2020). Here, we consider the task proposed by Baly et al. (2020) based on 3 classes (left, center, right). A similar task was also considered in Li and Goldwasser (2021), but their dataset is not available for comparison. In addition, Baly et al. (2020) explore methods that prevent the model from using media-related information while remaining based on other lexical and syntactic ones (see section 3). They report at best 51.41% in accuracy.

Contrary to previous studies based solely on lexico-syntactic information, we hypothesize that document-level organization is crucial. Rather than relying on low-performing discourse parsers, we test Liu and Lapata (2018)'s approach: structural dependencies over sentences are induced while encoding the document. Their results indicate that the learned representations, without ever exposing the model to linguistic annotations or an external parser, achieve competitive performance on a range of tasks while arguably being meaningful. This approach is effective for summarization with the learned structures, while less complex than classical ones, capturing consistent information (Liu et al., 2019; Isonuma et al., 2019; Balachandran et al., 2021). A similar approach was shown to be effective for detecting fake/real news articles (Karimi and Tang, 2019). While focused on discourse-level phenomena, previous studies use sentences as basic units. We experiment with a fine-grained level, discourse segments, provided by a state-of-the-art segmenter.

3 Model

In Liu and Lapata (2018), the sentences in each document are composed of sequences of static word embeddings that are fed to a bi-LSTM to obtain hidden representations used to compute the sentence representations, that are then passed through another bi-LSTM to compute the document representation. At both levels, representations are built using the structured attention mechanism allowing for learning sentence dependencies, constrained to form a non-projective dependency tree. Finally a 2-layer perceptron predicts the distribution over class labels.

We modify the model to include the improvements proposed by Ferracane et al. (2019). In particular: (i) we remove the document-level bi-LSTM, (ii) for the pooling operation, we aggregate over units using a weighted sum based on root scores, instead of a max pooling, (iii) we perform several additional levels of percolation to embed information from the children's children of the tree, and not only direct children.

On top of that, we skip the sentence-level structure attention as it adds an unnecessary level of composition that was found to have a negative empirical impact on the results.

Segmentation The learning of a latent structure is supposed to let the model leverage rhetorical and argumentative processes that can reflect the author's political orientation. We change the relevant textual units from sentences to more discourse-oriented ones, as given by a discourse segmenter (Muller et al., 2019). Discourse segmentation is the first stage of discourse parsing, identifying text spans called Elementary Discourse Units (EDU) that will be linked by discourse relations.

Adversarial Adaptation Some specific cues (e.g. media name, common patterns) can reveal the media source. Since most articles from a media share the same political label, the classifier decisions are biased towards the source and models easily overfit the training set. But removing these cues is a costly, hard to generalize preprocessing step. Baly et al. (2020) suggest two approaches: adversarial adaptation, or AA (Ganin et al., 2016), and triplet loss pre-training (Schroff et al., 2015), and chose the latter based on preliminary results. On the contrary we found AA more promising: it works by adding a media classifier within the architecture whose loss will be maximized using a gradient reversal layer. The model thus learns to be discriminative for the main task while being media independent.

As the training set contains many media sources, with a long tail distribution, we only consider the 10 most frequent sources (74% of the data) for the adversarial part of the model.

4 Dataset and Settings

Allsides Dataset The articles are crawled from the Allsides website,[2] with 192 news sources covering 109 topics. Allsides is a platform that offers an analysis of the political leaning of various English-language media at the article level by annotating them with 5 political classes that cover the whole political spectrum from the Left to the Right. The published version of the dataset[3] used in Baly et al. (2020) does not match their paper as it includes resp. $2,817$ and 119 additional articles and media. Although it complicates results comparison, we kept the published dataset which is large and seems well designed.[4] This dataset comes with two organizations: article-based or media-based. We chose the latter ($30,246$ articles) where media present at training time are excluded from evaluation, which avoids evaluating the model on articles that come from media already seen during training. For complexity reasons, we removed from the training set the longest articles in terms of number and size of segments, using a threshold of 100. The final dataset contains $27,146$ articles, see Table 1. Note that the original Allsides data are divided into 5 classes, but Baly et al. (2020) merged the two Left (resp. Right) classes.

Segmentation We kept the pre-processed data as in Baly et al. (2020) but we experimented with both sentence- and EDU-segmented texts (see Section 3). We rely on the DISRPT2019 shared task winner (Muller et al., 2019) that only needs plain text as input.[5] The model is based on the BERT pretrained transformer language model, fine-tuned for sequence tagging on plain documents from the GUM corpus (Zeldes, 2016), the English dataset which has the most varied document types. We end up with an average of 49 EDUs per article, and an average of 19 words per EDU.

	Left	Center	Right	Total
Train	$9,618$ (41%)	$6,683$ (28%)	$7,189$ (31%)	$23,490$
Valid.	98 (4%)	618 (26%)	$1,640$ (70%)	$2,356$
Test	599 (46%)	299 (23%)	402 (31%)	$1,300$

Table 1: Statistics about the dataset (media-based split).

Settings We built on Ferracane et al. (2019)'s implementation,[6] itself based on Liu and Lapata (2018)'s. We adapted the code according to the modifications and additions proposed in our approach as detailed in Section 3. Hyper-parameters were set using grid search: 200 for the hidden size of bi-LSTM and 2-layer perceptron, 0.01 for learning rate, 0.5 for dropout and 8 for batch size. We used pretrained 300D GloVe vectors. For Adversarial Adaptation, best results used a weighting factor $\lambda = 0.7$ for the adversarial part of the loss. Training is done with Adagrad optimizer, on a Nvidia GeForce GTX 1080 Ti GPU card.

Evaluation We evaluate four versions: (i) keeping only the bi-LSTM (Ours Base), (ii) full architecture with structural attention and sentence segmentation (Ours+SA/Sent), (iii) full architecture but with EDU segmentation (Ours+SA/EDU), and (iv) full architecture but keeping only the first 512 tokens of each text as in Baly et al. (2020) (Ours: 512t, +SA/EDU). We report standard measures but also the mean absolute error (MAE) as this is an ordinal problem. We compare to scores reported in Baly et al. (2020) on the same split for their LSTM and BERT versions (limited to 512 tokens).

5 Results and Analysis

Results obtained by the different models are given in Table 2. We also report scores per class in Table 3 (best model) to control that the model does

[2] http://allsides.com/

[3] https://github.com/ramybaly/Article-Bias-Prediction

[4] Note that the original version is not available.

[5] Recent approaches reported improvements (Zeldes et al., 2021), but require more preprocessing, e.g. syntactic parses.

[6] https://github.com/elisaF/structured/

Model	Acc.	Macro F_1	MAE
Ours Base	46.97	44.41	0.69
Ours+SA/Sent	48.76	45.84	0.67
Liu&Lapata+SA/EDU	51.01	48.61	0.72
Ours+SA/EDU	54.39	51.36	0.57
Ours: 512t, +SA/EDU	50.04	45.23	0.70
Baly 20: 512t, LSTM	46.42	45.44	0.62
Baly 20: 512t, BERT	51.41	48.26	0.51

Table 2: Accuracy%, macro-F_1%, Mean Absolute Error (MAE, lower is better) on the test set for different versions of the model. "Baly 20" refers to the results reported in Baly et al. (2020), we did not replicate their experiments. "512t" means that only the first 512 tokens of the inputs were used to train the model. "SA" = for Structured Attention, and "Sent"/"EDU" is for inputs segmented in sentence or discourse units. We also evaluate on the original model proposed by Liu and Lapata (2018) without the improvements added in our version of the model. The 95% binomial proportion confidence interval for the best model classification accuracy is 2.9%

not overpredict most represented classes. We observe significant differences in performance between models that use structured attention ("+SA") gaining about 7.4 points in accuracy and 6 in macro F_1 for the best version (+SA/EDU). Our full model, using GloVe, obtains higher scores that those reported in Baly et al. (2020) (LSTM version), +8 points acc. and +6 in F_1, and also a +3 improvement in both over their best BERT-based system.

We performed a control experiment on the size of the input as Baly et al. (2020) only consider the first 512 tokens of the articles, as this is a hard constraint on the BERT model. Reducing the input size (line 4 in Table 2) decreases model performance, showing the importance of considering the whole text and which represents an important limitation of BERT. The experiments with EDUs show the importance of having fine-grained level discourse phenomena: SA based on sentences only improves results by less than 2 points, while SA based on EDUs is much more efficient. In addition, we show the benefits of modifications made to the implementation of Liu and Lapata (2018) that include those proposed by Ferracane et al. (2019) with a +3 points improvement in accuracy. The detailed results by class show that our approach does not overspecialize, although the center class is harder to predict.

As said above, dataset differences and the lack

Side	Prec.%	Recall%	F_1%
Left	67.39	27.19	38.75
Center	39.59	72.76	51.28
Right	66.53	61.74	64.05

Table 3: Scores per class (best model): Ours+SA/EDU.

of detailed results per class means the comparison with Baly et al. (2020) should be considered with caution. In particular, since they do not yet provide an implementation to replicate their experiments, we cannot control the overspecialization issues.

Regarding biases towards the topics covered, we rely on the analysis by Baly et al. (2020) for their dataset: they showed that topics covered are fairly represented in each class and thus that it should not significantly impact the model decisions.

We also want to give here some insights into the model by an analysis with interpretablity methods at the lexical level but also with respect to the induced structure.

Saliency Map A saliency map in NLP is a method for visualizing a deep learning model by computing relative importance of each token (word) in the input based on gradients (Ribeiro et al., 2016; Murdoch et al., 2018). It allows us to identify the lexical cues that provide partial understanding of the decisions made by the model. Here, we considered the vanilla gradient approach (Simonyan et al., 2014), focusing on the gradient of the loss with respect to each token embedding. From these, we can first clearly assess the positive impact of the AA method. Lexical cues used by the model without AA, such as the name of the media source, are no longer as relevant for the prediction, although still present. We notice that the model focuses on specific lexical fields depending on the political orientation of the article, such as health, numbers/statistics, economy, for left, center and right leaning articles respectively. We found that crucial information for the model are the mentions or quotes of political figures (e.g., Donald Trump, Hillary Clinton, @realDonaldTrump, Barack) by media sources of the same political side, but they also represent an important source of errors when it appears in articles of the opposite side as the model tends to use this information alone without considering its context.

It also confirms our intuition that there is relevant information in the middle and at the end of articles, even though the model usually focuses on small portions of text, and it explains why reducing the entry size results in a loss of performance. An example is provided in appendix A as heatmap.

Structured Attention Regarding structured attention, we extracted the maximum spanning trees from the attention scores using the Chu-Liu-Edmonds algorithm (Chu and Liu, 1965; Edmonds, 1967). An example of dependency tree is given in appendix A. For a first qualitative analysis, we looked at some statistics following Ferracane et al. (2019) methodology. In particular, we measure the average height of trees (10.68), the average proportion of leaf nodes (0.77), and the average normalized arc length (0.35). Statistics per class are equivalent. The learned trees have complex (non-flat) structures which show that relevant information to the model has been encoded in them in contrast to the results obtained by Ferracane et al. (2019). We observed that they have marked differences with "natural" structures, such as distant links and it could be interesting to add more constraints.

6 Conclusion

We proposed an original approach for predicting the political orientation of newspaper articles based on learning a latent structure showing the importance of considering elementary discourse units over sentences to include the argumentative dimension, allowing for large improvements over past approaches. We provide preliminary qualitative results on interpreting the predictions to characterize bias. Further work will focus on relying on contextual pretrained models while overcoming limitations on document size, and improving output structures and analyses.

7 Acknowledgments

Nicolas Devatine's work is supported by the SLANT project (ANR-19-CE23-0022). This work was partially supported by the ANR (ANR-19-PI3A-0004) through the AI Interdisciplinary Institute, ANITI, as a part of France's "Investing for the Future — PIA3" program. This work is also partially supported by the AnDiaMO project (ANR-21-CE23-0020). Chloé Braud and Philippe Muller are part of the programme DesCartes and are also supported by the National Research Foundation, Prime Minister's Office, Singapore under its Campus for Research Excellence and Technological Enterprise (CREATE) programme.

8 Ethical considerations

We used the same data as Baly et al. (2020) for comparison purposes. They consist in news articles referenced by the Allsides website, which also assigns political orientation to media sources based on their expertise and some polling.[7] While the exact method is undisclosed, they allow user feedback, which is a way of validating the labels. The fact remains that political labelling is potentially subjective, evolving, and labelling the source is not the same as labelling an article from the source. We train models on that approximate information nonetheless, and it can affect the prediction performance. Also, we merged all labels from the same "side" (left/right) to have only 3 classes instead of Allsides 5 categories. The dataset is not entirely balanced between left/center/right classes, but it's not possible to tell if the distribution is representative of the whole set of potential journalistic sources.

This study is not intended to provide an accurate tool for predicting the political orientation of a news article. The prediction model is a means to analyze differences in linguistic expressions of different biases, with post-hoc analysis of the model internal representations. While revealing orientation of media sources could be a legitimate goal in itself (and is the purpose of the Allsides website), note that current models do not make reliable predictions, and their results should not be taken as such without evidence supporting their decision. This is why part of our work is to analyze and look for linguistic regularities with respect to political orientation. As existing clues are currently either shallow (lexicon) or subject to further validation (structure analysis), it does not dispense of human judgement to decide if a text if showing a bias, openly or not, towards a position on the political spectrum.

[7]https://www.allsides.com/media-bias/media-bias-rating-methods

References

Vidhisha Balachandran, Artidoro Pagnoni, Jay Yoon Lee, Dheeraj Rajagopal, Jaime Carbonell, and Yulia Tsvetkov. 2021. StructSum: Summarization via structured representations. In *Proceedings of the 16th Conference of the European Chapter of the Association for Computational Linguistics: Main Volume*, pages 2575–2585, Online. Association for Computational Linguistics.

Ramy Baly, Giovanni Da San Martino, James Glass, and Preslav Nakov. 2020. We can detect your bias: Predicting the political ideology of news articles. In *Proceedings of the 2020 Conference on Empirical Methods in Natural Language Processing (EMNLP)*, pages 4982–4991, Online. Association for Computational Linguistics.

Eric Baumer, Elisha Elovic, Ying Qin, Francesca Polletta, and Geri Gay. 2015. Testing and comparing computational approaches for identifying the language of framing in political news. In *Proceedings of the 2015 Conference of the North American Chapter of the Association for Computational Linguistics: Human Language Technologies*, pages 1472–1482, Denver, Colorado. Association for Computational Linguistics.

Dallas Card, Amber E. Boydstun, Justin H. Gross, Philip Resnik, and Noah A. Smith. 2015. The media frames corpus: Annotations of frames across issues. In *Proceedings of the 53rd Annual Meeting of the Association for Computational Linguistics and the 7th International Joint Conference on Natural Language Processing (Volume 2: Short Papers)*, pages 438–444, Beijing, China. Association for Computational Linguistics.

Wei-Fan Chen, Khalid Al Khatib, Benno Stein, and Henning Wachsmuth. 2020. Detecting media bias in news articles using Gaussian bias distributions. In *Findings of the Association for Computational Linguistics: EMNLP 2020*, pages 4290–4300, Online. Association for Computational Linguistics.

Yoeng-Jin Chu and Tseng-Hong Liu. 1965. On the shortest arborescence of a directed graph. *Scientia Sinica*, 14:1396–1400.

Giovanni Da San Martino, Alberto Barrón-Cedeño, Henning Wachsmuth, Rostislav Petrov, and Preslav Nakov. 2020. SemEval-2020 task 11: Detection of propaganda techniques in news articles. In *Proceedings of the Fourteenth Workshop on Semantic Evaluation*, pages 1377–1414, Barcelona (online). International Committee for Computational Linguistics.

Stefano DellaVigna and Ethan Kaplan. 2007. The Fox News Effect: Media Bias and Voting*. *The Quarterly Journal of Economics*, 122(3):1187–1234.

Jack Edmonds. 1967. Optimum branchings. *Journal of Research of the national Bureau of Standards*, 71:233–240.

Elisa Ferracane, Greg Durrett, Junyi Jessy Li, and Katrin Erk. 2019. Evaluating discourse in structured text representations. In *Proceedings of the 57th Annual Meeting of the Association for Computational Linguistics*, pages 646–653, Florence, Italy. Association for Computational Linguistics.

Anjalie Field, Doron Kliger, Shuly Wintner, Jennifer Pan, Dan Jurafsky, and Yulia Tsvetkov. 2018. Framing and agenda-setting in Russian news: a computational analysis of intricate political strategies. In *Proceedings of the 2018 Conference on Empirical Methods in Natural Language Processing*, pages 3570–3580, Brussels, Belgium. Association for Computational Linguistics.

Yaroslav Ganin, Evgeniya Ustinova, Hana Ajakan, Pascal Germain, Hugo Larochelle, François Laviolette, Mario March, and Victor Lempitsky. 2016. Domain-adversarial training of neural networks. *Journal of Machine Learning Research*, 17(59):1–35.

Felix Hamborg, Karsten Donnay, and Bela Gipp. 2019. Automated identification of media bias in news articles: an interdisciplinary literature review. *Int. J. Digit. Libr.*, 20(4):391–415.

Masaru Isonuma, Junichiro Mori, and Ichiro Sakata. 2019. Unsupervised neural single-document summarization of reviews via learning latent discourse structure and its ranking. In *Proceedings of the 57th Annual Meeting of the Association for Computational Linguistics*, pages 2142–2152, Florence, Italy. Association for Computational Linguistics.

Mohit Iyyer, Peter Enns, Jordan Boyd-Graber, and Philip Resnik. 2014. Political ideology detection using recursive neural networks. In *Proceedings of the 52nd Annual Meeting of the Association for Computational Linguistics (Volume 1: Long Papers)*, pages 1113–1122, Baltimore, Maryland. Association for Computational Linguistics.

Hamid Karimi and Jiliang Tang. 2019. Learning hierarchical discourse-level structure for fake news detection. In *Proceedings of the 2019 Conference of the North American Chapter of the Association for Computational Linguistics: Human Language Technologies, Volume 1 (Long and Short Papers)*, pages 3432–3442, Minneapolis, Minnesota. Association for Computational Linguistics.

Johannes Kiesel, Maria Mestre, Rishabh Shukla, Emmanuel Vincent, Payam Adineh, David Corney, Benno Stein, and Martin Potthast. 2019. SemEval-2019 task 4: Hyperpartisan news detection. In *Proceedings of the 13th International Workshop on Semantic Evaluation*, pages 829–839, Minneapolis, Minnesota, USA. Association for Computational Linguistics.

M. Lee and N. Solomon. 1990. *Unreliable Sources: A Guide to Detecting Bias in News Media.* Lyle Smart, New York.

D. G Levasseur. 2008. Media bias. In L. L. Kaid, editor, *Encyclopedia of political communication*. Thousand Oaks, CA: Sage Publications.

Chang Li and Dan Goldwasser. 2021. Mean: Multi-head entity aware attention networkfor political perspective detection in news media. In *Proceedings of the Fourth Workshop on NLP for Internet Freedom Censorship, Disinformation, and Propaganda (NLP4IF)*.

Yang Liu and Mirella Lapata. 2018. Learning structured text representations. *Transactions of the Association for Computational Linguistics*, 6:63–75.

Yang Liu, Ivan Titov, and Mirella Lapata. 2019. Single document summarization as tree induction. In *Proceedings of the 2019 Conference of the North American Chapter of the Association for Computational Linguistics: Human Language Technologies, Volume 1 (Long and Short Papers)*, pages 1745–1755, Minneapolis, Minnesota. Association for Computational Linguistics.

Fred Morstatter, Liang Wu, Uraz Yavanoglu, Stephen R. Corman, and Huan Liu. 2018. Identifying framing bias in online news. *Trans. Soc. Comput.*, 1(2).

Philippe Muller, Chloé Braud, and Mathieu Morey. 2019. ToNy: Contextual embeddings for accurate multilingual discourse segmentation of full documents. In *Proceedings of the Workshop on Discourse Relation Parsing and Treebanking 2019*, pages 115–124, Minneapolis, MN. Association for Computational Linguistics.

W. James Murdoch, Peter J. Liu, and Bin Yu. 2018. Beyond word importance: Contextual decomposition to extract interactions from lstms. *CoRR*, abs/1801.05453.

Marta Recasens, Cristian Danescu-Niculescu-Mizil, and Dan Jurafsky. 2013. Linguistic models for analyzing and detecting biased language. In *Proceedings of the 51st Annual Meeting of the Association for Computational Linguistics (Volume 1: Long Papers)*, pages 1650–1659. Association for Computational Linguistics.

Marco Tulio Ribeiro, Sameer Singh, and Carlos Guestrin. 2016. "why should i trust you?": Explaining the predictions of any classifier.

Dietram A. Scheufele and David Tewksbury. 2007. Framing, agenda setting, and priming: The evolution of three media effects models. *Journal of Communication*, 57(1):9–20.

Florian Schroff, Dmitry Kalenichenko, and James Philbin. 2015. Facenet: A unified embedding for face recognition and clustering. *CoRR*, abs/1503.03832.

Andrey Simonov, Szymon K Sacher, Jean-Pierre H Dubé, and Shirsho Biswas. 2020. The persuasive effect of fox news: non-compliance with social distancing during the covid-19 pandemic. Technical report, National Bureau of Economic Research.

Karen Simonyan, Andrea Vedaldi, and Andrew Zisserman. 2014. Deep inside convolutional networks: Visualising image classification models and saliency maps.

Amir Zeldes. 2016. The GUM corpus: Creating multilayer resources in the classroom. In *Proceedings of LREC*.

Amir Zeldes, Yang Janet Liu, Mikel Iruskieta, Philippe Muller, Chloé Braud, and Sonia Badene. 2021. The DISRPT 2021 shared task on elementary discourse unit segmentation, connective detection, and relation classification. In *Proceedings of the 2nd Shared Task on Discourse Relation Parsing and Treebanking (DISRPT 2021)*, pages 1–12, Punta Cana, Dominican Republic. Association for Computational Linguistics.

Longyin Zhang, Yuqing Xing, Fang Kong, Peifeng Li, and Guodong Zhou. 2020. A top-down neural architecture towards text-level parsing of discourse rhetorical structure. In *Proceedings of the 58th Annual Meeting of the Association for Computational Linguistics*, pages 6386–6395, Online. Association for Computational Linguistics.

A Example Appendix

Analysis As mentioned in Section 5, it is clear from this example that there is relevant information in the middle and at the end of articles, even though the model focuses on small portions of text, which confirms the value of keeping the whole text. Political figures play an important role for the model, with entities such as "Trump" or "Mattis" (from the Right) having high scores. Furthermore, the model focuses on words or, more generally, on lexical fields that relate to the main subject of the article and that seem to be particularly sensitive for the political side considered here.

President Trump ' s decision late Friday to ban transgender Americans from serving in the U.S. military was blasted by House Minority Leader Nancy Pelosi , who called the move " cowardly " and " disgusting . " The Trump administration issued a memorandum that bars people with a history of " gender dysphoria , " which would require medical treatment , from being admitted to the U.S. military " except under certain limited circumstances . " Pelosi , a San Francisco Democrat , immediately released a statement slamming the memorandum and condemning the Trump administration . " The President ' s ban is a cruel and arbitrary decision designed to humiliate transgender Americans who have stepped forward to serve our country , " she said in a statement . " This bigoted ban weakens our military readiness and our country , and shows this president ' s stunning lack of loyalty to those who risk all to defend our freedoms . " We will continue to fight this discriminatory action , which has no place in our country . House Democrats will never allow hate and prejudice to dictate our national security . " The current policy was based on recommendations made by Defense Secretary James Mattis , who said the Pentagon found that exempting transgender people from military standards could undermine its readiness for combat . " Exempting such persons from well - established mental health , physical health , and sex - based standards , which apply to all Service members , including transgender Service members without gender dysphoria , could undermine readiness , disrupt unit cohesion , and impose an unreasonable burden on the military that is not conducive to military effectiveness and lethality , " read the recommendation that was included in a court filing . DOJ ASKS SUPREME COURT TO TAKE UP CASE OF MILITARY TRANSGENDER BAN The Trump administration asked the Supreme Court to issue an unusually quick ruling on the Pentagon 's policy of restricting military service by transgender people in a bid to bypass lower courts that previously ruled against the administration and its policy barring transgender recruits . The Pentagon initially lifted its ban on transgender troops serving openly in the military in 2016 under the orders of the Obama administration . Trump reversed the policy , prompting outrage and lawsuits , which were ruled against the Trump administration .

Figure 2: Article from "Fox News" (right-leaning) correctly predicted: "Pelosi blasts Trump's move to bar transgender troops, calls it 'disgusting' and 'cowardly'". The darker it is, the higher the relevance of the word to the model.

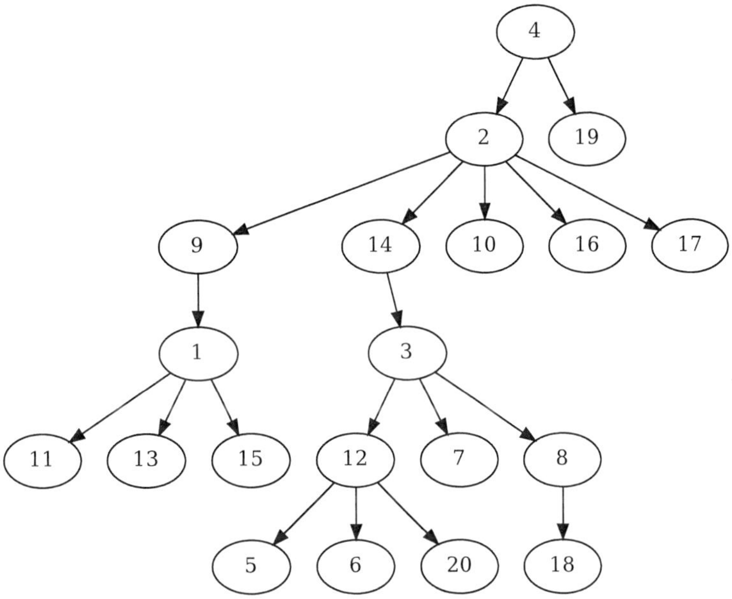

1 - President-elect Donald Trump has chosen Republican National Committee chairman Reince Priebus his new chief of staff.
2 - He also named conservative media executive Stephen K. Bannon as his senior counselor.
3 - "I am thrilled to have my very successful team continue with me in leading our country", Trump said in a statement.
4 - Trump's transition team made the announcement, Sunday, in the first steps toward solidifying the President-elect's administration.
5 - Priebus, is a Washington veteran with deep ties to Republican leadership, particularly House Speaker Paul Ryan, The Associated Press reports.
6 - "It is truly an honor to join President-elect Trump in the White House as his Chief of Staff", Priebus said in the statement.
7 - "I am very grateful to the President-elect for this opportunity to serve him and this nation
8 - as we work to create an economy that works for everyone, secure our borders, repeal and replace Obamacare and destroy radical Islamic terrorism.
9 - He will be a great President for all Americans."
10 - Bannon is believed to have been in the running for the position, but will now serve as chief strategist and senior counselor.
11 - He ran the conservative website Breitbart News before joining the presidential campaign during the general election.
12 - "Steve and Reince are highly qualified leaders who worked well together on our campaign and led us to a historic victory.
13 - Now I will have them both with me in the White House
14 - as we work to make America great again",
15 - Trump said.
16 - The campaign's statement described Bannon and Priebus as "equal partners".
17 - "Bannon and Priebus will continue the effective leadership team they formed during the campaign, working as equal partners to transform the federal government,
18 - making it much more efficient, effective and productive", it said.
19 - According to CNN, Trump's picks signal that he will look to build bridges in Washington and keep continuity with the Republican party's agenda.
20 - "We will have that same partnership in working to help President-elect Trump achieve his agenda", Bannon said.

Figure 3: Example of a tree induced by the structured attention mechanism. Article from "CBN" (leaning-right) correctly predicted: "Donald Trump Names Reince Priebus as Chief of Staff"

Attention Modulation for Zero-Shot Cross-Domain Dialogue State Tracking

Mathilde Veron[1,2] and **Guillaume Bernard**[2] and **Olivier Galibert**[2] and **Sophie Rosset**[1]

[1]Université Paris-Saclay CNRS, LISN, Orsay, France; [2]LNE, Trappes, France;

[1]{name.lastname}@lisn.fr; [2]{name.lastname}@lne.fr

Abstract

Dialog state tracking (DST) is a core step for task-oriented dialogue systems aiming to track the user's current goal during a dialogue. Recently a special focus has been put on applying existing DST models to new domains, in other words performing zero-shot cross-domain transfer. While recent state-of-the-art models leverage large pre-trained language models, no work has been made on understanding and improving the results of first-developed zero-shot models like SUMBT. In this paper, we thus propose to improve SUMBT zero-shot results on MultiWOZ by using attention modulation during inference. This method improves SUMBT zero-shot results significantly on two domains and does not worsen the initial performance with the significant advantage of needing no additional training.

1 Introduction

Task-oriented dialogue systems aim to provide information and perform tasks requested by a user during a dialogue (*e.g.*, booking a train ticket or finding a restaurant). As the dialogue progresses, the user may add some criteria or change its goal, so the system needs to track the current goal of the user at each dialogue turn for the dialogue to succeed. The associated task is called Dialogue State Tracking (DST) and consists, in its most studied form, in updating the slots mentioned by the user (see Figure 1). State-of-the-art models rely on deep learning models. However, a highly desirable feature of dialogue systems is the ability to scale to new domains without retraining but by taking advantage of knowledge already acquired in previous domains. Thus in this paper we study "leave-one-out" cross-domain zero-shot transfer. For each domain, a model is trained on dialogues that do not contain slots of the target domain and is then evaluated on dialogues containing slots of the target domain.

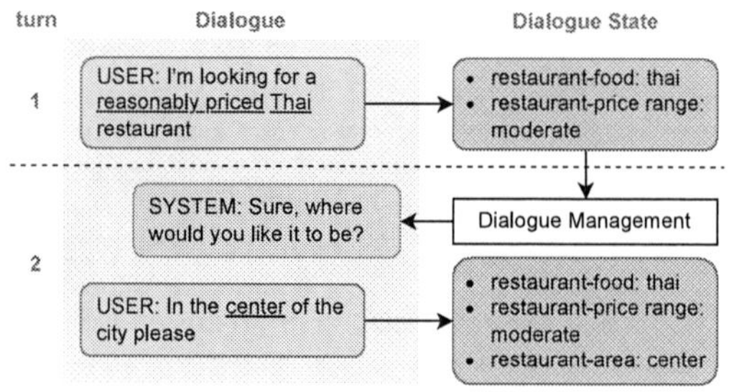

Figure 1: Example of dialogue along with the dialogue state at each turn.

Zero-shot cross-domain transfer studies on DST are relatively recent and are mainly conducted on the MultiWOZ dataset (Budzianowski et al., 2018)[1]. Such zero-shot learning was first applied to TRADE and SUMBT models (Campagna et al., 2020), where TRADE (Wu et al., 2019) relies on an RNN and SUMBT (Lee et al., 2019) on the pre-trained language model BERT (Devlin et al., 2019) and an RNN. Instead of building new architectures, recent state-of-the-art models leverage large generative pre-trained language models like GPT-2 (Radford et al., 2019) or T5 (Raffel et al., 2020), and work on the form of the input itself by incorporating slot descriptions (Lin et al., 2021b; Zhao et al., 2022), showing labeled examples (Gupta et al., 2022), or considering a slot as a question (Li et al., 2021; Lin et al., 2021a).

However, no further work has been conducted on understanding and improving the results of first-developed models. Thus in this paper we propose different architectural variants of SUMBT and introduce attention modulation to improve cross-domain zero-shot results on MultiWOZ 2.0.

[1]Schema-Guided Dialogue dataset (Rastogi et al., 2020) is also used but distinguishes only seen and unseen data, and thus does not allow cross-domain transfer analysis.

Proceedings of 3rd Workshop on Computational Approaches to Discourse, pages 86–91
October 16 – 17, 2022. ©2022 International Conference on Computational Linguistics

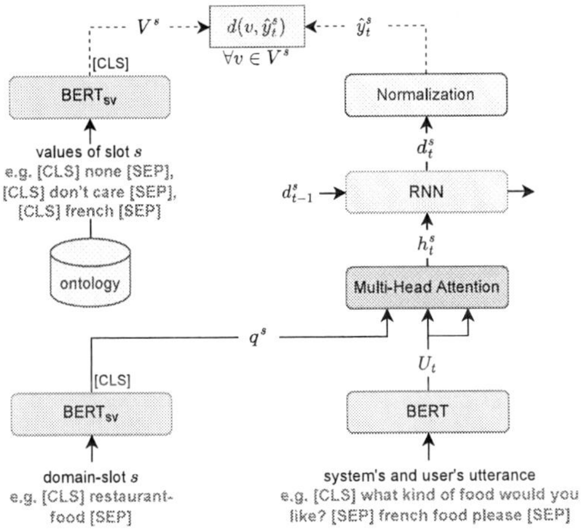

Figure 2: Architecture of SUMBT (Lee et al., 2019)

2 SUMBT

The main idea of SUMBT is to match each slot-name to a slot-value from an ontology given a dialogue turn (a system's and a user's utterance). The architecture of the model is illustrated in Figure 2[2]. During inference, any domain/slot-name pair can be used as query input as long as the ontology contains the list of values associated with the domain/slot-name pair. Trained SUMBT models can thus be applied to new domains after updating the ontology, and the models can predict new slots never seen during training.

We re-implemented our own version of SUMBT and conducted zero-shot cross-domain experiments. Transfer is measured by computing the Joint Goal Accuracy (JGA) only on the slots of the target domain. It consists of the percentage of turns from all dialogues where all targeted slots-names are associated with the correct slot-value. All experiments are run on 5 random seeds. In the first line of Table 1, we can observe that SUMBT performs poorly even if its ontology is updated before testing with the slot-value list of each slot-name from the target domain. Looking more closely at the model's predictions, we notice that SUMBT generally tends to predict the slot-value `none` more than it should. In fact, the proportion of `none` values in training data is 71%, while the model predicts 78% of the times the value `none` on test data of the domains used during training. When applying the model to unknown domains, the proportion increases on average to 88% and can even get to 99% in the case of the attraction domain. It shows that this tendency intensifies when a new slot never seen during training is queried.

[2]See Appendix A for further information.

3 Attention Modulation

Motivated by previous observations, we propose a method called *attention modulation* to push the model to predict the slot-value `none` less frequently for unknown slots. Specifically, this would apply when predicting the dialogue state of a dialogue turn that refers to an unknown domain. However, doing this could lead the model to predict any other value except the correct one. Thus we also describe two variants of SUMBT, aiming to take advantage of similarities that naturally exist between the slots of the different domains. We hypothesize that it would help the model to increase transfer between domains and that our method would be more effective on these variants.

3.1 Method

SUMBT relies on a multi-head attention layer, which basically repeats the Scaled Dot-Product Attention multiple times (Vaswani et al., 2017)[3]. This layer enables the model to draw its attention to tokens related to the queried slot. The attention mechanism takes as input three matrices: Q a set of queries, K a set of keys, and V a set of values. In our case, we have $Q \in \mathbb{R}^{1 \times d}$, where Q corresponds to q^s the domain/slot-name pair encoded by $BERT_{sv}$ and d denotes the dimension of the BERT model. $K \in \mathbb{R}^{sl \times d}$ and $V \in \mathbb{R}^{sl \times d}$ both correspond to the concatenation of a system's and a user utterance (a dialogue turn) encoded by $BERT$ also noted $U_t = \{u_{t,i}\}_{i \in [\![0,sl]\!]}$, where t denotes a unique turn index over all dialogues and sl the maximum number of tokens that can be encoded by $BERT$ including the special tokens `[CLS]` and `[SEP]`. The attention mechanism is formalized as follow:

$$Attention(Q, K, V) = (w_{t,i}^{d^s}) \cdot V \quad (1)$$

$$\text{with } (w_{t,i}^{d^s})_{i \in [\![0,sl]\!]} = softmax\left(\frac{s_{t,i}^{d^s}}{\sqrt{d}}\right) \quad (2)$$

$$\text{and } (s_{t,i}^{d^s})_{i \in [\![0,sl]\!]} = Q \cdot K^T \quad (3)$$

Where d^s denotes the domain associated to the slot s and $w_{t,i}^{d^s}$ corresponds to the attention weights applied to U_t (the values matrix V) after normalizing the attention scores $s_{t,i}^{d^s}$.

[3]For illustration purposes in this paper, the dimensions do not take into account the number of heads.

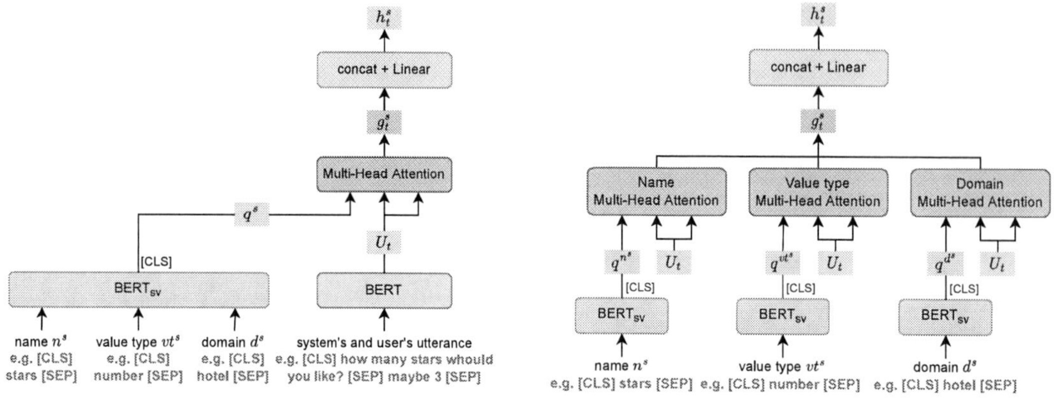

(a) triple query (b) triple attention

Figure 3: Variants of SUMBT. After h_t^s the architecture remains the same than the original model in Figure 2.

In their paper, SUMBT authors found out that the attention weights were high on the special tokens `[CLS]` and `[SEP]` when the slot-value `none` was predicted. To push the model to predict values other than the value `none`, we can then simply reduce the attention weights on these special tokens. We call this method *attention modulation* and defined it as follow:

$$(w_{t,i}^{d^s})_{i \in [\![0,sl]\!]} = softmax\left(\frac{\alpha_{t,i}^{d^s} \cdot s_{t,i}^{d^s}}{\sqrt{d}}\right) \quad (4)$$

$$\text{with } \alpha_{t,i}^{d^s} = \begin{cases} 0 & \text{if } d^s \in ND \text{ and } u_{t,i} \in ST, \\ 1 & \text{otherwise.} \end{cases} \quad (5)$$

Where ND is the set of new domains never seen during training, and ST is the set of special tokens `[CLS]` and `[SEP]`. This method is simple yet attractive since it does not need any additional training and can be directly applied to the model during inference.

3.2 Model Variants

Regarding SUMBT zero-shot results, it seems that it is not able to take advantage of the similarities that exist between each domain. In fact, some slots can share the same name, the same type of values, or even the same values. To boost cross-domain transfer, we describe each slot with its domain, its name, and the type of its values following (Lin et al., 2021b) "slot type" descriptions. We suppose that variants of SUMBT incorporating these descriptions should benefit more from attention modulation than the original model. We thus propose two main variants of SUMBT:

- **With triple query** (Figure 3a): The query q^s consists here in a matrix of 3 vectors corresponding to the name, the type of values, and the domain of the queried slot, the three being encoded by $BERT_{sv}$. Since we now have $q^s \in \mathbb{R}^{3 \times d}$, the multi-head attention layer outputs $g_t^s \in \mathbb{R}^{3 \times d}$. We thus reshape the output by concatenating the three vectors and by using a linear layer $h_t^s = g_t^s W + b$ with $W \in \mathbb{R}^{3*d \times d}$ followed by ReLU activation (Nair and Hinton, 2010).
- **With triple attention** (Figure 3b): We use 3 independent multi-head attention layers and input respectively the name, the type of values, and the domain of the queried slot, the three being encoded by $BERT_{sv}$. The outputs of each multi-head attention layer is then concatenated, and the resulting vector is reshaped the same way as previously. We suppose the independent training to favor more transfer.

For these two variants, as well as the original SUMBT model, we also add variants where the weights of the utterance encoder $BERT$ are fixed during training. We suppose this could help the model to generalize to unknown domains. Fixing its weights also has the advantage of reducing the computation cost per epoch considerably.

3.3 Experiments and Results

In these experiments, we used an oracle to detect the domain associated to the dialogue turn. The attention modulation is applied only on the query or the attention layer related to the domain, respectively for the *triple query* and the *triple attention*

Version	Modulation	Attraction	Hotel	Restaurant	Taxi	Train
Original	none	23.57 ±0.86	14.51 ±1.23	17.19 ±0.84	60.41 ±0.12	21.31 ±0.91
	on slot attn.	25.03 ±3.04	14.23 ±1.07	17.81 ±1.07	**60.48** ±0.15	21.25 ±0.88
		+1.46 ±2.19	−0.28 ±0.24	+0.62 ±1.46	+0.08 ±0.11	−0.06 ±0.05
+ frozen BERT	none	23.29 ±0.25	15.09 ±0.31	14.94 ±1.26	60.29 ±0.17	22.61 ±0.18
	on slot attn.	28.00 ±1.06	15.62 ±0.48	17.30 ±0.88	60.28 ±0.17	22.62 ±0.19
		+4.71 ±1.02	+0.53 ±0.22	+2.36 ±1.12	−0.01 ±0.03	+0.01 ±0.02
w/ triple query	none	23.56 ±2.09	16.02 ±1.17	18.16 ±1.19	56.11 ±3.60	21.42 ±1.59
	on domain query	25.40 ±1.78	16.14 ±0.95	**19.13** ±0.80	56.26 ±3.71	21.43 ±1.62
		+1.85 ±2.88	+0.12 ±0.41	+0.97 ±0.64	+0.15 ±0.26	+0.01 ±0.04
+ frozen BERT	none	24.52 ±1.07	15.92 ±0.78	15.58 ±0.32	58.17 ±1.75	22.61 ±0.33
	on domain query	25.58 ±1.36	15.90 ±0.70	16.99 ±0.58	58.13 ±1.77	22.63 ±0.31
		+1.06 ±1.23	−0.02 ±0.46	+1.40 ±0.68	−0.04 ±0.10	+0.02 ±0.03
w/ triple attn.	none	23.70 ±4.51	16.06 ±0.90	16.41 ±2.46	56.88 ±3.31	22.54 ±0.32
	on domain attn.	28.53 ±4.99	16.37 ±0.88	18.29 ±2.00	56.96 ±3.38	22.58 ±0.33
		+4.83 ±2.42	+0.31 ±0.09	+1.88 ±1.63	+0.08 ±0.08	+0.04 ±0.05
+ frozen BERT	none	23.32 ±1.64	15.55 ±0.90	15.65 ±1.20	59.68 ±0.83	**22.74** ±0.07
	on domain attn.	**29.83** ±1.57	**17.09** ±1.37	16.80 ±1.30	59.72 ±0.84	**22.74** ±0.07
		+6.51 ±0.87	+1.54 ±0.68	+1.15 ±0.60	+0.04 ±0.06	−0.00 ±0.03

Table 1: JGA of different variants of SUMBT on MultiWOZ 2.0 cross-domain zero-shot experiments with and without modulation. The columns denote the target domain and the ± sign denotes the standard deviation.

variant. The results are shown in Table 1. First, if we look at the results without modulation, it seems that the proposed variants do not increase cross-domain transfer in a general manner. On the attraction domain, the results of the different variants are similar to the SUMBT original ones. On the hotel and train domains, all variants perform better than the original. However, on the restaurant and taxi domains, almost all variants perform worst than the original, except the *triple query* variant on the restaurant domain. We also observe that fixing BERT weights during training does help the variant around half of the time to perform better than when fine-tuning BERT, so we cannot state that it is beneficial for transfer. Note that overall, fixing BERT weights gives less variation in the results.

Now, when looking at the results with modulation, we observe that the variant *triple attention* with a frozen BERT and modulation gets the overall best results on the attraction and the hotel domain with respectively a high increase of 6.26 and 2.58 points compared to SUMBT original without modulation. On the restaurant domain, the variant *triple query* with a fine-tuned BERT and modulation gets the best results with an increase of 1.94 points compared to SUMBT original without modulation. However, modulation does not seem to impact the taxi and train domains.

In order to better observe the actual benefit of modulation, we compute for each model trained on a specific seed the difference in its performance with and without modulation. The resulting differences are averaged across variants and domains and correspond to the third line of each variant in Table 1. In a general manner, we can see that modulation increases performance. In fact, the difference is almost always positive, and if not, it is contained in the standard deviation or close to it. On the attraction and hotel domains, the *triple attention* variants benefit more from modulation than the *triple query* ones. This suggests that the fact that the name, the type of values, and the domain of the queried slot have their own attention mechanism is more beneficial for transfer. More precisely, on these two domains the variant *triple attention* with a frozen BERT is the one that benefits the most from modulation with an increase of respectively +6.51 and +1.54. Surprisingly, modulation seems to work fine on SUMBT original with a frozen BERT on the attraction and restaurant domains. On the restaurant domain, the *triple query* and *triple attention* variants seem to benefit similarly from modulation. However, on taxi and train domains, modulation has a negligible impact on the performance of all variants. Apart from these two domains, modulation seems to have a better impact when BERT is frozen (two-thirds of the time).

4 Conclusion and Future Work

In this paper we proposed different variants of SUMBT and introduced *attention modulation*. This method successfully improves SUMBT original cross-domain zero-shot results on the attraction and the hotel domains by respectively 6.26 and 2.58 points with the *triple attention* variant, while not needing any additional training and never worsening original results. For further work, we plan to analyze in detail the results and conduct additional experiments to understand better the impact of attention modulation on the different domains. For example, we plan to introduce a variable β in place of the value 0 in equation 5 to study how changing the value of β can affect evaluation results with modulation. We also plan to study the possibility of extending the attention modulation to other architectures.

Reproducible Research

In the spirit of reproducible research, we release our code as open source available at https://github.com/mathilde-veron/attention-modulation-zero-dst.

Acknowledgements

This work has been funded by French ANRT under CIFRE PhD contract # 2019/0628. It was also possible thanks to the Saclay-IA computing platform and was performed using HPC resources from GENCI-IDRIS (Grant 2022-AD011012609R1).

References

Paweł Budzianowski, Tsung-Hsien Wen, Bo-Hsiang Tseng, Iñigo Casanueva, Stefan Ultes, Osman Ramadan, and Milica Gašić. 2018. MultiWOZ - a large-scale multi-domain Wizard-of-Oz dataset for task-oriented dialogue modelling. In *Proceedings of the 2018 Conference on Empirical Methods in Natural Language Processing*, pages 5016–5026, Brussels, Belgium. Association for Computational Linguistics.

Giovanni Campagna, Agata Foryciarz, Mehrad Moradshahi, and Monica Lam. 2020. Zero-shot transfer learning with synthesized data for multi-domain dialogue state tracking. In *Proceedings of the 58th Annual Meeting of the Association for Computational Linguistics*, pages 122–132, Online. Association for Computational Linguistics.

Jacob Devlin, Ming-Wei Chang, Kenton Lee, and Kristina Toutanova. 2019. BERT: Pre-training of deep bidirectional transformers for language understanding. In *Proceedings of the 2019 Conference of the North American Chapter of the Association for Computational Linguistics: Human Language Technologies, Volume 1 (Long and Short Papers)*, pages 4171–4186, Minneapolis, Minnesota. Association for Computational Linguistics.

Raghav Gupta, Harrison Lee, Jeffrey Zhao, Yuan Cao, Abhinav Rastogi, and Yonghui Wu. 2022. Show, don't tell: Demonstrations outperform descriptions for schema-guided task-oriented dialogue. In *Proceedings of the 2022 Conference of the North American Chapter of the Association for Computational Linguistics: Human Language Technologies*, pages 4541–4549, Seattle, United States. Association for Computational Linguistics.

Hwaran Lee, Jinsik Lee, and Tae-Yoon Kim. 2019. SUMBT: Slot-utterance matching for universal and scalable belief tracking. In *Proceedings of the 57th Annual Meeting of the Association for Computational Linguistics*, pages 5478–5483, Florence, Italy. Association for Computational Linguistics.

Shuyang Li, Jin Cao, Mukund Sridhar, Henghui Zhu, Shang-Wen Li, Wael Hamza, and Julian McAuley. 2021. Zero-shot generalization in dialog state tracking through generative question answering. In *Proceedings of the 16th Conference of the European Chapter of the Association for Computational Linguistics: Main Volume*, pages 1063–1074, Online. Association for Computational Linguistics.

Zhaojiang Lin, Bing Liu, Andrea Madotto, Seungwhan Moon, Zhenpeng Zhou, Paul Crook, Zhiguang Wang, Zhou Yu, Eunjoon Cho, Rajen Subba, and Pascale Fung. 2021a. Zero-shot dialogue state tracking via cross-task transfer. In *Proceedings of the 2021 Conference on Empirical Methods in Natural Language Processing*, pages 7890–7900, Online and Punta Cana, Dominican Republic. Association for Computational Linguistics.

Zhaojiang Lin, Bing Liu, Seungwhan Moon, Paul Crook, Zhenpeng Zhou, Zhiguang Wang, Zhou Yu, Andrea Madotto, Eunjoon Cho, and Rajen Subba. 2021b. Leveraging slot descriptions for zero-shot cross-domain dialogue StateTracking. In *Proceedings of the 2021 Conference of the North American Chapter of the Association for Computational Linguistics: Human Language Technologies*, pages 5640–5648, Online. Association for Computational Linguistics.

Vinod Nair and Geoffrey E Hinton. 2010. Rectified Linear Units Improve Restricted Boltzmann Machines. In *ICML*.

Alec Radford, Jeff Wu, Rewon Child, David Luan, Dario Amodei, and Ilya Sutskever. 2019. Language models are unsupervised multitask learners.

Colin Raffel, Noam Shazeer, Adam Roberts, Katherine Lee, Sharan Narang, Michael Matena, Yanqi Zhou, Wei Li, and Peter J. Liu. 2020. Exploring the limits of transfer learning with a unified text-to-text transformer. *Journal of Machine Learning Research*, 21(140):1–67.

Abhinav Rastogi, Xiaoxue Zang, Srinivas Sunkara, Raghav Gupta, and Pranav Khaitan. 2020. Towards scalable multi-domain conversational agents: The schema-guided dialogue dataset. In *Proceedings of the AAAI Conference on Artificial Intelligence*, volume 34, pages 8689–8696.

Ashish Vaswani, Noam Shazeer, Niki Parmar, Jakob Uszkoreit, Llion Jones, Aidan N Gomez, Ł ukasz Kaiser, and Illia Polosukhin. 2017. Attention is all you need. In *Advances in Neural Information Processing Systems*, volume 30. Curran Associates, Inc.

Chien-Sheng Wu, Andrea Madotto, Ehsan Hosseini-Asl, Caiming Xiong, Richard Socher, and Pascale Fung. 2019. Transferable multi-domain state generator for task-oriented dialogue systems. In *Proceedings of the 57th Annual Meeting of the Association for Computational Linguistics (Volume 1: Long Papers)*. Association for Computational Linguistics.

Jeffrey Zhao, Raghav Gupta, Yuanbin Cao, Dian Yu, Mingqiu Wang, Harrison Lee, Abhinav Rastogi, Izhak Shafran, and Yonghui Wu. 2022. Description-driven task-oriented dialog modeling. *ArXiv*, abs/2201.08904.

A SUMBT

We describe here the Slot-Utterance Matching Belief Tracker (SUMBT) (Lee et al., 2019) architecture as well as the way it is trained and how it works during inference . The main idea of SUMBT is to match each slot-name to a slot-value from an ontology given a dialogue turn (a system's and a user's utterance). The architecture of the model is illustrated in Figure 2.

The text corresponding to the domain/slot-name pair is first encoded by a BERT model (Devlin et al., 2019) $BERT_{sv}$ and the output of the `[CLS]` token is retrieved to obtain a overall representation of the domain/slot-name pair as a vector q^s. The text corresponding to the system's and the user's utterance is also encoded by a BERT model $BERT$ so that each token of the utterance are represented of contextual vectors, resulting in the matrix U_t. Note that the utterance encoder $BERT$ is fine-tuned during training but that the weights of $BERT_{sv}$ are fixed . The encoded domain/slot-name pair is then used as query in the multi-head attention layer and the encoded utterances as key and value. It enables the model to draw its attention to the tokens that are related to the queried slot and outputs an overall representation of these tokens. Since DST is about updating the current state of the dialogue, the model needs information about the past state of the dialogue. This is performed thanks to the RNN. Finally, each slot-value from the ontology corresponding to the queried slot is encoded by $BERT_{sv}$, resulting in a matrix V^s, and the euclidean distance between each vector v of V^s and the normalized output of the RNN $\hat{y}_t^s$ is computed.

During training, the model learns to minimize the distance between $\hat{y}_t^s$ and y_t^s the vector of the target slot-value of the queried slot and to maximize the distance with the other slot-values vectors $v \neq y_t^s$ by using the cross-entropy loss. During inference, the predicted slot-value for the queried slot consists in the slot-value which gives the smallest distance to $\hat{y}_t^s$.

An Empirical Study of Topic Transition in Dialogue

Mayank Soni[†] **Brendan Spillane**[†] **Leo Muckley**[†] **Orla Cooney** [‡] **Emer Gilmartin**[†]

Christian Saam[†] **Benjamin R. Cowan** [‡] **Vincent Wade**[†]

[†]ADAPT Centre, [†]Trinity College Dublin
leo_muckley@hotmail.com, {sonim, spillab, saamc, gilmare, vincent.wade}[†]@tcd.ie,
{benjamin.cowan, orla.cooney}[‡]@ucd.ie,

Abstract

Although topic transition has been studied in dialogue for decades, only a handful of corpora based quantitative studies have been conducted to investigate the nature of topic transitions. Towards this end, this study annotates 215 conversations from the switchboard corpus, perform quantitative analysis and finds that 1) longer conversations consists of more topic transitions, 2) topic transition are usually lead by one participant and 3) we found no pattern in time series progression of topic transition. We also model topic transition with a precision of 91%.

Turns	Dialogue Text
Turn 1: A: All right um well [laughter-uh] let's see i'm twenty Turn 2: B: How old are you Lisa. Okay that i'm older Turn 3: A: Yeah how old are you. Older [laughter] Turn 4: B: Older than you [laughter-are] Turn 5: A: [laughter-okay]	
Turn 6: B: Okay we are supposed to talk about places we like to go so i'm gonna and where are you from where are you calling from ? Turn 7: A: I'm calling from uh Provo Utah but I'm from Plano Texas Turn 8: B: Oh you are from Plano my sister lives in Plano yes her husband is the new Director of Admissions at uh University of Texas at Dallas Turn 9: A: Oh really. Oh wow my dad used to work at UTD also	
Turn 11: B: Yeah so I [vocalized-noise]. Anyway so where's your favorite place to go ? Turn 12: A: Um. Generally we just go on family vacations to Arizona my grandparents live there that's generally our usual summer vacation	

Figure 1: Hand-picked example of topic transition in the Switchboard corpus. Colors represent segments of conversation about the same topic

1 Introduction

Human conversation consists of multiple natural topic transitions, from introductions, to topics of interest, and on to leave talking, and thus relies on topic change and shading mechanisms to allow participants to maintain and change topics[1]. An example of topic transition can be seen in Figure 1, participants first begin by talking about each others age, then move on to the places they want to visit and finally move on to talking about the state of Arizona in the USA. Although topic transition has been studied in linguistics for decades (Gardner, 1984; Lambrecht, 1996; Riou, 2015; Van Dijk, 1977a), there are only a few corpora based studies investigating the nature of topic change. This is because of the labour intensive task of manually annotating datasets. Even though the task of annotation is labour intensive and manual, it is necessary to empirically understand how human participants engage in topic transition in a conversation.

Towards this end, this work annotates 215 conversations from the Switchboard (Godfrey and Holliman, 1993) corpus and studies different aspects of topic transition. To the authors best knowledge, this is the the largest quantitative study conducted on the nature of topic transition in social conversations till date. The dataset curated and code utilized can be found at [2].

2 Background Theory

Definitions of topic in the literature fall into two categories; sentence level (Lambrecht, 1996) and discourse level (Van Dijk, 1977a). Gardner (1984) emphasizes the presence and identification of a topic to be a *intuitive* phenomenon answering the question of 'being about'. Multiple Sentence-level topics about the same thing may consist of a discourse-level topic (Van Dijk, 1977b). As this study is concerned with discourse level topic annotation, we adopt the definition of Bonin et al. (2012) which maintains that topic at a discourse level is the *"segments of the discourse sharing coherent information (about the same thing)"*.

Topic transition has been categorized by Gardner (1984), whose model of topic development in

[1]Our annotated dataset and models do not differentiate between the types of topic transition (change, shift, shading, fading etc.) depicted in Gardner's model (Gardner, 1984). For simplicity, this paper uses 'topic transition' to describe all forms. Where necessary, it uses specific terms to differentiate.

[2]github.com/Mayanksoni20/topictransitiondialog

Proceedings of 3rd Workshop on Computational Approaches to Discourse, pages 92–99
October 16 – 17, 2022. ©2022 International Conference on Computational Linguistics

spoken interaction details the multiple means by which humans introduce, maintain, and change topics. Two areas which have received particular attention in the literature are topic change and topic shift. They have been defined as the point between two pieces of discourse which are considered to have different topics. Bublitz (1988) differentiates between topic change and topic shift as having low and high degrees of connectivity respectively to the previous topic. Topic shift includes both topic shading and topic fading (Maynard, 2009; Brown and Yule, 1983; Garcia and Joanette, 1997). Topic change includes reintroduction and full blown change. We annotate all such topic transitions under one common label.

3 Related Work

Related work in the literature is primarily found in the domains of *manual topic annotation* and *automatic topic segmentation*.

3.1 Manual Annotation or Segmentation

Early work to manually annotate topic transition was mainly done for the purpose of conversation analysis. Planalp and Tracy (1980) were among the first to annotate topic transition. They showed that information integration by the interlocutors impacts their topic transition strategies. Crow (1983)'s analysis of topic shift in couples' conversations showed that it occurred fairly frequently; every 48 seconds on average. Later work by Ries (2001) showed that speaker initiative and style can also be indicative of topic transition. Recently, Konigari et al. (2021) annotated a subset of the switchboard corpus (Godfrey and Holliman, 1993) into *major*, *minor* and *other* topics. Sevegnani et al. (2021) introduced a one-turn topic transition corpus by asking annotators to produce bridging sentence connecting two sentences of different topics.

3.2 Automatic Segmentation

There have been many studies to segment text based on topic or detect topic transitions. Unsupervised methods utilize annotated topic transition dataset for testing the algorithms while supervised methods train and test an algorithms on an annotated dataset. Our annotated dataset will be useful in both approaches. A detailed overview of early work is provided by Purver et al. (2011). Among the earliest relevant works is that of Reynar (1994) who proposed a method of identifying topic boundaries based on lexical cohesion and dot plots. Hearst (1997) developed an unsupervised method to separate texts into multiple paragraphs representing subtopics. Passonneau and Litman (1997) developed two algorithms that use utterance features to segment dialogue by topic. Boufaden et al. (2001) used Hidden Markov Models to segment transcriptions of telephone conversations into topics. Galley et al. (2003) tackled the difficult problem of topic segmentation in multiparty speech by focusing on the content of the transcripts and their form, *i.e.* the linguistic cues in the speech. Hsueh et al. (2006) built on the work of Galley et al. (2003) by combining Automatic Speech Recognition (ASR) with existing text based methods of topic segmentation. Arguello and Rosé (2006) also adopted a hybrid approach by combining linguistic features with local context indicators in the text. Sapru and Bourlard (2014) demonstrated that latent topic features are effective predictors of topic transition in transcripts of multiparty speech from office meetings. Joty et al. (2011) developed a supervised method of segmenting topic in email conversations. More recently, Zhang and Zhou (2019) introduced a method based on BERT and Temporal Convolution Network (TCN) . Xing and Carenini (2021) introduced an unsupervised method for topical segmentation of dialog by utterance-pair scoring. There are other relevant techniques and we skip them in the interest of brevity.

4 The Annotation Framework

We annotate 215 conversations from the Switchboard-1 Release 2 corpus (Godfrey and Holliman, 1993). Annotations are based on previous studies demonstrating that naive annotators are capable of annotating topic transition with success. (Mann et al., 1977; Passonneau and Litman, 1997; Planalp and Tracy, 1980).

Switchboard Corpus The Switchboard-1 Release 2 Corpus consists of recordings of about 2400 telephone conversations between 543 distinct speakers who did not know each other (Calhoun et al., 2010). All interlocutors spoke American English. They choose a topic from a list of about 70 topics and were connected to another interlocutor by a switchboard robot. About 50 of the 70 topics were chosen regularly. The conversation is not limited to the initial topic and participants could transition topics at any time. The individual conversation transcripts have been transcribed and annotated to the utterance level and include conversation IDs, time stamps, and label for speakers identity.

Annotation Framework 215 conversations were drawn at random from the switchboard corpus are annotated at sentence-level. The annotation were performed for start *(S)* and end *(E)* of the conversation, greeting and leave taking *(GIL)*, topic, topic transition *(C)*, and failed topic transition *(X)*. Detailed annotation guidelines can be seen in appendix D. This manually annotated corpus consists of $20,566$ turns from 215 conversation. The average number of turns per conversation is 96 with the shortest conversation lasting 33 turns and the longest conversation lasting 242 turns. Mean turns per conversation were found to be 8 and mean turns per topic were observed to be 12. The conversations were annotated by two annotators. The inter-annotator agreement (Cohen 's Kappa) obtained on a sample of five conversations is 0.64, signifying substantial agreement.

5 Empirical Studies of Topic Transitions

Having obtained an annotated corpus of 215 corpus, we conducted quantitative analysis on some aspects nature of topic change. The empirical findings are discussed in the subsections below.

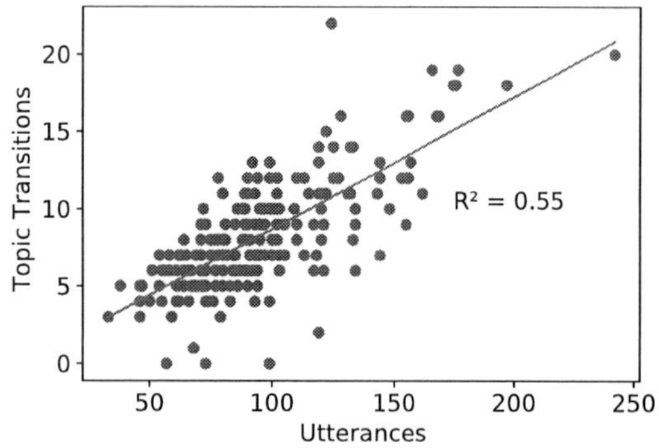

Figure 2: Scatter plot of number of topic transitions and length of conversations

Length of A Conversation and Number of Topic Transitions Longer conversation are a sign of successful and engaging conversation. We wanted to examine if longer conversation consist of more topic transitions than shorter conversation or the number of topic transitions remains similar and some topics are conversed for more turns than others. Towards investigating this relationship, we calculate number of topic transitions per conversation and plot it in Figure 2. The value of Pearson correlation coefficient is found to be 0.74, indicating a positive correlation between length of a conversation and number of topic transitions. We also plot a linear regression line and observe a R^2 value of 0.55 ($p << 0.001$). Figure 2 further highlights that number of topic transitions increase as length of a conversation increases. Most conversations consist of five to thirteen topic transitions. Thus, it is observed that longer conversations have more topic transitions.

Share of Topic Transition by Participants We wanted to explore further if the topic transitions are carried out evenly by both participant or if, one participant carries out more topic transitions. To investigate this, we first calculate the difference in number of topic transitions carried out by each participant for each conversation. We observe that only about 38% of conversations had an equal or only one more topic transition than the other per participant. In about 62% of conversations, one participant initiated at least two more topic transition than the other. It is thus observed that topic transitions are unequally carried out between participants ($\tilde{\chi}^2 = 403.41, p << 0.005$).

Time Series Analysis of Topic transition Next, the study investigate the distribution of utterances per topic as the conversation progresses. Mean and standard deviation of turns/topic is computed for all conversations. It is observed that standard deviation from mean of number of utterances is significant for all topics within a conversation. Hence, we use median to construct a line chart as median is a better measure of central tendency when there are outliers. The correlation between topic time series and number of utterances is observed to be 0.21 signifying only a weak correlation. Figure 3 shows a line plot of the number of turns per topic across the manually annotated dataset. Thus, this study did not find any pattern topic transition time series and number of utterances (($\tilde{\chi}^2 = 11.27, p = 0.98$)).

6 Modelling Topic Transition

In addition to the empirical studies performed, we also modelled topic transition on the manually annotated switchboard corpus, described in section 4. Before describing the modelling in detail, we briefly describe the approaches to model topic transition in literature.

Figure 3: Line plot of turns/topic in a conversation

Approaches to topical segmentation in dialogue include unsupervised and supervised methods. Unsupervised algorithm work on finding similarity or dissimilarity between segments of text, TextTiling (Hearst, 1997) is a seminal work in unsupervised topic segmentation. Supervised approaches work with hand-crafted features or deep learning based methods such as used (Arguello and Rosé, 2006; Xing and Carenini, 2021; Konigari et al., 2021). Following the related research work, we formulate topic transition turn detection as a binary classification problem. We implement TextTiling Hearst (1997) as a baseline and then proceed to implement classical machine learning as well as deep learning based classification algorithms

Since, dialogue is inherently context based *i.e.* the next utterance is influenced by previous utterances and a topic can span across multiple turns, consecutive utterances are grouped by speaker and termed *turn*.

TextTiling (Hearst, 1997) is implemented (employing the code from NLTK (Bird et al., 2009)). Turns are formatted as paragraphs separated by two line breaks ($\backslash n \backslash n$) as required by TextTiling which works with Lexical Cohesion. The last turn of a paragraph, obtained from Texttiling, is labelled as topic transition turn and all other turns are labelled as topic continuation turns. Additionally, as classic machine learning classifiers, Naive Bayes and LightGBM are implemented. Finally, utilizing modern deep-learning based classification algorithms, XLNet (Yang et al., 2019) is implemented using Hugging Face's Transformers (Wolf et al., 2019).

Results and Error Analysis Results in table 1 show that turns where topic transitions occur can be differentiated from turns where topics are continued. Evaluation is performed on a test set which is a subset of annotated switchboard corpus (described in section 4.2). It is observed from this study that TextTiling (Hearst, 1997) is more suitable for expository text since it works with lexical cohesion and requires input text to be in paragraphs, which is a property of expository text and not necessarily of a text conversation. Previous studies Konigari et al. (2021) have also demonstrated that TextTiling (Hearst, 1997) is more suitable for text with clearly defined topics. In terms of precision, LightGBM performs better than other algorithms with a precision of 0.91. In terms of recall and f1 score, XLNet-base performs better than other algorithms. XLNet is state-of-the-art in text classification tasks (Minaee et al., 2020). XLNet-base is fine-tuned with 4 epochs using AdamW (Adam with weight decay) optimizer with Learning Rate of $1e-5$. More than 4 epochs reduce the train error rate but the difference in valid and train error rate increases. The fine-tuning was done on a single GPU. One epoch took about 28 minutes to complete. The performance of algorithms is evaluate against macro averaged precision, recall and f1 score. Precision is a metric indicating how accurately topic transition turn is detected and the values obtained can be seen in Table 2.

Model	Precision	Recall	F1
Naive Bayes	0.55	0.57	0.40
LightGBM	**0.91**	0.50	0.46
TextTiling	0.58	0.59	0.58
XLNet-base	0.68	**0.61**	**0.62**

Table 1: Evaluation scores for various algorithms on test set

7 Limitations and Future Work

Future work will include the application of insights derived from empirical studies to apply them in open-domain dialogue systems such as using the topic transition trained to re-rank responses on topicality. A limitation of this work is the inter-annotator agreement could only be obtained on a small sample of conversation. Future work will include obtaining inter-annotator agreement for all 215 Switchboard.

8 Conclusion

Empirical study on how participants engage in topic transitions in a dyad is presented. It is observed that longer conversations have more topic transitions, topic transition is generally carried out more by one participant and there is no particular pattern observed in time series of topic transition. This study was also able to detect topic transition in dialogue with 91% precision.

Acknowledgments

This work was conducted with the financial support of the Science Foundation Ireland Centre for Research Training in Digitally-Enhanced Reality (D-REAL) under Grant No. 18/CRT/6224 and Science Foundation Ireland (SFI) under Grant Agreement No. 13/RC/2106 at the ADAPT SFI Research Centre at Trinity College Dublin. The ADAPT SFI Centre for Digital Media Technology is funded by Science Foundation Ireland through the SFI Research Centres Programme and is co-funded under the European Regional Development Fund (ERDF) through Grant Number 13/RC/2106. We would like to thank anonymous reviewers from CODI 2022 for their valuable comments.

References

Jaime Arguello and Carolyn Rosé. 2006. Topic-segmentation of dialogue. In *Proceedings of the Analyzing Conversations in Text and Speech*, page 42–49.

Steven Bird, Ewan Klein, and Edward Loper. 2009. *Natural Language Processing with Python*, 1st edition. O'Reilly Media, Inc.

Francesca Bonin, Nick Campbell, and Carl Vogel. 2012. Laughter and topic changes: Temporal distribution and information flow. In *2012 IEEE 3rd International Conference on Cognitive Infocommunications (CogInfoCom)*, pages 53–58. IEEE.

Narjès Boufaden, Guy Lapalme, and Yoshua Bengio. 2001. Topic segmentation: A first stage to dialog-based information extraction. In *In Natural Language Processing Pacific Rim Symposium, NLPRS'01*. Citeseer.

Gillian Brown and George Yule. 1983. *Discourse Analysis*. Cambridge University Press. Google-Books-ID: ZUnEAgAAQBAJ.

Wolfram Bublitz. 1988. *Supportive Fellow-speakers and Cooperative Conversations: Discourse Topics and Topical Actions, Participant Roles and "Recipient Action" in a Particular Type of Everyday Conversation*. John Benjamins Publishing. Google-Books-ID: d85TIjf7odQC.

Sasha Calhoun, Jean Carletta, Jason M. Brenier, Neil Mayo, Dan Jurafsky, Mark Steedman, and David Beaver. 2010. The nxt-format switchboard corpus: a rich resource for investigating the syntax, semantics, pragmatics and prosody of dialogue. *Language resources and evaluation*, 44(4):387–419.

B Crow. 1983. *Topic shifts in couples' conversations*. SAGE Publications, Inc.

Michel Galley, Kathleen McKeown, Eric Fosler-Lussier, and Hongyan Jing. 2003. Discourse segmentation of multi-party conversation. In *Proceedings of the 41st Annual Meeting on Association for Computational Linguistics - Volume 1*, ACL '03, page 562–569. Association for Computational Linguistics. Event-place: Sapporo, Japan.

Linda J. Garcia and Yves Joanette. 1997. Analysis of conversational topic shifts: A multiple case study. *Brain and Language*, 58(1):92–114.

Roderick Gardner. 1984. Discourse analysis: implications for language teaching, with particular reference to casual conversation. *Language Teaching*, 17(2):102–117.

John J. Godfrey and Edward Holliman. 1993. Switchboard-1 release 2 - LDC97s62 - linguistic data consortium.

Marti A Hearst. 1997. Texttiling: Segmenting text into multi-paragraph subtopic passages. *Computational linguistics*, 23(1):33–64.

Pei-Yun Hsueh, Johanna D. Moore, and Steve Renals. 2006. Automatic segmentation of multiparty dialogue. In *11th Conference of the European Chapter of the Association for Computational Linguistics*. Association for Computational Linguistics.

Shafiq Joty, Giuseppe Carenini, Gabriel Murray, and Raymond T Ng. 2011. Supervised topic segmentation of email conversations. In *Fifth International AAAI Conference on Weblogs and Social Media*.

Rachna Konigari, Saurabh Ramola, Vijay Vardhan Alluri, and Manish Shrivastava. 2021. Topic shift detection for mixed initiative response. In *Proceedings of the 22nd Annual Meeting of the Special Interest Group on Discourse and Dialogue*, pages 161–166.

Knud Lambrecht. 1996. *Information Structure and Sentence Form: Topic, Focus, and the Mental Representations of Discourse Referents*. Cambridge University Press. Google-Books-ID: bsXLCgAAQBAJ.

William C. Mann, James H. Carlisle, James A. Moore, and James A. Levin. 1977. *An Assessment of Reliability of Dialogue-Annotation Instructions*. ISI/RR-77-54.

Douglas W. Maynard. 2009. Placement of topic changes in conversation. *Semiotica*, 30(3-4):263–290.

Shervin Minaee, Nal Kalchbrenner, Erik Cambria, Narjes Nikzad, Meysam Chenaghlu, and Jianfeng Gao. 2020. Deep learning based text classification: A comprehensive review. *arXiv preprint arXiv:2004.03705*.

Rebecca J. Passonneau and Diane J. Litman. 1997. Discourse segmentation by human and automated means. *Comput. Linguist.*, 23(1):103–139.

Sally Planalp and Karen Tracy. 1980. Not to change the topic but...: A cognitive approach to the management of conversation. *Annals of the International Communication Association*, 4(1):237–258.

Matthew Purver, Gokhan Tur, and Rento De Mori. 2011. *Topic segmentation*, page 291–317. John Wiley 'l&' Sons.

Jeffrey C Reynar. 1994. An automatic method of finding topic boundaries. *arXiv preprint cmp-lg/9406017*.

Klaus Ries. 2001. Segmenting conversations by topic, initiative, and style. In *Information Retrieval Techniques for Speech Applications*, Lecture Notes in Computer Science, pages 51–66. Springer, Berlin, Heidelberg.

Marine Riou. 2015. A methodology for the identification of topic transitions in interaction. *Discours. Revue de linguistique, psycholinguistique et informatique. A journal of linguistics, psycholinguistics and computational linguistics*, (16).

Ashtosh Sapru and Hervé Bourlard. 2014. Detecting speaker roles and topic changes in multiparty conversations using latent topic models. In *INTERSPEECH*, page 2882–2886.

Karin Sevegnani, David M Howcroft, Ioannis Konstas, and Verena Rieser. 2021. Otters: One-turn topic transitions for open-domain dialogue. *arXiv preprint arXiv:2105.13710*.

Teun A. Van Dijk. 1977a. Sentence topic and discourse topic. *Papers in slavic philology*, 1:49–61.

Teun A Van Dijk. 1977b. Sentence topic and discourse topic. *Papers in Slavic philology*, 1(1977):49–61.

Thomas Wolf, Lysandre Debut, Victor Sanh, Julien Chaumond, Clement Delangue, Anthony Moi, Pierric Cistac, Tim Rault, Rémi Louf, Morgan Funtowicz, et al. 2019. Huggingface's transformers: State-of-the-art natural language processing. *ArXiv*, pages arXiv–1910.

Linzi Xing and Giuseppe Carenini. 2021. Improving unsupervised dialogue topic segmentation with utterance-pair coherence scoring. *arXiv preprint arXiv:2106.06719*.

Zhilin Yang, Zihang Dai, Yiming Yang, Jaime Carbonell, Ruslan Salakhutdinov, and Quoc V. Le. 2019. Xlnet: Generalized autoregressive pretraining for language understanding.

Leilan Zhang and Qiang Zhou. 2019. Topic segmentation for dialogue stream. In *2019 Asia-Pacific Signal and Information Processing Association Annual Summit and Conference (APSIPA ASC)*, pages 1036–1043. IEEE.

A Utterance Count Per Topic

In addition to plotting median utterances per topic, we also plot mean, minimum and maximum number of utterances as topic order progresses.

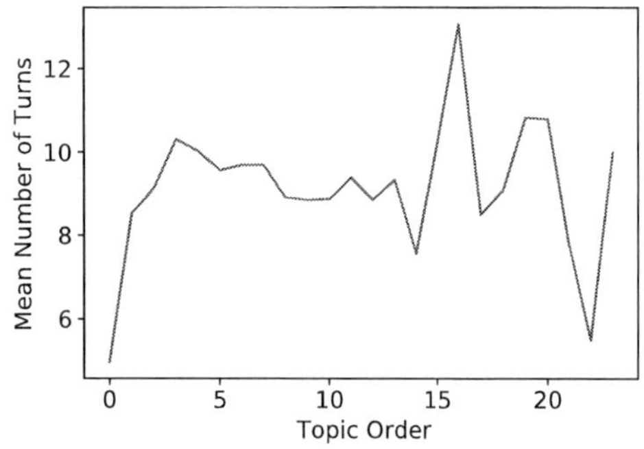

Figure 4: Line plot of mean utterances per topic

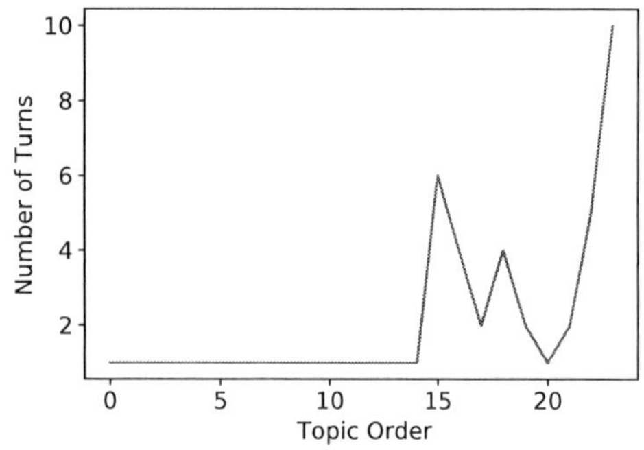

Figure 5: Line plot of minimum utterances per topic

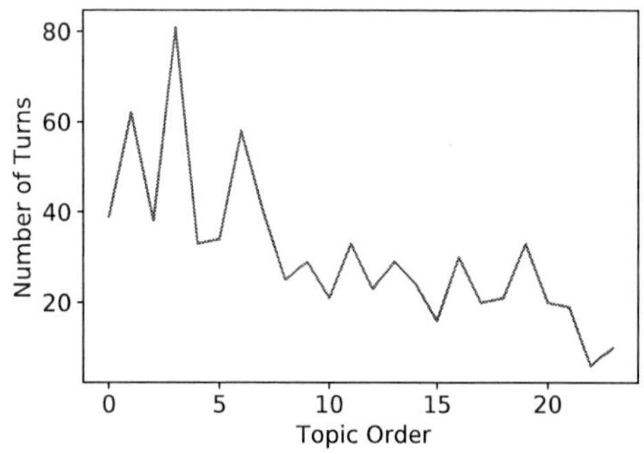

Figure 6: Line plot of maximum utterances per topic

B Share of topics by participants

Below we plot difference of topic transitions per participants across conversations. Figure below shows a bar plot of topic transition difference and percentage of conversations with such difference.

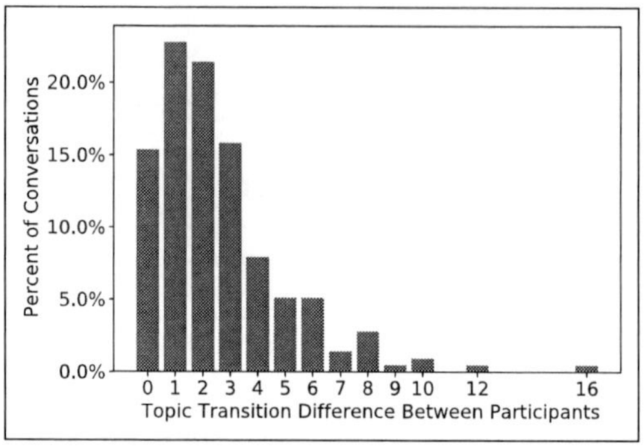

Figure 7: Share of topics per participants across conversations.

C t-SNE Visualizations

To empirically understand the separation of topic transition turns and topic continuation turns, we visualize the two classes using a t-SNE plot.

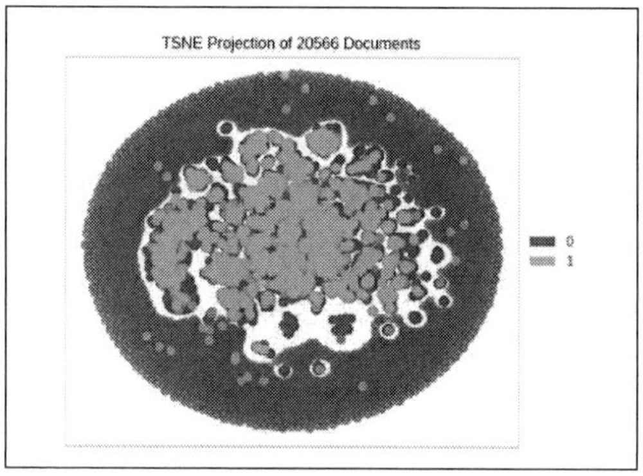

Figure 8: t-SNE visualization of utterances

D Annotation Guidelines

For a conversation, first, a topic is identified and then the topic transition is marked. For some conversation, it could be more difficult to mark the topic transition and may require reading the whole conversation.

start of topic: The first utterance, pertinent to a conversation, is marked as 's'. Here the first utterance is "[noise]" and therefore not pertinent. But the next line, a topic is introduced and therefore pertinent. This will be the starting a point for the conversation so will be marked with an "s". Non-pertinent utterances include greetings/introductions and leave-taking (GIL) as this is not the focus of this part of the project.

topic transition: This is the point when a new topic is introduced. For example, if Speaker B

H	I
"[noise]"	
"{alrighty} uh i guess our topic today is air pollution and we are to just discuss what substances do you think contribute most to air pollution"	s
"as well as what society can do to improve the air quality of the atmosphere around us"	
"right"	

introduces a new topic and then speaker A complies with the change in topic by either contributing or acknowledging the change in topic. This point of topic shift/change is marked with a "c". Here is an annotated example.

H	I	J
"yeah"		recycling
"or it ends up costing a lot more to recycle it than it does just to make it so "		recycling
"yeah {noise} well uh do you have a recycling program where you live"	c	recycling program
"oh yeah uh I go to Indiana University here and its real big and all the buildings are recycling bins for all kinds of materials"		recycling program

This example shows the point of topic transition. This can be seen when the point of the conversation changes from being about "recycling" to being about "recycling programs". This is then marked with a "c".

"well reduce reuse and recycle right [laughter]"		recycable products
"right [laughter] words to live by"		recycable products
"[laughter] that's right i try to remember them_1 i guess we've covered it"	e	recycable products
"[laughter]"		gil
"okay"		gil
"[noise] it was nice talking to you bye-bye now"		gil
"you too bye-bye"		gil
"[noise]"		na

end of a topic: We also denote the end of a topic. This is like beginning the topic where utterances may not be pertinent. When marking the end of the topic, it is marked with an "e" on the last utterance pertinent to the current topic. Here is an example.

Author Index

Association for Computational Linguistics
209 N. Eighth Street
Stroudsburg, Pennsylvania 18360

ISBN 978-1-7138-6148-5

CURRAN ASSOCIATES INC.
proceedings.com